Sandford Fleming

England and Canada

A summer tour between old and new Westminster, with historical notes

Sandford Fleming

England and Canada
A summer tour between old and new Westminster, with historical notes

ISBN/EAN: 9783337329341

Printed in Europe, USA, Canada, Australia, Japan

Cover: Foto ©Andreas Hilbeck / pixelio.de

More available books at **www.hansebooks.com**

ENGLAND AND CANADA.

A SUMMER TOUR

BETWEEN

OLD AND NEW WESTMINSTER

WITH HISTORICAL NOTES.

BY

SANDFORD FLEMING, C.E., C.M.G., Etc.

LONDON:
SAMPSON LOW, MARSTON, SEARLE & RIVINGTON.
1884.

Entered according to Act of Parliament of Canada, in the year 1884, by
SANDFORD FLEMING,
in the Office of the Minister of Agriculture.

GAZETTE PRINTING COMPANY, MONTREAL.

TO

The Right Honourable the Marquis of Lorne, K.T.

G.C.M.G., P.C., &C., &C.,

ONE OF CANADA'S TRUEST AND WARMEST FRIENDS,

WITH SINCERE RESPECT

THIS RECORD OF A JOURNEY FROM THE IMPERIAL CAPITAL TO THE PACIFIC OCEAN, THROUGH CANADIAN TERRITORY,

IS DEDICATED.

CONTENTS.

CHAPTER I.
INTRODUCTORY.

CHAPTER II.
HALIFAX TO LIVERPOOL.

Halifax—Cunard Line—Intercolonial Railway—Truro—Travelling by Pullman—New Brunswick—Miramichi—Great Fires in New Brunswick—Salmon Fishing—Micmac Indians—Rimouski—S. S. Parisian—The first Ocean Steamer the Royal William—Incidents of Ocean Voyage—Arrival.......Page 11

CHAPTER III.
ENGLAND.

Willie Gordon—Custom House Annoyances—Cable Telegram—Post Office Annoyances—London—Spurgeon's Tabernacle—An Ancestral Home—English and United States Hotels—English Reserve—A Railway Accident—The Land's End—A Deaf Guest............................Page 33

CHAPTER IV.

ENGLAND (Continued).

Marquis of Salisbury—Classical Studies—Henley Regatta—Red Lion—London Dinner to Lord Dufferin—His Speech—Greenwich—Fisheries Exhibition—Bray—The Vicar—The Thames—Minehead—The Polynesian.......................Page 58

CHAPTER V.

ENGLAND TO CANADA.

The Ocean Voyage—Its Comfort—Moville—Mail Coach Road of Old Days—Impressive Service on Deck—Comfort on the Vessel—Rimouski—Halifax........................Page 84

CHAPTER VI.

NOVA SCOTIA.

Early Colonization—De Monts—Champlain—Sir William Alexander—Capture of Quebec—The Treaties—The Acadian Evangeline—Louisbourg—First Capture—Peace of Aix la Chapelle—Boundary Disputes—The Final Struggle—Deportation of the Acadians—Nova Scotia constituted a Province. Page 102

CHAPTER VII.

HALIFAX TO QUEBEC.

Home in Halifax—Start for the Pacific—The Intercolonial Railway—Major Robinson—Old Companions—The Ashburton Blunder—Quebec—The Provincial Legislature—Champlain—The Iroquois. ....Page 119

CHAPTER VIII.

QUEBEC, MONTREAL, OTTAWA.

Montreal—Ship Channel—Hon. John Young—St. Lawrence Canals—Indifference of Quebec—Quebec Interests Sacrificed—Need of a Bridge at Quebec—Montreal Trade in Early Times—Beauty of the City—Canadian Pacific Railway—Ottawa—The Social Influence of Government House—Kingston............Page 131

CHAPTER IX.

TORONTO TO LAKE SUPERIOR.

Toronto—Collingwood—Georgian Bay—The Sault St. Mary—Navigation of the Great Lakes—Manitoulin Islands—Lake Huron—Arrival at the Sault............Page 147

CHAPTER X.

LAKE SUPERIOR TO WINNIPEG.

Lake Superior—Early Discoverers—Joliet and La Salle—Hennepin—Du Luth—Port Arthur—The Far West—The North-West Company—Rat Portage—Gold Mining—Winnipeg.
Page 161

CHAPTER XI.

WINNIPEG, HUDSON'S BAY COMPANY, LORD SELKIRK.

Early Explorers of the North-West—Du Luth—De la Verendrye—Mackenzie—Hudson's Bay Company—Treaty of Utrecht—North-West Company—Lord Selkirk—War in the North-West—Union of the Rival Companies—The North-West Annexed to Canada............Page 179

CHAPTER XII.
WINNIPEG TO CALGARY.

Winnipeg—Great Storm—Portage-la-Prairie—Brandon—Moose Jaw—Old Wives' Lakes—The Indians—Maple Creeek—Medicine Hat—Rocky Mountains. ....Page 201

CHAPTER XIII.
CALGARY TO THE SUMMIT.

Start for the Mountains—The Cochrane Ranche—Gradual Ascent—Mount Cascade—Anthracite Coal—Sunday in the Rockies—Mountain Scenery—The Divide. ....Page 221

CHAPTER XIV.
DOWN KICKING-HORSE VALLEY.

The Descent—Summit Lake—The Kicking-Horse River—Singular Mountain Storms—An Engineering Party—A Beaver Meadow—A Dizzy Walk........................Page 237

CHAPTER XV.
TO THE SUMMIT OF THE SELKIRKS.

The Eagle Pass—Kicking-horse River—Valley of the Columbia—The Selkirk Range—The Columbia River—Summit of the Selkirks—Major Rogers' Discovery.................Page 252

CHAPTER XVI.
DOWN THE ILLE-CELLE-WAET.

The Descent of the Selkirk Range—Glaciers—The Last of our Horses—Devil's Clubs—The Ille-celle-waet—A Rough Journey—A Mountain Storm—Slow Progress—A Roaring Torrent—Skunk Cabbage—Marsh—A Long Ten Miles' Journey.
Page 271

CHAPTER XVII.

DOWN THE ILLE-CELLE-WAET.—Continued.

A Difficult March—Cariboo Path—Organization of Advance—Passing Through the Canyon—Timber Jam—A Gun-shot heard — The Columbia again—Indians—Disappointment—The Question of Supplies becomes Urgent—No Relief Party Found—Suspense...Page 284

CHAPTER XVIII.

THROUGH THE EAGLE PASS.

The Kamloops Men at Last—No Supplies—On Short Allowance—An Indian Guide—Bog-wading—The Summit of the Pass—Bluff Lake—Victoria Bluff—Three Valley Lake—Eagle River—Shooting Salmon—The *Cached* Provisions—Pack-horses again—Road Making—The South Thompson—Indian Ranches.
Page 295

CHAPTER XIX.

KAMLOOPS TO THE COAST.

Lake Kamloops—Savona's Ferry—Irrigation—Chinese Navvies—Chinese Servants—Lytton—The Fraser River Canyon—Old Engineering Friends—Sunday at Yale—Paddling Down the Fraser—An English Fog at New Westminster.......Page 311

CHAPTER XX.

ON PACIFIC WATERS.

New Westminster—Enormous Forest Trees—English Broom—Port Moody—Down Burrard Inlet—Sea Fog—Navigation by Echo—Straits of Georgia—The St. Juan Archipelago—Seamanship—Victoria.....................................Page 329

CHAPTER XXI.

BRITISH COLUMBIA.

Sir Francis Drake—Mears—Vancouver—Astor—Hudson's Bay Company—Gold Discoveries—Climate—Timber—Fisheries—Minerals—Mountain Scenery.....................Page 340

CHAPTER XXII.

HOME BY THE NORTHERN PACIFIC.

Puget Sound—The Columbia—Portland—Oregon and San Juan Disputes—Arid Country—Mountain Summits—The Yellowstone—The Missouri—The Red River—Chicago—Standard Time Meeting—The British Association—Home.....Page 355

CHAPTER XXIII.

THE INDIANS.

Indian Population—The Government Policy—Indian Instincts—The Hudson's Bay Company—Fidelity and Truthfulness of Indians—Aptitude for Certain Pursuits—The Future of the Red Man...................................Page 380

CHAPTER XXIV.

THE CANADIAN PACIFIC RAILWAY.

Rapid Construction—Travelling Old and New—Beginning of Pacific Railway—Difficulties—Party Warfare—The Line North of Lake Superior—The United States Government—Mountain Passes—Soil and Climate—National Parks—Pacific Terminus.
Page 394

CHAPTER XXV.

CONCLUSION.

England and Canada—Old and New Colonial Systems—Political Exigencies—The High Commissioners—Lord Lorne's Views—The Future—The French Element in Canada—Colonial Federation—The Larger Union..........................Page 420

ENGLAND AND CANADA.

CHAPTER I.

INTRODUCTORY.

If we carry ourselves in imagination to that part of North America nearest to Europe, we find that we have reached the most easterly coast of the Island of Newfoundland, an outlying portion of the continent. Standing on Cape Bonavista and looking from this promontory over the waste of waters, we discover that between the Equator and Greenland the Atlantic Ocean is generally of much greater width in every other parallel than opposite our present position: that its breadth rapidly increases as we proceed southward, if but a few degrees of latitude, and that, in the parallels of New York or Philadelphia, the ocean is more than double the width. Towards the continent of Europe the first land the eye rests upon is that of the British Islands. Four centuries back the first recorded discoverer of Newfoundland sailed from those shores, and from the time of the Tudor monarchs this stretch of ocean has been unceasingly traversed by European ships. It has thus been the cradle of ocean navigation. Adventurous men, who planted the early settlement of America, crossed to the new world on this narrow belt. The vessels which carried them were indeed frail craft compared with the creations of modern ship-building. But, step by step, they were enlarged and developed to the magnificent clipper, which again has been supplanted by the still more magnificent ocean steamer.

In old days, even in a sailing vessel of large tonnage, a sea voyage was frequently accompanied with much misery. It was not uncommon for emigrants to be detained at sea as many weeks as now days are needed for the voyage. Ships might be retarded or driven back by adverse gales, or they might remain in mid-ocean, becalmed in water as unruffled as a mirror of glass. Steam has revolutionized these conditions. Instead of ships being turned far from their course by contrary winds, or with flapping canvas waiting for a fair breeze, we behold on the waters of the Atlantic fleets of swift steamers, carrying thousands of passengers to and fro with the regularity of the daily post between two neighbouring cities. However formidable the voyage once was, its greater drawbacks are now removed. A steam ferry has been practically established between the two continents, and transportation is effected with scarcely less regularity than between opposite banks of a navigable river. The path of the ocean steamer has in reality become, as it were, the Queen's highway; and were anything wanting to facilitate intercourse, we possess it in the telegraph. If this belt of ocean has been the nursery of the ocean steamers, it has also given birth to ocean telegraphy. In no part of the world are so many submarine cables laid along the ocean bed as in this direction. We live in a period when instantaneous communications from continent to continent are as easily effected as from county to county. Year by year the facilities of intercourse, both by steamship and by telegraph, are increasing in a manner to bind closer than ever, by the ties of mutual benefit and common interest, the different members of the British family. On the one hand, the Canadian is enabled to visit the old land, where his traditions have been gathered, and where there is a history in which he can claim an inherited participation. On the other, it provides the youth of the Mother Country with an outlet by which he may gain a home with a kindred people, who revere the same memories, and who will cordially welcome his labour and energies to aid in strengthening and consolidating the institutions of that portion of the Empire.

From a multiplicity of causes, there are different shades of character and thought to distinguish the several members of the British family. They are called into being by geographical position, by race, by climate and other influences. Diversities exist, and why should it not be so? It is a shallow and unwise pretension which would ignore the fact. The inhabitants of neighbouring counties, even the members of one family, have not the same characteristics or identical likes and dislikes. As in the family so in the state. It is natural, and in some respects advantageous, that varieties of character and power should be traceable; on the other hand, as the family likeness may be seen in a group of individuals, however in many respects they may differ, an essential unity of national life and sentiment may be found one and the same amid characteristics the most divergent. The people of Canada and of England differ as the current coin of the realm differs. While in the currency there are dissimilarities of name, of value, of colour and of metal, all are impressed with the stamp of the one sovereign; so in the people there are diversities, but all can be recognized as British subjects.

If we turn our eyes in the direction opposite to Europe, we find Newfoundland situated as a barrier between the outer ocean and an inner sea; the Gulf of St. Lawrence. Whatever its destiny, Newfoundland is the one portion of British North America which has not allied her fortunes with the Canadian Dominion. Geographically, the island stands as a gigantic breakwater to shelter from the surges of the Atlantic the continent to the west, and to protect the entrance of the St. Lawrence.

INTRODUCTORY.

The Gulf of St. Lawrence has been compared to the Baltic, but, unlike the Baltic, having but one narrow channel of entry, it is approachable from the ocean by two wide navigable openings. These passages—the Straits of Belle Isle and St. Paul—lie to the north and south of Newfoundland. Around this inner Baltic-like sea we behold the Maritime Provinces of Nova Scotia, New Brunswick and Prince Edward Island, to which may be added the eastern portion of Quebec. These Provinces occupy an extensive coast line, indented with bays and capacious harbours, presenting all the facilities for shipping, commerce and fisheries. They are bound together, and to the other Provinces of the Dominion, by one trade, one tariff and by one common nationality; on the other hand, they have each distinct local institutions for their own domestic government.

Continuing our glance westward, a thousand miles from Bonavista, beyond the ancient fortress of Quebec, we behold Montreal, the commercial metropolis of the Dominion. Here are seen ocean steamers of the largest class discharging cargoes loaded twelve days back in Liverpool, Glasgow and other parts of Europe. Advancing our view another thousand miles, over cultivated fields and flourishing cities and lakes of unrivalled magnitude, our vision carries us through deep forests beyond the Province of Ontario to the confines of Manitoba, in the middle of the continent. Still another thousand miles to the west, across prairies abounding with a fabulous fertility of soil, we reach the foot-hills of a snow-capped mountain range, concealing the country which lies beyond it. To penetrate this barrier we must advance by the known passes, and for hundreds of miles follow deep defiles, traversing further mountain ranges, until we reach the wide grassy plateau interspersed with picturesque lakes in the heart of British Columbia. We may still pierce another serrated wall of mountains by a deep and rugged valley, and, by following a tortuous and foaming river to its mouth, we meet the flow of tide of another ocean far greater in extent than that which lies behind us.

Carrying our vision beyond the shore of the western mainland, across a strait similar to that separating England from Europe, we see the Island of Vancouver, washed by currents warmed in the seas of Asia. Vancouver Island is not quite so large as England, but it enjoys the same climatic conditions, and possesses in profusion many of the same mineral treasures.

British Columbia is the youngest colony of the Empire, and until recently was practically the most distant from the Imperial centre. Its chief city bears the name of Her Majesty. The sun does not rise on Victoria, the capital of British Columbia, until eight hours after it gilds the towers of Westminster. One-third of the complete circle of the globe separates the Imperial capital from the capital of the Pacific Province, but no land intervenes which is not British, and the whole distance is under the shadow of the one national flag.

In imagination we first glanced across the ocean at its narrowest limit. Turning our glance landward, we have looked across a continent at its greatest width. All we have scanned, from sea to sea, is Canada. The vast proportions of the Dominion, its varied features, its lakes and rivers, mountains and plains, its sources of wealth and magnificent scenery, are but little known to Englishmen. A country to be known must be seen. It is not enough to examine a terrestrial globe or ponder over maps and geographies in order to form an estimate of the character of half a continent. They suggest but a faint idea of territorial extent. You must traverse its different sections, and bestow time in examining its fields and forests, its natural landscape, its cities and its civilization.

There are few, indeed, who possess anything like an adequate conception of the immense extent and resources of the Dominion. It is scarcely possible even for Canadians themselves to conceive the wealth of territory and the varied magnificence of scenery and the productive capacity of the land, the destinies of which it is their privilege to control.

During the past summer (1883), circumstances

induced the writer to visit England, to recross the Atlantic, and make a journey through the whole extent of Canada to the Pacific coast. The railway took him to the base of the Rocky Mountains. From thence he entered the passes, and by pack-horse and on foot he followed the route proposed to be taken by the Canadian Pacific Railway through British Columbia.

As is customary in such circumstances, the writer sent home, at convenient opportunities, a diary of his daily progress. He is aware that the notes of travel which have interest for a circle of intimate friends, have often but slender claim to public attention. These notes, however, give a sketch of the first continuous journey ever made, indeed the only one yet attempted, through the whole longitudinal extent of the Dominion by the route taken. From the interest which has been attached to his notes of travel, the writer has been prevailed upon to prepare them for publication, and, with the view of supplying such information as the future traveller may desire, a few historical notes have been included in the narrative.

Canada is certainly not within the actual geographical limits of the Mother Land, yet it is no mere rhetorical phrase to say that this half of the North American continent has become an integral part of the Empire. Seventeen years ago, when the British North American Act of 1867, creating the Dominion, passed the Imperial Parliament,

British and Canadian statesmen laid the foundation of a great future for the confederated provinces. From that date Canada has steadily, step by step, done her part to realize all that was then foreshadowed of her future. She undertook to establish a highway for commerce through her forests, prairies and mountains, to connect the most distant Provinces. In a short time the national highway will be opened from the Atlantic to the Pacific, and Canada will become a recognized central commercial link between England and Asia.

The writer ventures to think that the record of the journey he made, will show how closely England and Canada are brought together by the modern agencies of steam and electricity. Equally it will be obvious, how easily the British subject in Canada may revivify old associations; and how the denizen of the United Kingdom can, without discomfort, visit the whole extent of the Dominion, to enjoy the varied scenery in the many forms in which it is presented. The writer sincerely hopes that what he ventures now to submit may be instrumental in leading others to enjoy what proved to him a delightful summer tour by sea and land. It is not without diffidence that he yields to the wish expressed for the publication of his notes. He is desirous, however, of establishing that such a journey as he has accomplished presents many other points of attraction independent of the beauty of the scenery and novelty of the associations. There is much to repay enquiry in the examination of our system of government and of the institutions of the several Provinces; in ethnological developments; and in geological and kindred scientific researches. It will be found, too, that there is a past history which gives attraction to many a scene, and in all that constitutes and promotes the advance of nations there is presented much of varied interest worthy of investigation.

The writer does not hide from himself the fact that, in describing scenes and events, he may say much that is well known to many. He makes no pretension to original research. His endeavour is simply to present the notes of his journey side by side with some leading historical facts, in a way which may admit of generalization and be useful to the ordinary reader. Hence it is not impossible that the professional *littérateur* may, with a certain cynicism, consider that the following pages contain much that is not worth the record.

The two voyages across the ocean and the journey over the continent embraced a total distance travelled of about 14,000 miles, the eastern and western portions of which began and ended at Halifax.

CHAPTER II.

HALIFAX TO LIVERPOOL.

Halifax—Cunard Line—Intercolonial Railway—Truro—Travelling by Pullman—New Brunswick—Miramichi—Great Fires in New Brunswick — Salmon Fishing — Micmac Indians—Rimouski—S. S. Parisian—The first Ocean Steamer the Royal William—Incidents of Ocean Voyage—Arrival.

Halifax, selected for its excellence as a harbour in connection with its geographical position, is well known throughout the world as one of the most important stations for the British Navy. For upwards of a century it has been pre-eminently the Admiralty port for the British fleet in North Atlantic waters, and it was its superiority as a harbour in all respects which determined the demolition of Louisburg in 1756. It was held that no second naval arsenal was required in proximity to Halifax, and consequently not one stone was left standing upon another at Louisburg after its second capture. The enterprise of the city has intimately connected its name with the history of the navigation of the ocean. Ships of Nova Scotia may be seen on every sea, and it is here that the centre has been, around which the commerce of the Province revolved. It was in Halifax that the

Cunard Steamship Company took its origin, under the distinguished family who have so long lived there: an organization which may well be considered one of the most successful known. For nearly half a century the record of their immense fleet shows that not a passenger has been lost or a letter miscarried. The irreverent Frederick the Great was wont to say that Providence was generally on the side of large armies. His own good fortune in the field was owing, however, mainly to his supervision of the simplest detail and attention to discipline. In a similar manner the unprecedented success and the perfect organization of the Cunard Company must be traced to the unwonted care and vigilance continually observed in connection with the enterprise. The principle laid down by Mr. Cunard was that nothing was to be left to chance; that the best of all material and workmanship was to be obtained in the construction of his steamers; that the crew were to be subjected to the strictest discipline; and that no possible care or precaution, even in the simplest detail, was to be omitted. The result of these efforts from the initiation of the company is seen in the magnificent Cunard fleet: a noble monument to the name it bears.

My connection with Halifax sprang from my relationship with the Intercolonial Railway, the explorations of which I was appointed to conduct in 1863, and of which I remained Chief Engineer

HALIFAX.   13

until its completion in 1876. My acquaintance with this locality consequently extends back twenty years. I have formed there many warm friendships, which I am happy to think I still retain, and scarcely a year goes by without my passing some portion of the summer months at that delightful suburb of Halifax known as the "Northwest Arm."

In common with all who have been connected with Halifax, I must express my humble view of the charm which the place possesses. Its scenery of wood, hill and dale; its ample expanse of water in all forms; its healthy climate and fresh air; its cool evening breezes in the heat of summer; its pleasant drives and the varied features of its daily life; all leave an impression not easily forgotten. But when to these recognized advantages the social elements of Halifax are added, it is held by common consent that there are few cities more attractive. And when we remember the well-bred, travelled men, many of whom also highly educated, to be met among the officers of the garrison and on board the ships at the station, with their continuous efforts to return the hospitalities of the citizens, we all must acknowledge that Halifax, in its social aspects, possesses features and a charm peculiar to itself.

A line of steamers runs from Halifax to Liverpool, but I had taken my passage by the steamer "Parisian," of the Allan Line. The weekly steamer of this line, as a rule, leaves her moorings in front of Quebec at a fixed hour on the forenoon of Saturday. The traveller ordinarily goes on board the tender an hour earlier. But a train leaves Toronto, 480 miles west of Quebec, on the evening of Friday, connecting at Montreal on Saturday morning with an express mail train for Rimouski, a point on the St. Lawrence about 200 miles below Quebec. By this means letters can be posted at Toronto, indeed at nearly all the cities in Canada west of Quebec, to the last moment. This express mail, which makes rapid time, reaches Rimouski late on Saturday night. By it, passengers who have been unable to embark at Quebec may take the steamer, as it always remains off Rimouski to receive the mail. Travellers to Europe from the Maritime Provinces may also embark at Rimouski by taking the regular train over the Intercolonial Railway from St. John or Halifax. The latter is the route which I followed.

On the afternoon of the 15th June I said good-bye to my family at the station at Halifax, and with my youngest daughter I started for England. The day was bright and beautiful; indeed, although sea fogs prevail at certain seasons of the year, I know no latitude where the air is purer than it is in Nova Scotia, or where nature, during summer, is more attractive. There were several of my friends on the train, and when the sadness of parting passed away there was everything to make the trip cheerful.

TRURO. 15

After leaving Halifax we have supper at Truro, a large, clean-looking Nova Scotian town, situated on one of the heads of the Bay of Fundy. Truro, however, was not always so clean and cheerful looking as it is to-day. At one time it was conspicuous for its dark and dingy appearance, and it has to thank the visit of the Prince of Wales, nearly a quarter of a century back, for the change. The Prince had landed at Halifax, and was expected to pass through Truro in a few days. Meetings were held to devise means to do honour to the Royal visitor. I think it was Mr. Hiram Hyde who said that "evergreen arches would be out of place unless the town presented a clean face." He moved a resolution, which was unanimously adopted, that a schooner load of lime lying in the bay should be secured, and every one be obliged to turn out with whitewash brushes. In forty-eight hours Truro was so metamorphosed as not to seem the same place, and so well satisfied were the inhabitants that they have kept its face clean ever since.

To continue. We are at the Truro refreshment room. One never criticizes railway meals too severely, at least those who are much accustomed to travel. The golden rule on such occasions is to open your mouth, shut your eyes, and take what is placed before you. If things are to your liking, then you can "give them the painted flourish of your praise."

Our route passes over the Cobequid Mountains, and at Amherst, on another inlet of the Bay of Fundy, you may have further refreshments at ten o'clock. Then comes the night's rest in the Pullman. To the denizens of this continent the Pullman is a necessity. In a country of narrow geographical limit nothing is more pleasant than a few hours in an ordinary first class English carriage. But we do not count our trips by hours on the western continent. Often we do so by days. Sitting up all night in one of the old carriages, which many yet from circumstances are obliged to do, was one of the small miseries of life. The want of rest, the cramped position, the foul air, the banging of doors, frequently the crowd of passengers, had all to be endured; and who of that date cannot remember the extreme discomfort to which the traveller was compelled to submit as best he could. With a Pullman you have comparative quiet, and with well-mannered and competent officials, who keep the car heated only to an endurable temperature and properly ventilated, you have all the auxiliaries of comfort. What dream is there in the Arabian Nights equal to the realization of finding yourself in a comfortable bed, with all the accessories of home, travelling at the rate of forty miles an hour?

Soon after leaving Amherst we crossed the Missiquash, the river which separates Nova Scotia from New Brunswick. It has some historic import of which I will speak hereafter. Our course is now through New Brunswick to the River Restigouche, on the north side of which lies the Province of Quebec. The whole distance through the three Provinces embraces a variety of scenes of great interest to me, as many years of my life were passed in the construction of the Intercolonial Railway.

It was not until after the American Revolution that New Brunswick was looked upon as a colony. Five thousand of the United Empire Loyalists arrived at St. John in the British fleet in 1783, one hundred years ago. It became a Province in 1786. No little of its history is in connection with its terrible fires. That of Miramichi in 1825 ; of St. John in 1837, when, in the heart of a rigorous winter, nearly the whole business part of the city was destroyed; and again of St. John in 1877, when, in the short space of nine hours, 200 acres of buildings were levelled to the ground, and fully two-thirds of the entire city laid in ashes. During the night the train passes through the scene of the first disaster, which left some 6,000 square miles in a state of devastation. The summer had been unusually hot and dry. On the first day of October, 1825, the inhabitants of the valley of the Miramichi were disturbed by immense forest fires in the neighbourhood of the settlements. The smoke with great heat continued for seven days, when the fire extended to the settlements, defying all efforts to extinguish it, and sweeping away all that lay before it. The town of Newcastle was consumed, as also Douglastown with all the smaller outlying settlements. The devastation continued along the northern side of the river for one hundred miles. Hundreds of settlers and thousands of cattle were lost. The number of wild animals which were burned was also very great. Even the salmon perished in the smaller streams, owing to the intense heat. To this date the trace of the fire is distinctly seen in the character of the trees which have grown upon the burnt district. A gale increased the violence of the fire, so that its fury was uncontrollable. In many cases the inhabitants, not looking for such a calamity, were suddenly awakened in their beds by the alarm of danger. A few minutes' delay would have led to their destruction. Many were unable to save themselves. Not a few owed their preservation to the fact that their farms were near the river, in which they threw themselves, and escaped by clinging to logs. The loss of life to those at a distance from the river, where escape was impossible, must have been serious. Many of the survivors were dreadfully mutilated, and in the distant settlements few escaped to tell their dreadful experience.

In the morning we reached Campbellton, on the Restigouche, at the head of the Bay Chaleur, and we have a royal breakfast of salmon fresh from the nets. Some of our friends on the train are enthusiastic fishermen. Col. Chalmers, recently from India, and the Rev. Mr. Townend, Garrison Chaplain at Halifax, are among the number. They are bound for the fishing pools on the Restigouche, and are in high spirits. They learn here that the run of salmon up the river is unprecedentedly large, and their excitement is intense. My sympathies are with them, for fishing to me is a most pleasant recreation. If I am not a skillful, I am at least a devout, disciple of Isaac Walton.

At the station I met some of my old Micmac Indian friends, some of whom I have known for twenty years, and who accompanied me in my various wanderings in the wilds of New Brunswick. I have a strong and kindly feeling for these children of the forest. Personally I have found their simplicity of character not the sham which many claim it to be. There are exceptions, but, as a rule, in their relations to me, they have proved honest and faithful. Although perfectly undemonstrative, they never forget a kind act or word. Such is my experience, and I have had much to do with Indians of nearly every tribe between the Atlantic and the Pacific. It has been my invariable good fortune to come in contact with those among them to whom I could at any time have trusted my life. We shook hands all round. Breakfast, however, has only left time for a few words. The train starts, and as it leaves the station I receive from my dusky friends a hearty *bô jou! bô jou!*

We are still in New Brunswick, but in half an hour we cross the Restigouche and enter the Province of Quebec near the Metapedia station. Here our friends of the rod leave us with our best wishes for their success. The Railway now follows the River Metapedia, and the run up the valley is all we could wish. The day was fine; no morning could be more bright. The curves in the track are frequent but unavoidable, and how few who whirl over them ever think of the labour bestowed in order to reduce them to a minimum! In the Metapedia many splendid salmon pools are found. Mr. George Stephen, President of the Canadian Pacific Railway Company, has the most pleasant of fishing boxes here, pleasantly situated within sight of the passing train at Causapscal. H. R. H. Princess Louise and Prince Leopold remained for some weeks here three years ago. Mr. Stephen is himself a keen sportsman, and never lets a season pass without spending a holiday at Causapscal. He had arrived the day previous with a party of friends.

In the middle of the afternoon we reached Rimouski, where we left the train and placed ourselves in the hands of Madame Lepage, who keeps a comfortable *pension* at this place. This landlady's untiring devotion to the comforts of her guests is on a par with the glow of her sparkling black eyes. She is the mother of a large family, some of whom are grown up, yet she retains all her youthful vivacity and *naiveté*.

Rimouski is a large straggling French Canadian town, the last of any importance in the Province of Quebec to the east, if we except the thriving village of Matane. It is chiefly remarkable for its ecclesiastical and educational institutions. There is another peculiarity; the largeness of the family in many households. It is no uncommon matter to find a family of from fifteen to twenty children. Not long ago I heard of a case of a family of eighteen, and there was a question of an orphan to be taken, for whose nurture nothing was to be paid, its parents having died under circumstances of privation and poverty. " Let it come and take its chance with our children," said this excellent French Canadian mother, and it was so resolved.

Travellers to Europe, like ourselves, have their letters and telegrams directed to Rimouski in case of more or less last words being necessary. I was very glad to find good news in those I received. I went to the station to meet the train for the south. There I found more fishermen bound for the Restigouche, New Yorkers, who now come yearly to our waters, a class who do not fish for the pot, but are sportsmen. Among them were Mr. Dean Sage and Mr. Worden, with a party of friends.

At 10 o'clock p.m., the mail train having arrived,

we took the tender for the steamer, which lay off in the stream. Sir Alex. Galt was on the train, on his way back from Halifax, where he had taken part in a public banquet given to his successor as High Commissioner for Canada in London; Sir Charles Tupper. I was in hopes that he, too, was starting for England, but to my disappointment he continued his journey to Montreal.

We reach the wharf on the branch railway, where the tender is lying. The arrangements are not quite perfect. The wharf itself is of unusual length, but it only reaches shallow water at low tide. In consequence the capacity of the tender is limited, and, although strongly built, it rolls disagreeably in rough weather, to the discomfort of passengers who are indifferent sailors.

We embarked on the "Parisian," and at once found our way to the cabins allotted to us. A friend had previously consoled us by saying that they were the worst in the ship. They were directly under the scuppers used for pouring the ashes overboard, the disagreeable noise of which operation we were expecting to hear every hour in the night. We did not, however, experience much inconvenience on this score, as for the greater part of the voyage, our cabin was on the windward side, which is never used at sea for the discharge of refuse.

The passenger list placed in our hands contained several familiar names. There were Canadian Cabinet Ministers and Montreal merchants, with their wives and families, and there were friends whom we expected to meet, some of them we found in the saloon before retiring for the night.

Trips by ocean steamers have much the same features, and, while the changes and vicissitudes of fog, rain and fine weather are all important in the little floating community, they have little concern for the outer world. To sufferers from sea-sickness, an ocean trip is a terror. Medical men say, in a general way, that the infliction should be welcomed, for it brings health, but I have seen those prostrated by it who have been so depressed that I can not but think that if this theory be true the improvement to health will be dearly purchased by the penalty. Such, however, are the exceptions. With most people one or two days' depression is generally the extent of the infliction Personally I cannot complain. Nature has made me an excellent sailor. With no remarkable appetite, I have never missed a meal on board ship, nor ever found the call to dinner unwelcome.

Our first morning commenced with fog, but it cleared away as we coasted along the somewhat bold shore of Gaspé in smooth water. There is always divine service on these vessels on Sunday. The Church of England form is as a rule adhered to, which is read by the captain or doctor if no clergyman be present. If a clergyman be found among the passengers he is generally invited to conduct divine service, and any Protestant form is admitted. On the present occasion the Rev. C. Hall, Presbyterian minister of Brooklyn, N. Y., officiated. The service was simple and appropriate, and the sermon admirable. The day turned out fine, and the water so smooth that in the afternoon every passenger was on deck. Our course being to the south of the Island of Newfoundland, we passed the Magdalen Islands and the Bird Rocks, and we think of the vast number of ships which have ploughed these waters on their way to and from Quebec and Montreal. It is now fifty years since "The Royal William" steamed homewards on the same course we are now following. Much interest begins to centre in "The Royal William." It is claimed that she was one of the pioneers of steamers, if not the very first steamer which crossed the Atlantic under steam the whole distance. She was built in Canada. She left Quebec on the 18th August, 1833, coaled at Pictou, in Nova Scotia, and arrived at Gravesend on the 11th September. She did not return to Canada, as she was sold by her owners to the Spanish Government. Her model is preserved by the Historical Society of Quebec. Some of these particulars I had from the lips of one of the officers of "The Royal William," who died a quarter of a century ago.

There is but one counter claim to the distinction. A ship named the "Savannah" crossed the Atlantic from the port of that name in the Southern

United States to Liverpool in 1819. She had machinery for propulsion of a somewhat rude description, which seemed to be attached as an auxiliary power to be used when the wind failed. There is nothing to show that it was continuously employed. I have recently heard from a friend in Savannah on the subject, and I quote from his letter: " She was 18 days on the voyage. She resembled very much in mould an old United States war frigate. The hull was surmounted with a stack and three masts—fore, main and mizzen— and was provided with side wheels of a primitive pattern, left wholly exposed to view, and so arranged that they could at any time be unshipped and the vessel navigated by sails only."

On Monday before 2 a.m. we pass out of the Gulf by the Strait of St. Paul into the open Atlantic, and still the water continues perfectly smooth. There is a slight fog, which passes away, and we behold nothing but the world of waters around us. The moon appears, and we have an evening on deck long to be remembered. Everything stands out clear and distinct, but the shadows are dark and heavy. The moon casts its line of rippling light across the waves, and the ship glides onward, almost weird-like in its motion.

One of the pleasures, as well as penalties, of travelling is to be asked to make one at whist. It is a pleasure to take part in a single rubber if played without stakes, but to one indifferent to cards, who does not want to win his friend's money or lose his own, to join such a party is often no little of a sacrifice. Your reply when asked to play may take the conventional form, "With pleasure," and in a way you feel pleasure, for you like to oblige people you care for, and you may be in an extra genial mood; but how often I have wished some other victim could have been found at such times. On this occasion I left the deck when I would have willingly remained, and took my seat at the card table.

The fog returned, and the ship went at half speed for the night. When next day came there was no fog, but there was some little rocking, which, to me, during the previous night, was but a pleasant incentive to sleep, for I did not once hear the fog whistle in its periodic roar—no pleasant sound—nor was I sensible of the dreaded rattling of the ashes emptied overboard, a nightly and unavoidable duty, and by no means a musical lullaby.

I find that several ladies are absent from breakfast this morning. A breeze springs up; a sail is hoisted; and occasionally we have fog, and now and then a cold blast, with alternations of damp and moist air. Such is the general experience in crossing the Banks. As one passenger remarked, "It is hungry weather." The breakfast in most cases had been sparing, an enforced necessity in some instances, but the general feeling is one of being ravenous for lunch. The day passes pleasantly, possibly idly, and in the evening the whist table has its votaries. We leave the fog behind us, but the next day is cloudy. There is a light wind, and the sea is a little disturbed. Most of the passengers keep the deck. We fancy we see a whale. There is too much cloud for the moon to penetrate, so the passengers generally leave the deck to enjoy themselves quietly in the saloon. We have a bright midsummer day this 21st June after a glorious morning, and we advance eastward with all sail set. The spirits of all on board seem to rise, the sky is so blue, and the sea so bright. There is but slight motion, with which, most of the passengers are becoming familiar.

We are now half way across. We begin to calculate when we shall arrive, and what trains we shall take at Liverpool. I have many times crossed the Atlantic, but I never could understand the restlessness with which so many look for the termination of the voyage. If there were some urgent necessity for immediate action on the part of those who are travelling this impatience could be accounted for. The majority, however, are tourists for pleasure or for health, and, as for business or professional men, I never could see how a few hours one way or the other could influence their operations. To some the voyage is simply imprisonment; the condition of being at sea is a penalty they pay at the sacrifice of health and comfort. These are the exceptions. There are a large number who feel as I do, and for my part, while it would be affectation to profess to be fond of storm and tempest, a sea voyage in ordinary fine weather is one of the most pleasurable experiences of my life. I have good digestion and good spirits, and I am satisfied with the pleasant change from a life on shore. I can generally read, and I can always remain on deck, and I always have a certain feeling of regret when I think that the voyage is soon coming to an end. We are all well cared for, we form pleasant associations, and anyone who can study human nature finds no little opportunity for doing so on shipboard.

Our library, it is true, is somewhat limited, but it has a few good books. I was somewhat struck on reading during this voyage almost the last words of the celebrated Mary Somerville, who, after a most distinguished career in science, died eleven years ago at Naples. These words appear more striking to me when read on board ship. "The blue peter has long been flying at my foremast, and, now that I am in my 92nd year, I may soon expect the signal for sailing."

We discuss our progress on all occasions There is a general thankfulness as we advance. Towards evening the motion of the ship has increased, but we can all walk the deck. On the following day we put on more canvas, for the breeze has increased and is more favorable, and our progress is much greater. There is now considerable motion, but we have all got familiar with it, and, as sailors say, we have our sea-legs. The wind is at north-west; the day clear and bright, with a warm-looking sky, speckled with fleecy clouds. The decks are dry. We appear to be achieving wonders in speed, and we are entering into all sorts of calculations as to what extent we shall make up the seven hours' detention by fog on the Banks of Newfoundland. Our run yesterday was 342 miles in 23½ hours. Reckoning by observed time, we lose half an hour daily by the advance made easterly. During the afternoon we have a fair breeze, with all sail set, followed by the same pleasant and agreeable evening. The passengers talk of leaving with much readiness. Well is it said that much of the pleasure of life is retrospective. "We are approaching land" is now the cry, and we commence early the next morning calculating when we shall reach Moville. Saturday afternoon is delightful. Bright gleams of sunshine appear in the intervals of occasional showers. In the evening there is a concert with readings from eight to ten. The collection is for the "Sailors' Orphanage" at Liverpool. On account of the concert our lights are allowed to burn until midnight, and many of us remain on deck nearly to that hour. The moon is three-quarters full; we have all sail set, and we can see the reflected light of the sun in the northern sky at midnight. To me there is a strange fascination in a scene of this character, with all its accompaniments. There is a movement in the sea and a freshness in the air which give a tingle to the blood, and we seem to walk up and down the deck with an elasticity we cannot explain to ourselves.

Next morning was Sunday. I was on deck half an hour before breakfast. The land on the west coast of Ireland was in sight. The morning was most fair, and it seemed to give additional zest to the excitement produced by the approaching termination of the voyage. We learn that we shall be at Moville at 2 o'clock. We have again divine worship. A Methodist minister read the Church of England service and delivered an admirable sermon. We reach Moville, and find we have been seven days and ten hours making the run from Rimouski. I took the opportunity here to send a cablegram home; it consisted of one word, but that word contained a page of family meaning.

We passed the Giant's Causeway, at which the passengers intently looked. We could also see Islay and the Mull of Kintyre.

In the evening we have a second service. Our eloquent friend from Brooklyn satisfied us so well the previous Sunday that we begged of him to give us another sermon. He complied with our wishes, and with equal success.

It is our last night on board; to-morrow we are to separate. Many of us on this voyage have met for the first time, and in all human probability few of us will again come side by side. There is always a feeling of sadness in thinking you do something for the last time. I can fancy even a convict leaving his cell where he has passed some years pausing upon the threshold while a rush of the old recollections, the long, sad hours cheered by gleams of hope, crowd upon him, when he will feel some strange sentiment of regret that it is the last time he looks upon the place. The feeling may last but a second, but it is an impulse of our nature which is uncontrollable;

On board ship, with a certainty of gaining port to-morrow, the last hours are passed in packing up and preparing to leave, and a feeling of regret creeps in that now so many pleasant associations are to end, and in spite of yourself some of the good qualities of those who are set down as disagreeable people come to the surface in your memory. Some few friendships are formed at sea which are perpetuated, but generally the pleasantest of our relations terminate with the voyage. It is too often the case, as in the voyage of life, that those we have learned to esteem are seen no more.

We had to lose no time in order to pass the troublesome bar at the mouth of Liverpool harbour. With vessels of the draught of the American steamers it can only be crossed at high water. The officers generally calculate what can be done from the hour they leave Moville, and regulate their speed accordingly, so as to approach it at the right moment.

No one knows better than the occupants of the cabin corresponding with our own on the opposite side of the vessel that a great many tons of ashes have been thrown overboard during the voyage: we all know that a large volume of smoke has passed out of the funnel, a proof of the great weight of fuel which has been expended in keeping the screw revolving. The draught of the ship is consequently considerably less than when we left the St. Lawrence.

There is now no fog; the weather is fine; there is everything to encourage the attempt to run in, and it proves successful. On this occasion, had we been twenty minutes later, we should have had to remain outside until another tide. The lights of Galloway and the Isle of Man were passed before the most of us retired last night. We all awoke early; at a quarter to five we had crossed the bar; the "Parisian" was in the Mersey; the tender came alongside the ship, and very soon afterwards I stood again on English ground.

CHAPTER III.

ENGLAND.

Willie Gordon—Custom House Annoyances—Cable Telegram—Post Office Annoyances—London—Spurgeon's Tabernacle—An Ancestral Home—English and United States Hotels—English Reserve—A Railway Accident—The Land's End—A Deaf Guest.

As I stood on the landing stage at Liverpool awaiting patiently and with resignation for the Customs officers to allow the removal of our luggage, a host of recollections ran through my mind. My thoughts went back twenty years to another occasion when I landed from an ocean steamer at an hour equally early. My memory has been aided by one of those works which appear so frequently from the New York press, so fertile in this species of encyclopædiac literature, endeavouring to embrace in a few pages the truths learned only by a life's experience. The small volume tells you what not to do, and it sententiously sets forth its philosophy in a series of paragraphs. There are ninety-five pages of this philanthropic effort, with about four hundred negative injunctions. The title of the book is "Don't." The injunction that struck my eye most forcibly may be taken as no bad type of the teaching of the book. It runs, "Don't" is the first word of every sentence. "Don't go with your boots unpolished, but don't have the polishing done in the public highways." These words met my eye as I was engaged in these pages, and they brought back the feelings which passed through my mind on the morning I left the "Parisian."

My thoughts reverted to my visit to the Mother Country after eighteen years' absence; the first made by me since I left home in 1845. I was a passenger on the "United Kingdom," due at Glasgow. She had passed up the Clyde during the night, and arrived opposite the Broomielaw in the early morning. The night previous the passengers were in the best of humour, and the stewards had been kept up late attending to us. We were all in high spirits, and without exception delighted at returning to Scotland. I was particularly impatient to get ashore, to touch the sacred ground of my native land. I arose that morning one of the first of the passengers, before the stewards were visible. The ship was in the stream off the Broomielaw. A boat came to the side. I jumped into her and went ashore. I strolled along the quay. My foot was not literally on "my native heath," but I enjoyed intensely the pleasure we all feel in revisiting our native shores, and in being near the scenes from which we have been long absent. Everything seemed so fresh and charming. I had no definite purpose in my wandering, but I was at home; it was Scotland. In my semi-reverie I was interrupted by a young voice in the purest Clydesdale Doric saying "hae yer butes brushed?" I looked down mechanically at my feet, and found that the cabin bootblack of our vessel had neglected this duty, probably owing to the irregular hours of the last night on board. Moreover, it was the first word addressed to myself, and I should have felt bound to accept the offer if it had been unnecessary in the fullest sense. I commenced conversation with the boy. He was very young. I summoned to my aid my best Scotch for the occasion. His name was Willie Gordon, and he told me his widowed mother was a washerwoman, that he had a number of brothers and sisters younger than himself, that his earnings amounted to about half a crown a week, and that between him and his mother they managed to earn ten shillings in that time. "And how do you live, Willie?" "Reel weel," replied the boy, with the cheeriest of voices. "And now, Willie," I said, when I had paid him his fee, "it is many years since I have been here. I want to see the places of greatest interest in Glasgow." "Ou, sir," he promptly said, "ye shuld gang ta see Corbett's eatin hoose." "Do you know the way there?" I asked. "Fine, sir. I ken the way vary weel. I'll gang wi ye tae the door," and his face looked even happier than before. I accepted his guidance, and, if my recollection is correct, the place was in Jamaica street. The boy walked by my side carrying his brushes and box, and chatted gaily of himself and his life. Apparently no prince could be happier. We reached the renowned establishment he had named It was a species of home which a benevolent citizen had instituted, on the same principle on which the coffee taverns are now established: to furnish an early hot cup of tea or coffee to men going to work, to offer some other refreshment than whiskey and beer, to give a meal at cost price with all the comfort possible with cleanliness good cheer and airy rooms, warm in winter. After some hesitation, and persuasion on my part, Willie shyly entered with me. The *menu* was on the wall. Porridge and milk one penny, large cup of coffee one penny, bread and butter, thick, one penny, eggs and toast one penny, &c., &c.; everything, one penny. I cannot say that I give a precise account of what appeared, but it was essentially as I describe it. We were a little early even for that establishment, so Willie and I sat down. The buxom matron gave us some account of the place and its doings. The Duke of Argyle had dined with her a few days before. She told us the establishment was well patronized and prosperous. The time soon came for our order, for we were the first to be served. I set forth what I required for myself, and that was no light breakfast, as I had a sea appetite, sharpened by the early morning walk. I directed the attendant to bring the same order in double proportions for the boy, so that we had a splendid *déjeuner*. My little companion was in ecstasies. Never was hospitality bestowed on a more grateful recipient. He would not leave me, and he seemed bound to make a morning of it, and from time to time graciously volunteered, "I'll tak ye ony gait, Sir" His customers were forgotten, but I trust he did not suffer from his devotion to me, for I did my best to remedy his neglect of professional duty. He followed me from place to place, carrying the implements of his day's work, and he seemed anxious to do something for the trifling kindness I had shown him and the few pence I had paid for his breakfast. But I was more than compensated by the pleasure I myself received. I listened to all he said with fresh interest, for he was open, earnest, honest and simple-minded. He was deeply attached to his mother, and was evidently proud to be able to add to her slender earnings, which were just enough to keep her and her family from want. He certainly seemed determined to do all in his power to make her comfortable. He never lost sight of me till I left by the eleven o'clock train, and my last remembrance, on my departure from Glasgow on that occasion as the train moved out, was seeing Willie waving his brushes and boot-box enthusiastically in the air. I often wonder what Willie's fate is. He appeared to me to be of the material to succeed in life. In Canada he certainly would have worked his way up. I never heard of him again, but I certainly shall not be greatly astonished to hear of Sir William Gordon, distinguished Lord Provost of Glasgow.

One of the nuisances of travelling throughout the world is the ordeal of passing the Custom House. Frequently the traveller from Canada thinks the infliction at Liverpool is pushed a little further than is requisite. What can we smuggle from Canada? I know quite well that there is generally a very loose conscience as to the contents of a lady's trunk, considered under the aspect of its fiscal obligations, but surely some form of declaration might be drawn up by means of which honourable men and women would be spared this grievous and irritating delay. Apart from the delay, it is no agreeable matter to open out your carefully packed portmanteau. To ladies it is particularly offensive to have their dresses turned over and the contents of their trunks handled by strangers. Canadians, while crossing their own frontier, find the Custom House officers of the United States, as a rule, particularly courteous, and, on giving a straightforward declaration that they have nothing dutiable, they are generally allowed to pass at once. Liverpool may not be alone in strictly exacting all that the law allows, but is this course at all necessary or wise? It cannot increase the revenue, for the additional expense of collection must more than absorb the trifling receipts. And one is not kindly impressed with this reception, especially when we feel that it is totally unnecessary. We cross the ocean from Canada with peculiar feelings of pride and sentiment to visit our Mother Land, and it is somewhat of a severe wrench to be treated as foreigners by the Customs authorities on our arrival; I will not say uncivilly or wrongfully, but as if we were adventurers going to England on some plundering tour. It is certainly no petty annoyance to Canadians, when they make their entry into a land they are taught to call "home," to have their sense of common honesty thus challenged at the threshold. Anything which is brought from Canada can only be some trifling present, such as Indian work, to some relative in the Old Country; and if, possibly, a few pounds be lost to the exchequer, it is made up a thousandfold by the good will arising from being courteously treated on the first landing on English soil. Would it not suffice if every ordinary passenger were required to make a declaration in some such form as the following?: "I am a Canadian subject. I declare upon my honour that my baggage contains nothing whatever for sale. I have with me my personal effects for my own use only." Or it may be added, "I have a few gifts for old friends, of little or no commercial value."

Perhaps some British statesman might not think these suggestions beneath his notice. Let him send a competent agent to examine and report upon this subject. He will probably discover that the whole nuisance can be swept away without inflicting the slightest injury on the national exchequer. It would form no discreditable sentence in a statesman's epitaph to read that "he did away with the needless and offensive restrictions imposed on British subjects from the outer empire visiting the Imperial centre."

Having at last passed the Custom House, I drove to Rock Ferry, one of the most pleasant suburbs of Liverpool, to visit a family I was acquainted with, and with them I passed a most enjoyable day. The greeting I received was most cordial and gratifying. In the afternoon I started for London, leaving my daughter behind me, and I found myself once more whirling through the green meadows and cultivated fields of England. I was alone, but I did not feel solitary. How charming everything looked! The air was fresh with passing showers, and the rain played for some quarter of an hour on the landscape only to make it look fresher and fairer, and, when the sun came out, more full of poetry. Why, we are at Harrow-on-the-Hill! Has time gone so quickly? There is so much to think about, so many fresh scenes to gaze upon, and so many events seem to crowd into the hours that the traveller, in his bewilderment, loses count of time.

I am again in London, at Batt's hotel, Dover street, and I walk to the Empire Club to learn if there are any letters for me. I am disappointed to find there is no cablegram. I despatched one from Moville, and one word in reply would have told me if all was well. I recollect well the depression I experienced at the time at not receiving news. It was an inexplicable feeling; not exactly one of impatience or disappointment, but rather of keen anxiety. "Why should there be silence," I murmur, when everything points to the necessity for a reply.

Next day my business took me to the city, and I returned as rapidly as I could. In the afternoon, to relieve my suspense, I went to the Geological Society's rooms, and mechanically looked over the books and specimens. I wandered into the rooms of the Royal Society, and found before me the well known features of Mary Somerville as they are preserved in her bust. I then strolled into the parks and down to the Club, and still no cablegram. These facts are of no interest to any but the writer, but possibly they may suggest, not simply to the transmitter of telegrams but to the officials who pass them through their hands, how much often depends upon their care and attention, and that there is something more required than simply receiving and recording a message. There is the duty of seeing to its proper delivery, and it was precisely on this ground that my trouble took its root.

I was three days in London when I received a telegram from Mr. George Stephen, President of the Canadian Pacific Railway Company, stating that he was desirous that I should proceed to British Columbia as soon as possible. It was my acceptance of this proposition which has led to the production of these pages, but at that hour I felt that Mr. Stephen's communication only increased my bewilderment. My telegraphic address was properly registered at the General Post Office in London, and it had been used over and over again during my annual visits to England. The cablegram I had just received bore the registered address, and yet I had received no message from my family in Halifax. I have often sent cablegrams, and never more than twenty-four hours elapsed before receiving a reply. Consequently I again telegraphed, plainly stating my anxiety, and then wandered out to call on some friends. Later in the evening I at last found an answer, and, in order that it might not again miscarry, the sender put on my address five additional words, held as quite unnecessary, at two shillings each, making ten shillings extra to pay. On my return to Canada I learned that no less than three cablegrams had been sent to me, each one of which remains to this day undelivered. Two of the despatches were sent before, one subsequently to, the message last mentioned. All were properly addressed. I felt it a public duty to write to the Secretary of the

Post Office Department in London, but no satisfactory explanation has yet been given. Life is a mass of trifles, as a rule. The exceptions are our griefs and our sufferings, our triumphs and joys; the latter, as a French writer says, "counting by minutes, the former by epochs." I passed three particularly unpleasant days during this period, my own personal affair, of course, and one in which the world may seem to have no interest. But the public has really a deep interest in having a more perfect system of Atlantic telegraphy than we now possess, and the facts I have described, have their moral. At least it is to be hoped that the authorities may remember that anyone separated by the ocean from his correspondents is not content that telegrams should be delayed for days, and still less content not to have them delivered at all.

I was a month in England, chiefly in London, remaining until the 26th of July. I must say that when in London I often thought of, although I can not fully endorse, the words of that enthusiastic Londoner who held that it was the "best place in the world for nine months in the year, and he did not know a better for the other three." In London you can gratify nearly every taste, and although it always takes money to secure the necessaries and luxuries of life, especially in great cities, still, if one can content himself with living modestly, it does not require a wonderfully large income to enjoy the legitimate excitements and amusements of London. In this respect it is a marked contrast to New York, where, generally speaking, a large income must be at your command for even a moderate degree of respectable comfort.

In London, to those who cannot afford a carriage, there is a cab, and those who have no such aspirations as a "hansom" can take the omnibus. It is not necessary to go to the orchestra stalls to see a performance, nor are you obliged to pay six guineas per week for your lodgings or one pound for your dinner. The reading room of the British Museum is open to every respectable, well-ordered person. You can look at some of the best pictures in the world for nothing, and, if you are a student of history and literature, there are localities within the ancient boundaries of the city which you cannot regard without emotion. You have two of the noblest cathedrals in the world; Westminster Abbey, with its six centuries of history, and with its tombs and monuments, setting forth tangibly the evidences of the past national life. Then you have Wren's classical masterpiece St. Paul's, one of the most perfect and commanding edifices ever erected anywhere. Its interior has never been completed. Will it ever be so? Yet, as Wren's epitaph tells us, if you wish to see his monument "look around you."

Again, in London, by way of recreation, you have public parks, river-side resorts, and by the river itself and underground railway you can easily reach many pleasant haunts about the suburbs. Indeed, by the aid of the steamboat or rail you can take the most charming outings any person can desire to have. London may be said to be inexhaustible.

As one of the directors of the Hudson Bay Company I had often to visit the city, and some very pleasant relationships grew out of my attendance at the various board meetings. I was constantly meeting Canadians, and certainly we hold together in a peculiar way when away from the Dominion. It is a strong link we are all bound by, and yet we would find it hard to explain why. Even men who are not particularly civil to one another in Canada will cross each other's path with pleasure when from home, and intimacies never anticipated are formed, and associations entered upon once thought impossible.

One of my visits was to Spurgeon's Tabernacle. The name is familiar to everyone, and as I had been many times in London without hearing this celebrated preacher, I was anxious not to return to Canada without making the attempt. I was told to be in good time, and, acting on the suggestion, I obtained a good seat, and formed, I should suppose, one of four thousand people. Just in front of me, strange to say, I beheld a familiar form, which I recollected last to have seen at Queen's College convocation, Kingston: the Premier of Ontario! Mr. Oliver Mowat was the gentleman who was seated two pews in front of me. He was the last person I expected to meet in such a place, as I did not even know he was in England. He was the only one in that vast assemblage I recognized. Spurgeon is, undoubtedly, worthy of his great reputation, and on this particular Sunday his sermon was forcible, marked by rare good sense, and perfectly adapted to his auditory. I felt fully rewarded for my effort to be present. When the service was over I had a few words with Mr. Mowat, but our interview was but short, for I had an engagement, and it was necessary for me to hurry to the Waterloo Station to take the train for Guildford, in order to reach —— Park, in its neighbourhood.

This was a most agreeable visit to me. I do not think there is any country but England where scenes and associations are known such as I there witnessed. At the station a carriage met us, for I found myself in company with a gentleman going to the same hospitable mansion. He was an Irish M. P. On our entering the grounds we passed amidst grand old elms, along a noble avenue, and through walks beautiful with roses, ivy and laurel. My welcome was most courteous and graceful. There were several guests, but it was my privilege to sleep in the haunted room. The walls were hung with tapestry; the floor was of oak; the fireplace was a huge structure of sculptured stone from floor to ceiling. No ghost disturbed my slumbers, and, in the words of Macbeth, "I slept in spite of thunder." I awoke at dawn, and drew back the heavy curtains to admit the light. It was about sunrise. Shall I ever forget that magnificent view from the old windows, with their quaint transoms and quarterings, and circular heads! the sight of those fine old trees, stately beeches, tall ancient elms, venerable blue beech, and many a noble oak of from two to three centuries' growth! It was one of those old ancestral domains, with glades, avenues and forest, which seem to take you out of the present world and back in thought to one altogether different, in many of its conditions, from the life of to-day. The most carefully developed homestead of old Boston, or one of the finest mansions on the Hudson, with the outline of mountain scenery, and its associate stream; any one of the well built halls south of the Potomac, elaborated with all the wealth of the planter; or even one of our own palatial Canadian residences; all appear a thing of yesterday as compared with that stately edifice, with its delightful lawns, walks and avenues, which bear the ancient impress of their date and of their early greatness. No doubt these paths were trod by men in the troublous times of Henry VIII. and his three children, men who then may have debated mooted points of history in this very neighbourhood. There is a tradition also that the virgin Queen has looked upon this same landscape "in maiden meditation fancy free."

The morning was peculiarly fine, and as I opened the window to admit the pure, fresh air I really breathed again to enjoy it, and inhale the perfume of foliage and of the garden flowers; flowers whose ancestors may have traced three centuries of life, at least the early known plants indigenous to English soil; while those of foreign origin could boast of sires, perhaps, the first of their genus brought from the Continent. The air was vocal with music; the trees seemed peopled with scores of blackbirds and mavis, and there was many a proverbial "early bird" busy with the yet earlier worm, who had gained so little by his rising. All nature seemed teeming with life and gladness. I can only here acknowledge the courtesy I received from my host and hostess. The hours passed away unclouded by the slightest shadow, and I know no more pleasant memory than that of my visit to this English ancestral home.

I was highly pleased, on my return to Batt's Hotel, to receive intimation that my daughter was shortly to join me in London. There is a certain solitude in a London hotel, which is much the opposite of the continental life, and entirely distinct from the *table d'hote* system of this continent. In England the desire is to secure extreme quiet and privacy, while on this side of the Atlantic every auxilliary is provided for publicity and freedom of movement. This is especially the case in the United States. In Canada it may be said that a middle course is taken. In many large hotels on this continent, in addition to the drawing and breakfast rooms, parlours and halls and writing and news rooms are open, where papers are furnished and sold, seats at the theatre obtained, telegrams sent, books, especially cheap editions of novels, purchased, with photographs of the professional beauties, leading politicians and other celebrated people. All of these places are marked by busy, bustling life. The dining room, from its opening in the morning till a late hour at night, is one scene of animation, be the meal what it may. Some of the *beau sexe* even visit the breakfast room with elaborate toilets, and many a pair of earrings glitter in the sun's early rays. A walk up and down the wide passage or hall at any hour is proper and regular, and it is stated that it is often the only exercise indulged in by many living in the great hotels of the United States, the street car furnishing the invariable means of locomotion. In the large cities the hotels are situated, as a rule, on the main streets. There are always rooms where one may from the windows look upon the crowds passing and repassing. Thus a drama of ever-changing life can be comfortably witnessed from an armchair placed at the right point of observation. There is no such thing as loneliness. Almost everyone is ready, more than ready, to converse with you. If you yourself are courteous and civil you will probably find those around you equally so, whether they be guests or belong to the establishment. With a little tact and judgment you can always obtain useful information. My experience likewise is that the information is invariably correct: for there never seems to be any hesitation in a negative reply when those you address are not acquainted with the particular point of inquiry. The gentleman who presides over the cigars, the controller of the papers and the photographs and the official of the bar, an important field of action in a high class hotel, each and all make it a point of duty impressively to patronize your local ignorance when you ask for information. In an English hotel the general rule is for no one person to speak to another. If you do venture on the proceeding, Heaven only knows what reply you may receive. In the class divisions of the Mother Country there may be social danger in not observing the lines defined by etiquette. There are always men of good address and appearance who are not unknown to the police, and whose photographs may be destined at no distant period to figure in the Rogues' Gallery. But such men are to be found in all countries. Whatever necessity there may be for prudence and circumspection, it has struck me that there is really no ground for that absolute uncompromising offensiveness of manner which often well-meaning men in England feel bound to show to any person who addresses them, as the joke goes, "to whom they have not been introduced."

If you are quite alone very little experience in the English hotel is enough to throw you back on yourself, and to depress even a gay and blithsome nature. You walk with a listless air through the corridors, you take your meals with a sort of mechanical impassiveness which you cannot help feeling, and you seem to drop into the crowd of reserved, self-contained individuals, who act as if they thought that courtesy to a stranger was a national crime. I do not speak of the clubs, where, if you are a member, you can always meet some acquaintance. But comparatively few Canadians visit England who are club men. I know no solitude so dreary, nor any atmosphere so wearying, as that of the London hotel in a first class lateral street when you have nobody to speak to, where you can see scarcely a living soul out of the window, where the only noise is the distant rumble of vehicles in the neighbouring thoroughfare, and where, when you are tired with reading or writing, you have no recourse but to put on your hat and sally out into the street.

A circumstance crosses my mind as I am writing which gives some insight into English life and character. It happened to a friend, now no more, with whom I had crossed the Atlantic. He was travelling from Liverpool to London, and took his place in the railway carriage, sitting on the back middle seat, while opposite in the corner seats were two gentlemen, each with a newspaper. The train had been an hour on its journey, but the silence was unbroken. At last my friend spoke. "Gentlemen," he said, "I am L—— D——. I have come from ————, and he named a city in the Dominion. I have been a merchant for fifty years, and now I am living in ease. I am eighty-three years of age, and, like the large majority of Canadians, I have two eyes and one tongue, and, like a great many of my countrymen, I feel a pleasure in using them. My eyes feel the period of time they have done me service. I cannot read from the motion, but I can take part in a conversation. My business in Britain is to see my daughters. One is married to an officer quartered at the Royal barracks in Dublin. I am just returning from a visit to her, and I am on my way to see my second daughter, whose husband is stationed at Woolwich. Having now introduced myself, I trust, gentlemen, you will not look upon me as a pickpocket or anything of that sort." One of the gentlemen carefully drew out his card-case and gave his card. This example was followed by his opposite neighbour. "What, gentlemen," my friend said, looking at the cards through his spectacles, which he deliberately put on, "you do not seem to know one another; let me introduce you."

At the same moment he crossed his arms and presented the card of the one to the other. The curtest and least definable bow was given. One query followed another, and my friend had a great deal to say and much to enquire about. He had occupied the highest position in the city he came from, and had mixed a good deal with the men of his world. The three or four hours which followed were most pleasing to the trio. My friend's fellow travellers were county men, and he was cordially invited to spend a week with each of them. The invitations were accepted, the acquaintance renewed, he met with the most cordial English welcome, and the visits proved to be particularly agreeable to all parties.

In my experience, and in that of others who come under the name of Canadians, whose fortunes now lie in the Dominion, whatever our place of birth, all that the Englishman wants to know regarding us is that we are Canadians; in other words, that we are not dubious members of an uncertain phase of English society. We then at once receive the most genial courtesy and kindness; real, true, honest, hospitable kindness. I reason from this that we must be outside the circle in which this frigid intercourse is observed as a protection. We are in England for a brief time; then we pass from the scene, and there is no fear entertained on the part of our English neighbours of forming an unpleasant and unprofitable, that is scarcely the word, an embarrassing, relationship. I have heard the explanation given for this peculiarity that its very defects spring from the loyalty of character which marks the high-bred Englishman. The theory is that, if he knows you once, he is always to know you. He wishes to run no risk of being placed in a false position, and hence avoids any intercourse which, although in a way agreeable to him, he will not accept at the cost of his own self-respect. And there are men who in no way incur blame for want of courtesy in a railway carriage, but they will pass their fellow traveller after a week's interval as if they had never seen him. It may be urged that those who live in the state of society which obtains in England are the best able to understand its conditions and the wisdom of its laws. It is quite possible that this mode of treatment of a stranger may be commended by experience. There are many examples where the opposite course has led to trouble, but prudence and good sense would surely avoid annoyance, and they are requisite under all circumstances. But is it not also advisable to avoid the extraordinary discourtesy with which sometimes a remark from a stranger is received, as if it were designed to serve some deliberate scheme of wrong, or to lead up to some act of swindling and imposture. Surely we may always be able to detect any attempt of this kind and protect ourselves; and in all conditions of life good manners cost little and entail no risk.

In one of my excursions from London I was travelling by the Great Western Railway. A lady and gentleman were in the same compartment. I made the third. Shortly after leaving Paddington the lady suffered from a spark in her eye, certainly a most painful annoyance. Her fellow passenger appeared much troubled and as much bewildered. Neither seemed to know what to do, and the lady did not conceal how much she suffered. I ventured to address the gentleman, and said, as was the case, that I had frequently experienced this unfortunate accident, and that if the eye was kept moist the pain would be lessened. He barely answered me. The lady continued in pain. The train stopped for three minutes at Swindon. I took my flask, made a rush to the refreshment room, carefully washed the cup, filled it with water, and brought it to the carriage. I offered it, I believe with ordinary good manners, to the gentleman, and suggested that a handkerchief moistened with cold water should be applied to the eye. My offer was curtly declined! There was nothing more to be done. I threw the water out of the window, replaced my flask in my travelling bag, and turned to my book. I did not forget the incident during my trip, nor, indeed, have I ever done so.

I continued on my journey, and proceeded to

visit some friends in the West of England, after which I found my way to the Land's End, which I felt a great desire to see. I went to Torquay, and the sight of so many invalids in Bath chairs made me melancholy; to Dartmouth, at the entrance of the River Dart, near the birthplace of the great Sir Walter Raleigh; to Totness, to Davenport and to Penzance; thence to the treeless, bleak-looking district of the Land's End, to look at a landscape which I shall always remember.

At a little inn on the most westerly point of England I found I could get a chop and a glass of ale. Having ordered luncheon, I strolled out in the meantime to have a look at the blue water and the wide expanse of ocean. The place is certainly solitary enough, but in its way the boldness of the landscape and the never-ceasing roar of the waves elevated it from dreariness. I returned to the room of the inn and found a gentleman seated at the table. I had a perfect recollection of my experience in the railway carriage a few days previously. But it seemed to me to meet a stranger at this spot, seldom visited, gave a guarantee of a certain similarity of tastes, and that it might possibly be agreeable to both to exchange a few words. Indeed, I thought it would be perfect folly for us to remain together in silence for about half an hour as if ignorant of the presence of each other. I therefore made up my mind that, at any rate, the fault should not be mine, and that I would make bold to break the ice. We were certainly not introduced, but at all risks I would make an effort to begin by saying some ordinary words about the weather. The sky was cloudy and the air cold, but I raised my voice to a cheerful tone and said, "It is rather raw to-day, sir." The gentleman addressed took not the slightest notice of what I had said! And how ridiculous and embarrassing it did seem to me at the time to think that two rational beings should be lunching together at a little round table in the last house in England in solemn silence! I fear that not a few disagreeable thoughts passed through my mind, but I could do nothing. In due time I was ready to return to Penzance. I entered the vehicle which had brought me hither, and at no great distance away from the inn we passed the individual I had lunched with, walking by himself. I took the opportunity, when out of hearing, of asking the driver if he knew who he was. I received the reply that he was a deaf and dumb gentleman who lived in the neighbourhood!

CHAPTER IV.

ENGLAND—(Continued).

Marquis of Salisbury—Classical studies—Henley Regatta—Red Lion—London Dinner to Lord Dufferin—His Speech—Greenwich—Fisheries Exhibition—Bray—The Vicar—The Thames—Minehead—The Polynesian.

I was exceedingly glad to be joined by my daughter in London, because much depended on her arrival. We had many places to see together, and she was to accompany me on a visit to some friends in the country, who had extended to us a very warm invitation. During this visit we met all the kindness we could have even fancied, at one of those English homes, standing among old trees, with ivy-covered walls, and gardens full of roses of all colours and in the greatest perfection.

We returned to London, as I had matters to attend to at the offices of the Hudson Bay Company, the Colonial Office, and the office of the High Commissioner for Canada.

Shortly after my arrival the Marquis of Salisbury distributed the prizes at King's College, and his remarks on the occasion struck me forcibly. Owing to my connection with Queen's University, Kingston, it had become my duty, however imperfectly I might have performed it, to approach the same question: the extent to which classical studies should form the basis of education. Lord Salisbury pointed out, with all the polish which marks his utterances, that intellectual capacity is as varied as any other of God's creations; that many minds have little inclination for study: and that to devote the best years of life to the acquisition of an imperfect acquaintance with Greek and Latin was most unwise and barren of good results. Lord Salisbury proceeded to say:

"I cannot but feel, in reading this list, how singularly privileged the present generation is in the studies they are invited to pursue. In my time, and before my time, for I was just at the end of the darker period, there were only two possible lines of study—classics and mathematics. Mathematics was looked upon in many quarters with considerable jealousy and doubt. Classics was the one food tendered to all appetites and all stomachs. I do not wish to say a word in depreciation of classics. It would be as sensible to speak in depreciation of wheat and oats because wheat will not grow in the North of Scotland and oats will not grow at the equator. But people are coming gradually, if they have not come fully, to the conclusion that the intellectual capacity is as various as any other of nature's creations, and that there are as many different kinds of minds, open to as many different kinds of treatment, as there are soils on the surface of the earth; and that it is as reasonable to try to force all minds to grow classics, or to grow mathematics, or to grow history, as it would be to force all soils to grow fruit, or grass, or corn. This is an enormous gain to the present generation. For what happened in the last generation, or two generations ago, was this, that those minds which were fitted for education in classics received full development, while those minds not fitted for that treatment were stunted and turned from intellectual pursuits altogether. There is no greater privilege of the present generation than the full conception at which we have arrived of the fact that almost every intellect is, if it be properly treated, capable of high development. But whether that development be reached or not depends upon the judgment with which its capacities are nurtured and its early efforts encouraged. Now, in this list I am very glad to see that modern history and the English language and literature occupy a very distinguished position.

"I have the greatest possible respect for the educational establishments in which I was brought up, but I never look back without a feeling of some bitterness to the many hours during which I was compelled to produce the most execrable Latin verse in the world. I believe that if a commission of distinguished men were appointed to discover what is the most perfectly useless accomplishment to which the human mind can be turned a large majority would agree that versification in the dead languages was that accomplishment. On that account, I suppose, we were compelled in the last generation, whether we were fitted or not, to devote a considerable time to it, and, if it is any compensation to you for the severe examination you have to undergo, think of the agonies of unpoetical minds set to compose poetical effusions, which you are happily spared."

Lord Salisbury dwelt upon the number of examinations to which everybody in the military and civil services is subjected, and instanced one official who had passed through thirty-six examinations. In his own able way he declared his opposition to the system of cramming, by which the mere surface of knowledge is floated over with facts, cunningly grouped together, soon to be forgotten and never of true value.

Hot weather is sometimes experienced in London, but it is a different heat from that of Canada, and by no means to be compared with it in temperature. Few people dress to meet the summer in England, and in winter the sole addition is the great coat. A fur cap is unknown. The round silk hat, so much abused, holds its own, summer and winter, against all attempts to banish it. Although the days are hot, the nights are generally cool. Any extraordinarily hot weather is exceedingly oppressive to the Londoner.

It was during the warm days that I went to Henley, to join a party who had engaged to be present at the regatta. With a Canadian friend I took the train to Maidenhead, thence by the branch railway to Henley, one of the most striking landscapes in the valley of the Thames, remarkable for its many beauties. The river here is broad, and runs between undulating hills covered with foliage. We cross the old stone bridge at Henley in order to find our friends among the many carriages. No more pleasant spectacle could have been seen. It presented only the sunny and holiday side of life. It was as different from the mixed mass of human beings of all classes and conditions you meet at the Derby or the other horse races near the metropolis as can be imagined. All was order, quietude and irreproachable respectability. There were no drinking booths, no gambling, no shrieking out the "odds," none of the professional rough element in search of a "good thing." We were among the most elaborate toilets. No one but looked her best. Probably nowhere do we see more thoroughly this one phase of English life than at the Henley regatta. The scenery is English, the people are English; we have the theoretical English staidness and propriety. The amusement is English. What struck me was the absence of all excitement. This indifference appeared to me remarkable. Indeed, the only exhibition of interest was that shown by the oarsmen, who were young men in perfect condition, with muscles well trained and developed, and who bent enthusiastically to their work. I did not hear a single cheer. I never before nor since beheld such an orderly crowd, if I may apply that word to an assemblage of so many distinguished people. I noticed that those who came under my observation were generally light-haired or brown, with fair complexions. It seemed to me, judging from appearances, as if the regatta was looked upon as a very ordinary affair in itself, and that it was more an occasion for the well-dressed mass of people to meet together. There evidently was a theory that some one boat must come in first, and, as it generally happened that there was a foregone conclusion as to who the winner would be, there was nothing to call for enthusiasm. Certainly none was shown.

We did not find our friends, although we searched diligently for them on both sides of the river. After giving up the attempt reluctantly, we resolved to take luncheon at the renowned old hostelry, the "Red Lion," celebrated as the inn where Shenstone wrote his lines in praise of an inn, perhaps his only lines now generally remembered. The "Red Lion" did not belie its ancient reputation. There is always a pleasure in visiting these haunts of a former generation. There is little of modern finery and frippery about them, but you find the actual comforts of life above criticism. Nowhere can be seen a whiter cloth, brighter glass, finer bread, sweeter butter, juicier meat or a more royal tankard of English ale, whose praises Chaucer might have sung.

We took the 6.10 evening train to Maidenhead, and then walked to our friends' place. We found that they had driven to Henley, excepting those who kindly received us. The party, however, came back in good time, having heard of us through a common friend, recently an Aide-de-camp on the General's staff in Halifax. We had met him at the regatta, and asked intelligence of the party. He had succeeded where we had failed, and had found those of whom we were in search.

We returned to London. Finding we had now about a fortnight to remain, we mapped out our plans in order to see what we could do in that time. We saw all the public sights which our engagements enabled us to do. I cannot say that I was greatly impressed with the pictures of the Royal Academy. Several were good, but I did not find a large number of surpassing excellence. I was much struck by a water-colour drawing of mountain scenery, with a bridge and stream, Kirbrücher Stadden in Switzerland, by Arthur Croft. We went to the theatre, and saw Irving in "The Bells" and "Impulse" at the St. James; to a promenade concert at the Botanical Gardens, Regent's Park and to Wimbledon. Through the courtesy of Col. Otter, in command of the Canadian camp, we were invited to an at home given by him, where we saw a great many Canadian friends. We also met some distinguished military people. We were gratified to learn all about the success of our marksmen. The rain, however, was exceptionally heavy during the whole day, and most unfortunately there was no going beyond the shelter of the canvas tents.

One event of no ordinary importance which we witnessed was the banquet to Lord Dufferin at the Empire Club. Lord Bury presided. Sir Charles Tupper and the Honourable Alexander Mackenzie both spoke very effectively. It struck me that in each case their speeches were admirable. Neither of them occupied more than ten or fifteen minutes, and what they said had the impress of careful consideration and finish, for it was dignified, concise and appropriate. I have no recollection of having heard either of those well known public men speak to better advantage, and it was a matter of great regret to all of us that their speeches were not reported. The dining room of the club is not large; it can hold no more than sixty at most, so the number who could attend was limited, much to the disappointment of many. We were all of us glad to see Lord Dufferin. He was quite unchanged. He had the same high-bred charm of manner, and that polished courtesy which becomes him so well and is never out of place. We did not sit down to dinner until 8.30, so it was late when we separated. There was something in Lord Dufferin's speech which made it more than a mere after-dinner address, something so striking, so statesmanlike, that I deem it my duty to include it in these chapters:

My Lords and Gentlemen,—If there is one thing more embarrassing than another to a person on commencing a public speech it is to find his oratorical ground suddenly cut away from beneath his feet. I had fully intended to claim your indulgence on the grounds so eloquently referred to by my noble friend, and I can assure you that that indulgence is as much needed as I have ever experienced it, for, however easy it may be to speak with an empty head, it is very difficult to do so with a full heart. In rising, however, to return my warmest thanks for the kind manner in which you have drunk my health, I cannot help asking myself with some anxiety what title I possess to the good-will of my entertainers. Your chairman has been pleased to refer in very flattering terms to my public services: but I fear that the reason of your cordiality is further to seek than anything which can be found in the indulgent observation, I hope, on the present occasion, of the members of the Empire Club, and I think I am not wrong in conjecturing that I am indebted for the signal honour which you have conferred upon me, not so much to my individual merits, as to the fact that for the last twelve years of my life I have been unremittingly occupied in promoting and maintaining the Imperial, as distinguished from the domestic, interests of our common country. In Canada, at St. Petersburg, at Constantinople and in Egypt, I can conscientiously say that home politics, with all their irritating associations, have faded from my view, and that my one thought by day and night has been to safeguard, to protect and to extend the honour, the influence and the commerce of England with the foreign Governments, or else to draw still more closely together those ties of affectionate regard by which she is united to one of her most powerful, most loyal and most devoted colonies. Well, then, gentlemen, under these circumstances, I think I may be pardoned if I have come to look at

England, this sceptred isle, this earth of majesty, this other Eden-beaming paradise, this happy breed of men, this precious stone set in a silver sea; not as she displays herself in the recriminatory warfare of parliamentary strife, or in the polemical declamation of the platform, but in an aspect softened by distance and regarded as the happy home of a noble and united people, whom it is an honour to serve, and for whose sake it would be a privilege to make the greatest sacrifices. I do not say this in any spirit of selfish and vulgar "Jingoism," although I must admit that by their profession ambassadors and colonial governors are bound to be a little "jingo." I have come to regard England in the same light as she is regarded by those great communities who are carrying her laws, her liberties, her constitutional institutions and her language into every portion of the world, many of whose most distinguished representatives are present here to-night, and to whom it is the especial function of this club to extend the right hand of brotherhood and affection. Gentlemen, I am well aware that many of our most influential thinkers are almost disposed to stand aghast at the accumulative responsibility and increasing calls upon our resources, and the ever-widening vulnerability entailed by England's imperial position. Certainly, the outlook counsels both prudence and, above all, preparation. After all, the life of nations and individuals in many respects resemble each other, and each of us is aware that his daily burden of care, anxiety and responsibility gathers weight and strength in proportion to the expansion of his faculties, the accumulation of his wealth, the energy of his endeavours and the extension of his influence. Why, gentlemen, even the children that people our homes are so many hostages given to fortune; and the wives of our bosoms—I say this beneath my breath—are very apt each of them to open a startling chapter of accidents; but what man of spirit has ever turned his back upon the opportunity, or refused to enter upon the tender obligations of a love-lit fireside for fear of increasing his responsibilities, entailed by a fuller, ampler and more perfect existence? But, my lords and gentlemen, even did she desire it, I believe that the time is too late for England to seek to disinherit herself of that noble destiny with which I firmly believe she has been endowed. The same hidden hand which planted the tree of constitutional liberty within her borders, and thus called upon her to become the mother of parliaments, has sent forth her children to possess and fructify the waste places of the earth. How a desert in every direction has been turned into a paradise of plenty those who are present can best tell. I believe that, great as have been the changes which have already occurred, our children are destined to see even still more glorious accomplishments. One of the greatest statisticians of modern times, a man of singularly sober judgment, has calculated that ere the next century has reached its close the English speaking population of the globe will have already exceeded one hundred millions of human beings. Of these, in all probability, forty millions will be found in Canada alone, and an equal proportion along the coast of Africa and in our great Australian possessions. If these great communities are united in a common bond of interest, if they are co-ordinated and impelled by a common interest, what an enormous influence, as compared with that of any other nationality, whether for good or evil, whether considered from a moral or material point of view, are they destined to exercise! But, gentlemen, that they will remain Englishmen who can doubt! The chops and changes on an accelerated momentum of human progress forbid all accurate prediction. These enormous forces, operating over such a large space, defy all pre-science and human wisdom to direct the current of events; but one thing, at all events, is certain, and that is that these great communities will be deeply impressed by English ideas, by English literature, by English institutions and by English habits of thought. That this shall long continue to be the case is, I am sure, the earnest wish of those whom I am addressing. It is their desire that our statesmen should so conduct the relations of this country with their colonial dependencies as to cherish and maintain those affectionate ties by which they are so remarkably and distinctly bound to the Mother Country. One thing, at all events, is certain: that the people of England will never again allow their Government to repeat the error which resulted in the separation of the United States. Whatever may be our present relations with the great transatlantic republic, it is certain that, had it not been for the violent disruption that occurred, those relations would now have been even more mutually advantageous. The catastrophe, unhappily, was brought about by the Ministry of the day being incapable of appreciating and understanding the force and direction of colonial sentiment. Now, my lords and gentlemen, I believe that statesmen can make no greater mistake than not accurately to comprehend the enormous part which sentiment plays in human affairs. By far the greater number of the wars which have devastated the globe have been produced and generated by outraged sentiment rather than by the pursuit of material advantages. Even commerce itself, the most unsentimental and matter-of-fact of interests, is wont for long periods of time to follow in the track of custom, habit and sentiment. This was a fact which for a long time the English people failed to comprehend. They failed to comprehend the desire which the colonies had to have their kinship recognised. Happily, however, the increased facilities of communication and the necessities and exigencies of trade have changed all this, and I believe that now there is not a man in England who does not understand, and to whose imagination it has not been forcibly brought home, that beyond the circuit of the narrow seas which confine this island are vast territories, inhabited by powerful communities who are actuated by ideas similar to our own, who are proud to own allegiance to Queen Victoria, whose material resources are greater than those possessed by his own country, and whose ultimate power may, perhaps, exceed the power of Great Britain. And yet these great communities of noble, high-spirited, industrious Englishmen, if only they are properly dealt with, and if only their feelings and just exigencies are duly considered, will never have a higher ambition than to be allowed to continue as co-heirs with England in her illustrious career, associated with her in her gigantic empire, and sharers in her fortunes, whether they be for good or evil, until the end of time. Gentlemen, such are the sentiments and opinions which I believe this club has been founded to encourage and propagate, and I felt that in rising to return thanks for the great and signal honour which you have done me, and for which really I cannot find words sufficient to thank you, I could not do so in a more acceptable manner than by telling you with what enthusiasm and with what sincerity of conviction I myself subscribe to these sentiments."

One of my pleasantest recollections of London dates about ten days before my departure for Canada. When the heat was tempered by a fresh breeze, a party of us met by appointment on one of the wharves near London Bridge. We owed the invitation to a Canadian who, like myself, was from the north of the Tweed. He introduced me to our host, one of his oldest friends, a friendship which had lasted from boyhood. Our host had engaged a steamer to take his guests down the river to the large establishment of which he is the leading mind. I believe I am safe in saying that thousands of people are employed in these works. We went through the various departments, and to do so took some hours. Some of the ladies of the party thought they had accomplished miles of pedestrianism. They were greatly interested in what they saw, and before they left were delighted, for our host, who has a heart as large as the business he controls, presented from the factory to each of our party a substantial mark of his regard.

We returned to Greenwich, the very name is redolent of fish dinners and whitebait to the Londoner, and twenty-one of us sat down at the great round table in the bow window of the "Ship Hotel." We were not in a mood to criticise our entertainment. Had we been so, we could only have found something additional to praise. We had good appetites, were in the best of humour, and felt prepared to do justice to the profusion of dainties set before us. Our host had visited Canada nearly half a century ago, and he spoke of his experience in what is now a highly cultivated district, but was then very thinly populated. His youthful days came back to him, and he referred to a pair of bright eyes he encountered at a picnic on the shores of Lake Simcoe which very nearly made him a Canadian. I do not know what prominent position amongst us he might not now have occupied had the possessor of the bright eyes affirmed her conquest.

We are not, in Canada, a people particularly demonstrative in our own land, but away from home, when those of us who are bound by friendly associations come side by side, no meeting can be more gay or pleasant. It was especially so on this occasion, and our host had the satisfaction of seeing all his good cheer thoroughly appreciated by his guests. It was ten o'clock before we separated, and found our way back to London.

The Fisheries Exhibition was then the event of the season. In London or Paris there is always something going on which everybody feels bound to see, and not to have the privilege or opportunity of seeing places you, in an undefined way, in such a secondary position that you appear to be excluded. The question is not always if the spectacle or exhibition, or other notoriety of the moment, will repay the time and attention given to witnessing it. The leading consideration is that it is something to be seen, and it is never of any use running counter to the tide of the community in which you live and move. Very often a good deal of trouble is taken, and frequently no small amount of money expended, to pass through some ordeal of this character, which brings no addition to our information and but little satisfaction.

The Fisheries Exhibition, however, was not of this character. Many must have been surprised at the part played in it by Canada, and at the richness and variety of her exhibits. Scarcely anything could have been designed to set forth better to the London world the vastness of the resources of the Dominion than this exhibition, and to bring before the English people an idea of the extensive fishing grounds it possesses. Many would then learn for the first time that our fisheries are not confined to the St. Lawrence and the lakes. Canada has an immense extent of sea coast in the Maritime Provinces frequented by shoals of fish, for which these waters have been famous since the first discovery of America. The almost virgin waters of British Columbia swarm with fish of the finest description, and Canada possesses the whole of Hudson Bay and the northern coast of America in which to develop her enterprise and industry. What country in the world can boast of such great and prolific fish fields on three oceans, all open to enterprise.

One of the agreeable associations connected with

the exhibition was the *fête* in aid of the English Church at Berlin, and in commemoration of the silver wedding of the Crown Princess of Germany, Her Majesty's eldest daughter. It seemed to me that there was a constant rush of visitors till midnight. The spectacle was a brilliant one, as much on account of the great crowd of people who were there as from the light and glitter of the scene itself. The newspapers mentioned the number present as 6,000, and they truly described it as a fairy scene. The whole place was bright with many-coloured lamps, Chinese lanterns and electric lights. One of the striking features was the tea party of the Chinese court, where a veritable Chinese grandee presided with her daughter. The Marchioness Tseng seemed to me a type of liberality. It could scarcely be political exigency which led this lady and her family to intervene in aid of an Anglican Church in the heart of a Lutheran population. The Duke and Duchess of Albany assisted her. Fans were sold here, the recommendation of which was that they had been specially painted by the Chinese Minister himself, and embroidered and worked by the Marchioness and her daughter. It struck me that if this display be typical of the industry of the Chinese family our western civilization is much behind in the path of productive labour. There were to be seen also an English refreshment room, and an "American" bar, under the direction of Mrs.

Lowell, attended by all the United States beauties in London, whose personal charms, supplemented by New York taste in dress, not a little influenced the price of what was served. The Countess of Dufferin was there. She seemed quite in her element, doing her best to promote the general gaiety and brightness of the scene. A distinguished naval officer, whose name has penetrated wherever the English language is spoken, Lord Charles Beresford, assisted Lady Dufferin. It was their duty to preside over the fish pond, where the small charge of five shillings was paid for the use of the rod and line. There seemed to be an unlimited supply of fish. The successful anglers generally brought up something which excited shouts of laughter. One fisherman would land a nightcap, another a toy of some sort, and so on. The Prince and Princess of Wales came about eleven o'clock, which added in no little degree to the excitement of the scene. What must strike strangers on British soil is the admirable order which prevails during an exhibition of this kind. It is seldom that any unpleasantness occurs We did not remain until the close, but it was late before we reached home.

It was my good fortune to spend some pleasant days with my friends at their charming and hospitable house within four miles of Windsor. A few hours in the country is always a congenial change even to the inveterate London-loving resident of the capital. It was equally so with myself. I awoke at my friend's pleasant home one bright Sunday morning. Some of the family started for the old church at Bray, and invited me to accompany them. We pass along a winding road, between hedges of hawthorn, with here and there fine old trees, some of them with trunks as much as five and six feet in diameter, relics of Windsor Forest. The country is somewhat flat, but it is rendered peculiarly attractive by its fertility and the richness of the foliage. Windsor Castle stands out boldly in the landscape, and to-day the Imperial Standard on the Round Tower shows that Her Majesty is at her ancient home.

We reached the cross roads, with a finger post directing us to Windsor and to Bray. Following the road to the latter, we came upon "Jesus Hospital," founded, we read on the inscription over the gateway in quaint old English characters, by William Goddard in 1627. His statue over the entrance looks upon a plot of garden flowers. On the inscription we further learn that "he hath provided for forty poor people forever." Then we are told that there is no admission for vagrants, or unlicensed hawkers, or dogs.

We attended service at Bray Church, an old edifice dating, in some parts, from the beginning or middle of the fifteenth century. The square tower tells a story of a later date.

Who has not heard of Simon Aleyn, the Vicar?

His memory is still as fresh as it was three centuries back, when he died. He lived from the time of Henry VIII. to that of Elizabeth, and was an Anglican, a Presbyterian or a Papist as was expedient. It does no harm to repeat old Fuller's words, although they appear in the guide book: "He had seen some martyrs burned at Windsor, and found this too hot for his tender temper. This Vicar being taxed by one with being a turncoat and an inconsistent changeling. 'Not so,' said he, 'for I have always kept my principle, which is to live and die Vicar of Bray." After the service we walked through the churchyard, and, Scotchman-like, I looked among the tombstones to see if there were any Dugalds, Donalds or Macs. There were none. I never before felt so much being in the heart of England. There was not a record of one Scotchman having died here, and I thought they had penetrated everywhere. I can well recollect making a trip to the west coast a few years back. It was during the period when the Honourable A. Mackenzie was Premier of Canada. I was then an officer of the Canadian Government on leave. I visited Truro, the most southern city in England, and on entering the principal business street the first sign I saw was that of Alexander Mackenzie & Co. I certainly thought then I was a long way from Scotland, and still further from all Canadian associations. I have been in many strange and remote corners of the globe on both continents, but I was never before in a place where there was no trace of the ubiquitous, enterprising and energetic north-countryman. And yet it was a Vicar of the church which I had just attended who curtly refused to pay a bill of James the First at Maidenhead. That monarch, on a certain occasion, having outrode his hunting escort, and being hungry, begged leave to join the Vicar and curate at dinner. His Majesty seems to have been in excellent humour. He told so many stories that the two listeners, who did not know their Royal guest, laughed as they seldom did. The bill came, the King had no money, and asked his companions to pay for him. The Vicar declined, it would seem, somewhat irately. The curate was more kindly disposed, and paid the bill. In the meantime the retinue arrived, and with it recognition of the Royal person. The Vicar threw himself on his knees, and asked pardon for his harshness. James told him he should not disturb him in his vicarage, but that he should always remain Vicar of Bray. The genial curate he would make a Canon of Windsor, so that he would look down on both him and his vicarage.

On returning from the church we strolled by the river, which, from Oxford to London, is renowned as boating water, and we saw many skiffs and pleasure boats upon it. It is here that Monkey Island is situated, so often visited from Windsor and Eton. The houses in the neighbourhood are all suggestive of comfort; they are surrounded with abundance of flowers, and have all a look of cleanliness, and an aspect both cheerful and inviting

We return home by another route. Our walk is a good mile and a half, in the course of which we are caught in the rain and take shelter in a cottage. Some one remembers that it is St. Swithin's Day, the 15th of July, and according to the tradition, if it rains on that day, it will rain for forty days. We revert in thought to those ancient historians, the most sceptical of whom, while they very summarily got rid of the portents and miracles of their own time, hesitated to reject the traditions of their ancestors. However there is a break in the clouds and we reach the house.

Even with the dread of the realization of the prophecy, we take an afternoon walk and return at five, just in time to escape another St. Swithin shower. In the evening we go again to church. I experience that which is not always the case in the Anglican service. The lessons are remarkably well read, the words properly and distinctly pronounced, the sentences not dropped in tone at the end and run into one another, and above all with an entire absence of affectation. I learn that the reader is Mr. Wallace, who has lately taken high honours at Oxford.

The weather at this time turned exceedingly cold, and the Londoner may recollect this exceptional wave of low temperature. The newspapers declared that the thermometer fell to a degree lower than it read on Christmas day. I never heard any explanation of this abnormal depression in July, but last year was marked by remarkable phenomena. The terrible earthquakes in the south of Europe and in the Indian Ocean betokened the activity of extraordinary forces. We are, indeed, fortunate in our experience throughout the British Empire that hitherto no portion of it has suffered by such terrible convulsions, and that the extent of them is limited to a fall of the temperature or an excess of rainfall.

I again receive a telegram to know when I will leave for Canada and proceed to British Columbia. I had already arranged to leave London by the 20th, but I felt that my plans must be altered, and that I would be obliged to give up the idea of spending a week in Scotland.

Previous to starting for Liverpool I had arranged to visit some friends in Somersetshire. The route is by the Great Western Railway and the branch line to Taunton. As I passed from Bristol to the latter place the appearance of the country reminded me of the reclaimed marsh land at the head of the Bay of Fundy; and the turbid water of the Bristol Channel was very much the same in colour as that of the bay. The country is admirably adapted for grazing, and large herds of beautiful cattle; Herefords, Devons, and Shorthorns were to be seen along the route.

We reached our destination at Minehead, and here our friends, who were originally from Nova Scotia, gave us that warm welcome which we everywhere received in England. Not the least of the pleasant associations connected with this visit was the charming scenery from the hills behind the town, which command a view of the Bristol Channel east of Ilfracombe and the distant mountains of South Wales. The foliage of the west of England is always particularly striking to anyone from Canada. Trees and plants which, with us, can only be raised under glass, are found in luxurious abundance. There is a profusion of walnut, myrtle, wistaria, laurestina, bay, ivy, and roses, which give a rich variety to the flora of the parks and gardens, leaving nothing to be desired. The drives are unrivalled: often through narrow lanes with high hedgerows blooming with flowers such as, at least, I have never seen out of England. One of our drives took us to Exmoor, the only district of England, as I was informed, where stag-hunting is still enjoyed yearly. At Exmoor I gathered a bunch of heather which, on the higher levels, has an extensive growth. On Sunday there was a christening at the church, in which we were all interested, and through which one of the names born by the humble writer of these pages may be remembered a few years after his own race is run. There was an old church in the neighbourhood which we visited, as a north country man would say, "in the gloaming." There was, however, light enough to see in the dusk a marble statue of Queen Anne near the altar, which might easily pass for the Virgin. There is a chained Bible on the stand as in the first days when the people were called to hear it read. I could not say what the date of the Bible was; whether one of Tyndall's or Archbishop Cranmer's, or one more modern. The pews were separated from each other by high divisions, five or six feet in height, so that those who desired to pray unseen could do so. Certainly they were not favourable to the display of any finish in dress worn by their occupants, and which now makes such a marked feature in what are called, I borrow the phrase, fashionable churches.

On Monday we had to leave, and it is often hard to say good-bye under such circumstances. Is it not one of the hardships of life that we have to undergo these separations? But often our pleasantest memories are crowded into the narrow space of such brief visits. Our destination is Liverpool; we leave by the morning train at eight o'clock, and reach Bristol to take the connecting train to Liverpool. We pass by the world-renowned Stratford-on-Avon, by Burton, for which place the unrivalled pale ale of Bass and Allsopp have obtained an almost equally extended reputation. As we crossed the silvery Trent I wondered if any calculation had ever been made as to the quantity of its water which had found itself transferred to every clime in the shape of bitter beer. We soon leave Birmingham behind and pass through the hills and dales of Derbyshire; a district celebrated for its loveliness and beauty. The panorama which is seen even from the carriage window is worth the trip. It is, indeed, something to say you have looked upon it. At half-past six we are again in Liveepool. Tuesday and Wednesday we enjoy the society of some old friends, and on Thursday we embark on the Allan line steamer "Polynesian," and start on our way over the western waters to Canada.

CHAPTER V.

ENGLAND TO CANADA.

The Ocean Voyage—Its Comfort—Moville—Mail Coach Road of Old Days—Impressive Service on Deck—Comfort on the Vessel—Rimouski—Halifax.

We are off this Thursday, 26th July, and underway at three p.m. As is usually the case we have a pleasant run down the Mersey to the Irish Sea. With few exceptions the passengers are all strangers, one to the other, and we remain on deck, no few of us speculating as to "who is who?" We dine at four the first day. There is a printed list of passengers on the plate of each as we take our seats at the tables which have been assigned to us, perhaps in some cases by a little pre-arrangement with the purser. In the evening we pass close to the Isle of Man with its bold headlands and picturesque coast line, but few of us appear to be inclined to stay up late. There is always an exictement, and consequent rebound, in leaving the land where we have passed some weeks, whatever the associations we have separated from, and whatever future may lie before us. The first night at sea is generally quiet; it is true you have always your inveterate whist player who wants to get up a rubber as if it was the one duty of life not to lose an opportunity of gaining the odd trick. And you have the perpetual smoker who looks upon leisure as specially designed for the enjoyment of the pipe or cigar, as if the sole charm of life lay in tobacco!

The whole conditions of an ocean voyage have, of late years, been much changed. A voyage in the modern steamship is more like a yacht trip. Indeed, excepting the yachts of men of colossal fortunes, the yacht suffers by comparison with the steamship. In the latter you have a bed clean and comfortable, with all the auxiliaries of the toilet. On nearly all the best ships you have hot and cold baths. Some vessels carry a professional barber; and I have known a chiropodist to be in attendance. If you want more bedding, or hot water, or any other *et cetera* you ask for and obtain it. You have a cabin as large and comfortable as it is possible to have under the circumstances, and if you chose to pay for it you can have it to yourself, and thus obtain all the privacy of an anchorite. Your state-room, as it is called, is cleaned daily, and it is open to you whenever you see fit to enter; you have a large saloon in which you take your meals, sit, read, or write, or play chess or whist; where ladies can group themselves in order to carry on their embroidery, or to undertake less pretentious, if more useful work. Generally there is a separate saloon, for ladies, in an airy part of the ship, where, if they are not free from nausea or depression, they can retire and be as private as they desire. You have the best of food, thoroughly and carefully cooked, with the most obsequious of attendants whom you are generally expected to reward at the end of the voyage, and you feel yourself second to no one in the world you are in. There are no troublesome experiences on points of etiquette or ceremony; you never receive a lesson of your insignificance, although if it be particularly sought for, it can be obtained. You have fresh air, bright skies, and the ocean that

> "Glorious mirror, where the Almighty's form
> Glasses itself in tempests."

is your constant monitor. All you seem to want is a sea-stomach and firmness on your feet. As a rule, a few days, often a few hours, will give you both. To those who are not sea-sick what life is more pleasant? You have all sorts of people on board, and the sea seems to act as a sort of leveller of individualism. Although there are men and women who are known to have spoken to nobody, and who have walked up and down during almost the whole voyage in perfect solitude, wrapped up in themselves, as if no contact with others were permissible. On seeing these people I have thought of Æsop's mountain in labour, and pitied the poor little mouse brought into the world with such effort.

There are storms at sea, naturally, but you have a crew in the highest state of discipline; you have a ship as strong as money and iron can make it; you have an engine of wondrous power and a marvel of perfection in machinery. Competition, energy, and enterprise, have so multiplied the means of travel that you may pass from one continent to the other with comfort, and for not much more money than the sum you pay for the same period of time at one of the high class hotels in London or New York. You have no extras to pay for in the steamship except wine or beer.

According to your feeling you can give a *douceur* to the steward who attends to your room, and if need be nurses you in sickness, and to the steward who waits upon you at table. The only items you have to pay extra for, as before stated, are beer and wine, if you choose to order either. You are not remarkable either in avoiding or using them, for never was there so unrestrained a matter of taste as in this respect at the saloon table.

It is Friday: we have passed the first night at sea, and we take an early tepid salt water bath. We are now steaming up Lough Foyle to Moville, where the mails containing letters posted in London on Thursday night, are put on board. Thus the clear business day of Thursday is gained by English correspondents. The weather is delightful. Some of the party go on shore as the steamer is seven hours in advance of the train with the mails.

There is nothing specially attractive on this part of the Irish coast it is true, still it is always pleasant to touch *terra firma* as a change, and it is always a break during the hours that we are lying at anchor. We remain at Moville until three o'clock, when the "Polynesian" starts. The weather continues bright and clear, the water smooth, all is pleasant on deck, where all the passengers are present. The only spectacle to which I can compare the scene is a garden party where everybody has but one thing to do, and that is to amuse and be amused, and look as charming as each one can. We all know that the best way to succeed in being genial and good-humoured is to endeavour to be so, and where can a day be better enjoyed than at sea? I am aware that tradition is against me. The poor sufferer from sea-sickness may remember this trying time, as the most dreary of his life, and this form of sickness is to many, even in a minor way, a most serious ordeal, but, as a rule, it soon passes away. I believe the best cure for those afflicted with this malady is to remain quiet, to eat sparingly, and avoid everything greasy; if there be nausea to take only toast and tea, and make the effort to get on deck Looking at the severities of the affliction in their strongest light they are certainly by no means what they were in the old days of sailing vessels of small tonnage, and with accommodation proportioned to the craft. There were then many discomforts and privations now happily unknown. Voyages were, at that period, counted by weeks instead of days, and to one unaccustomed to the sea the Atlantic trip was no little of a penalty. It is very much owing to the reminiscences of this period that the dread of the sea now prevails. The discomforts of land travelling in the past have now ceased to be even thought of. The bad roads, the ricketty coaches, the foul air in the inside, and the suffering from cold and wet on the outside of the coach, have all passed out of mind. Even the modern novel does not dwell upon them. All that is recorded is the cheery appearance of the old-time coach on a fine evening, driving through a town, with the guard arrayed in bright uniform, with his bouquet in his buttonhole, the cynosure of all the servant girls; while the coachman handled the ribbons to the admiration and envy of all the fast young gentlemen of the place. In its way there was bitter suffering in bad weather in the course of such a journey, but the ease and comfort of railway travelling have destroyed all remembrance of it. What greater contrast can there be between the torture felt in the inside of an old stage coach going from Liverpool to London and the luxury of sitting in a Pullman car travelling the same distance? What more striking difference can there be between railway life as it is now in the journey from Brighton to London, accomplished in an hour, and the same journey performed by the old stage coaches? Railway travelling has so insensibly crept into our system that the present generation does not think of the privations of half a century ago.

One of the causes doubtless of the continuance of the prejudice against ocean navigation is the poor and inefficient steamers still in use for crossing the English Channel. There is frequently bad weather, indeed, if all that is said be true, it seldom would appear to be otherwise, and an immense percentage of those now passing to the continent suffer the tortures of sea-sickness, much as was experienced on this route half a century back. One of the channel steamers, on a fine day when the run is made in calm weather, is a spectacle. Everybody is good-tempered and in the best of humour; even the most high-minded somewhat unbend and cease to be ungenial. They appear to feel that a great penalty has been escaped, that they have passed unscathed through what is generally considered a terrible ordeal.

To such as these, whose experience has been gained in this school of travel, the escape from sea-sickness may appear impossible. They will be exceedingly surprised to learn that many make an ordinary voyage across the Atlantic without any sea-sickness at all. Some may, it is true, have a slight qualm; but half a day's retirement and careful diet, are all that is necessary to bring back health, good spirits, and vivacity, and possibly a wonderful increase of appetite.

Such was the experience on Friday afternoon; all were pleasant and agreeable, and many, as they retired that night to rest, on the Atlantic Ocean, felt that the voyage was a delightful reality and that there was every prospect of their proving excellent sailors.

Saturday is equally pleasant, happy, and bright. The portholes are opened, and, as usual, many begin the day with a salt water bath. We pass the "Oregon," which left Liverpool at the same time we did, but our visit to Moville enabled her to sail onward as we entered Lough Foyle. A light breeze springs up, and the swell of the ocean gives movement to the vessel which causes more or less seasickness and depression. Many are walking about with comfort and ease, and a few are miserable. There is dinner at 6.30; one of those sumptuous, well-served dinners which no wise man will face every day of his life, even if he can manage to obtain it. There are one hundred and fourteen saloon passengers and five children on board, but only seventeen are at table, one of them a lady, Mrs. D., of Toronto. A great contrast to yesterday's experience. The deck is wet and uncomfortable, the rain is falling and there is a heavy fog. The planks are slippery, and with the unsteady motion of the ship, there is little to tempt one to abandon the shelter of the warm, cheery, well-lighted saloon.

On Saturday night there was a head wind, but on Sunday morning the ship was somewhat quieter, the decks were dry, and motion was practicable. There are on board two clergymen of the Anglican Church, so service is held in the saloon. We have also with us Bishop Rogers, the Roman Catholic Bishop of Chatham, New Brunswick, who holds a service in another part of the ship. We pass through a school of whales, some six of which rise above the water not far from the vessel. The majority of the ladies make an effort to appear on deck, and either sit on chairs or recline on couches extemporised with cushions, wraps and shawls; some few even attempt a promenade. Well does Shakespeare tell us that "Courage mounteth with occasion." There are those who shake their heads at the prediction of their immediate recovery. Some few achieve wonders and attend dinner. The evening turns out fine, the air is warm, so the Rev. H. Huleatt conducts a service on deck. He is an old army chaplain, and over his white surplice wears three medals for service in the Crimea, China and Abyssinia. I was bred in, and adhere to, the Presbyterian Church, in which the forms of the Anglican Church are certainly not taught, and by many of us not favourably regarded. The persecution of the Covenanters in the seventeenth century, having in view the establishment of Anglicanism, produced results which its projectors did not conceive possible. It cannot be said that persecution always fails in its purpose, for history furnishes painful examples to the contrary. But there are few instances of its failure more remarkable than this attempt to force on the people of Scotland a form of worship which they did not favour. With certain classes and individuals the feelings which the attempt left have long since died out, but the memory of them remained for many a year. I am not one who has been trained to regard the ceremonies of the English Church with marked reverence, especially when they turn towards the "high" development. With men like myself I venture the remark that the Church of England is never so strong as when she adheres to her simplest teaching. Her ritual is never so impressive as when stripped of strained formality; it is then that, in spite of ourselves, we must feel and admire all the strength and beauty of her liturgy. It is not easy to comprehend how thoughtful men can advocate the introduction of extreme ceremonies, which even many Anglicans themselves regard as theatrical accessories. It has been my good fortune to attend the English Church service in some of the noblest cathedrals in England; at Westminster, Canterbury, Chester and St. Paul's, unrivalled in its classic excellence: and I have at such times felt how decorous and impressive it can be made when the ritual is not encumbered with the observances which a strong party in the Church of England regard as unseemly, and which, with my feelings, I hold to be unnecessary. With this limitation this form of prayer, in my humble view, appears peculiarly adapted to the English mind and character. For more gorgeous ceremonial, I have witnessed the Mass at St. Peter's, one of the grandest temples erected by man for the worship of his Maker. Never in any church was I ever present at a scene and service more memorable than the evening prayer on the deck of the "Polynesian." The military chaplain, in his white surplice, appeared with the three medals on his breast and his Bible and prayerbook in his hand, walking slowly once or twice up and down the deck, by way, as he afterwards explained, "of ringing the bell." In this manner the passengers generally were collected into picturesque groups. He took an elevated position; his white dress and his long white hair moving in the breeze, formed a striking contrast to the dark funnel, masts and spars in the background. He repeated the simple words of the Anglican liturgy in a clear, natural voice. He spoke briefly and forcibly, as possibly he had often done on the eve of battle. He conducted the singing of some of those touching hymns common to all branches of the Christian Church. The congregation, consisting of all sects and beliefs, was unaffectedly serious and devout, and many voices joined in earnest praise.

We occupied the centre of the ocean, that marked emblem of the Everlasting. Above and around us the blue vault of heaven was frescoed with fleecy clouds, radiant with the rich hues of the evening sun. On every side the rolling waters added solemnity to the scene. There were few who did not feel the spectacle itself to be a sermon not soon to be forgotten. It spoke to us all against our littleness and selfishness. As we looked beyond the bulwarks of our ship, a point in God's endless creation, we could feel how imperfect was the teaching of sects and creeds, in view of the higher and nobler views we should aspire to: the faith which widens our sympathies as the warmth of summer expands the buds of our northern forests.

Monday again is a beautiful morning, and we are all on deck enjoying the fresh, healthful breeze and the sun, whose bright beams glitter on the face of the rolling waters, the blue sky above us with its passing clouds, and the sea in ceaseless motion all around us, wave chasing wave, chequered with varying light and shade. We are all so full of life that the afternoon is given over to games which, on shore, many of us might think somewhat undignified. At dinner the table is full. And what appetites most of us have! Some achieve perfect wonders as trencher men and women, and often in memory many of the passengers will revert to their powers in this respect. Wholly undisturbed by fears of dyspepsia, they ate with the best of appetites. The evening passed pleasantly with most of us in the saloon, which presented a scene of quiet comfort and amusement. The next morning is also enjoyable. We find we are now half way across, and we talk of making the Straits of Belleisle by Thursday. Our run at noon is 332 knots. There is a little fog, and the air is somewhat cold. The theory is expressed that we are near Greenland; that a cold blast may come from across its "icy mountains," told of by Bishop Heber in the hymn we have heard so often.

All the passengers, without exception, are now accustomed to the motion of the ship. Every one appears at home. The forenoon passes quickly, and we can hardly believe that the dinner hour is near. When we all sit down at the long and well-provided tables one can hardly conceive that he is not on shore at some famed hotel in Montreal or Toronto. I am aware that I run the risk of being charged with exaggeration, but I express the result of my convictions. I am sure that my remarks will be borne out by all who have made several trips across the Atlantic. There are stormy and particularly unpleasant voyages, I know. Such I have myself experienced, but they are generally in winter; in summer they are the exception.

The evening passes in the usual pleasant way, and we all separate reluctantly when bed-time comes.

We have again another fine day, and the forenoon is marked by sunshine. During the night we passed the steamer "Parisian," homeward bound. At noon we learn the run is 332 miles, the same as yesterday, and our chart shows us that we are due at the Straits of Belleisle at midnight. During the afternoon, at intervals, fog arises and disappears to return again, and when the fog is on the water we prudently go at half speed. We pass some icebergs, and they seem to have affected the temperature, for the air is cold. The passengers are in high spirits. The prospect of seeing land gives an impetus to the general hilarity. We expect to enter the northern passage to the St. Lawrence before morning. The trip so far has been most agreeable. The time has passed pleasantly. The group to which I was more particularly attached was always full of life and animation. One gentleman, who had retired from the army, and was going out to Canada on a sporting tour, proved to be an excellent artist, and made many amusing sketches. To another member of our group we owe particular acknowledgments for the life he inspired around him, and, if he cheered us by his unfailing good temper and charm of manner, we owe also no little to his brilliant and ready wit.

The evening was spent in asking riddles and playing card tricks. One effort led to another. Some of them were worth perpetuating. Indeed, a very interesting volume of a moderate size could be written descriptive of our trip, which would be read with no small amount of pleasure, and I have no doubt would lead to the removal of many prejudices regarding sea voyages.

We are now in the straits of Belleisle, having passed the light at five a.m. During the forenoon the weather is a little foggy, so we go at half speed. In the afternoon the fog clears away to be replaced by pleasant sunshine. There is to be an amateur concert this evening in aid of the funds of the Sailor's Orphanage at Liverpool. Those who are directors in this matter are particularly earnest. In the meanwhile some of us write letters to post at Rimouski. I take it into my head to count how many trips I have made across the Atlantic Ocean since I left Glasgow in April, 1845. I have crossed in every kind of vessel, from a sailing ship up to the "Great Eastern," and this present voyage I find to be my nineteenth, so I think I can speak with some confidence of what life on an ocean steamship truly is. My shortest passage was by the "Alaska," in October, 1882, from Sandy Hook, New York, to Liverpool, in seven days and five hours, but on this occasion we were detained inside the bar in the harbour of New York for two days, owing to fog. My longest voyage was by the ship "Brilliant," it occupied nearly six weeks.

The concert was, as usual, a success, at least everybody was pleased. Thirteen pounds sterling were collected. Those who ventured on supper partook of all the usual delicacies in vogue on these occasions, and the disciple of the pipe and cigar indulged himself for some time on deck. By half-past eleven the last of us had turned in.

It was wet the following day; we were steaming up the St. Lawrence as we took breakfast. Those who were to leave at Rimouski, of whom I was one, point out that it is the last time we may take this meal together, for we may arrive at Rimouski by night. In the afternoon we have fog, showers, and fine weather alternately. We overtake the "Hanoverian." She had passed us during the five hours we had lost in the fog. Night comes on, and at ten o'clock we run into a dense fog. Prudence dictates that we advance "dead slow," so I throw myself on my bed without undressing, to catch some little sleep in the interval before we are met by the Rimouski tender.

We are called at three o'clock on Saturday morning; we take a cup of coffee in the saloon, and I receive a batch of letters from my family and other correspondents. We enter the tender and arrive at the long Rimouski wharf just as dawn is breaking. My daughter and myself go southward to Halifax with three others, amongst them the venerable Bishop Rogers, of Chatham.

However pleasant the trip across the ocean has been, and although many of us found its associations most agreeable and we separate from them only by necessity, nevertheless all of us reach the shore with no little satisfaction. The fact is we are subjected to a new set of influences. We revive old associations. We see well-known scenes, and meet familiar faces. There is a change from our life of the last nine days to a new series of events and excitements. One of the first Canadians to give us a welcome was the young son of Madam Lepage, who had seen us off by the tender on 17th June.

The train carries us over the familiar Inter-Colonial Railway, nearly every spot along the line having a special claim on my recollection. The landscape is always striking in the neighbourhood of the Metapedia and Restigouche. There has been much rain and the vegetation is luxuriant. Bishop Rogers and myself revert to fifteen years ago when we crossed the Atlantic together. Then, as now, he was returning from a visit to the Holy Father at Rome. The Bishop insisted on acting as host at breakfast at Campbelton: he held that we had now entered his diocese and that he must consider us his guests. It would have pained the good old Bishop had we declined his courtesy

We learn that the fishing on the Restigouche this season has been excellent. As usual, we have the best of fresh salmon for breakfast. We say good-bye to the Bishop, who leaves us at Newcastle, and we proceed on our journey, arriving late at night safely at our home in Halifax.

We are now in Nova Scotia, where I am delayed a few days before starting on the long land journey over the western continent.

CHAPTER VI.

NOVA SCOTIA.

Early Colonization—De Monts—Champlain—Sir William Alexander—Capture of Quebec—The Treaties—The Acadian Evangeline—Louisbourg—First Capture—Peace of Aix la Chapelle—Boundary Disputes—The Final Struggle—Deportation of the Acadians—Nova Scotia constituted a Province.

The first attempt at the colonization of Nova Scotia which was made from France was singularly unfortunate. In 1598, we read, the Marquis de la Roche left Saint Malo with a crew, almost entirely composed of convicts. He landed forty of them at Sable Island until he could select a place fit for settlement, when a westerly storm drove his ship back to France. These settlers, if they can be so called, remained unnoticed for seven years, and when they were found twelve only remained. Had it not been for De Lery, who placed some live stock here in 1518, which in the interval had greatly multiplied, they must have starved. Their houses were built of the timbers of wrecked vessels, and it would seem no little of the fuel was derived from the same source. There is a letter from one John Butt to Henry VIII., which states that in 1527, seventy years previously, he met fifteen vessels in the harbour of Newfoundland, and there is every ground to warrant the belief that individual enterprise led to constant communication between the maritime nations of Europe and America from the early days of the discovery of Newfoundland, and that very many vessels penetrated to the shores of Nova Scotia and to the St. Lawrence before the days of Verazzano and Cartier. The object being alone that of trade with the Indians, and to obtain fish, no settlement followed, and doubtless many a wreck lay on the dreary shores of the exposed island where these unfortunate men had been landed.

The first well-considered attempt at European colonization occurred under the leadership of De Monts in 1604; in which we of Canada feel the greater interest, as the founder of Canada, the illustrious Champlain, took part in it. He has himself recorded the voyage, and Lescarbot, the first chronicler of the northern portion of the continent has fully related its history. It is mentioned that when De Monts arrived, he found a free trader in one of the bays whose name is preserved, Rossignol, a marked proof which I venture to adduce as showing the frequent intercourse between the two hemispheres at that date. De Monts entered the Bay of Fundy and passed up St. Mary's Bay, whence he proceeded to what is now known as Annapolis. Poutrincourt was of the party, and he commenced his chequered career by obtaining a grant of Port Royal from De Monts, founding a settlement there and giving it the name it bore for upwards of a century. De Monts himself passed over to Saint John whence he descended to Passamaquoddy Bay, where he built the Fort of Saint Croix. His crew suffered from scurvy during the winter. Hence he formed the opinion that the settlement was unhealthy, and accordingly he went as far south as the Penobscot. Finding the Indians unfriendly at this place, he returned to Port Royal. Here he met Pontgravé, known as the friend and associate of Champlain, who at this date first appears on the scene.

The leaders returned to France where strong influences were exercised against them. But they reappeared in 1606 and commenced in earnest to cultivate the land. A mill was constructed, and in the height of their efforts the following year notice was received from France that the monopoly of the trade in peltry given to De Monts was revoked. De Monts' future scene of labour was the Saint Lawrence, but Poutrincourt obtained the confirmation of De Monts' concession to him of Port Royal, accompanied by the condition that it should maintain a Jesuit Mission.

The influence which sustained this addition was all powerful, so the two Jesuits, Biard and Masse, arrived at Port Royal.* The Jesuits could not agree with the commander of the settlement and they departed to found a colony on the Penobscot River. But in 1613, Captain Samuel Argall, from James River, in Virginia, where a settlement had been established since 1606, sailed to fish for cod in the more northern waters. His pretensions were higher than that of a fisherman, for he carried fourteen guns and a crew of sixty men. Some Indians in perfect good faith set him on the track of the new settlements, which he at once attacked and destroyed.

No attempt was made to form a settlement from the Mother Country until 1621, when what in modern language are called the Maritime Provinces were granted to Sir William Alexander. A vessel with emigrants sailed in 1622, but owing to storms, was driven to Newfoundland. James I died in 1625, and his death led to the complications which followed on this continent. Charles I. had determined to assist the French Protestants then besieged in Rochelle, and as a portion of his operations, Kirke's celebrated expedition against Canada, took place in 1628. Quebec was taken. The French

---

* A stone inscription, dated 1609, was found in an old wall in the Fort at Port Royal, now Annapolis, by the late Judge Halliburton, author of "Sam Slick." Some fifteen years ago it was in the possession of his son, Mr. R. G. Halliburton, then in Halifax. That gentleman gave it as a loan to the writer to be placed in the Museum of the Canadian Institute. Thus the oldest stone inscription probably in America may be found in Toronto.

settlements still continued with small increments in what is known as Acadia: at Port Royal, Annapolis, to the country round Minas Bay, or the Basin of Minas from Chignecto to Cobequid, and south to Windsor and Cornwallis. There were some small settlements at Cape Sable, Cape la Have and at Canso. Fifty years after this date the total population was but little over 800, so settlement could only have taken place slowly and at intervals.

In 1632 all that is now known as British America, which lies beyond the valley of the St. Lawrence, was given over to the French by treaty. But Oliver Cromwell became Protector of England, and seized the forts of St. John and Port Royal, and, what is more, in the treaty of Westminster of 1655 held Nova Scotia as a possession. In 1658 the great Englishman died, and the discreditable days of the restoration followed. In 1662 the French Ambassador received instructions to demand restitution of the country. The English King, the pensioner of France, had no resource but compliance, although the people of Massachusetts, hearing of the proposition, sent a remonstrance against the proceeding. Its only effect was to lead to delay, for in 1667 a discreditable surrender was made by the treaty of Breda. The Governor was ordered to hand over Nova Scotia to French rule. The accession of William III. led to war, and in 1690 an expedition against Port Royal ended in its capture. But by the Peace of Ryswick, 1697, Nova Scotia was again transferred to France. Port Royal was occupied and placed in a condition of defence, and it was among the grievances of the New Englanders that it was the resort of pirates who preyed on Massachusetts commerce. War again broke out in 1702. The early attempts to capture Port Royal were not successful. Had the Governor, Subercase, been sustained from France, the conquest might have been perhaps stayed. But the support he asked was not extended, and in 1710 the place was again taken. The English Government had learned some terrible lessons on the necessity of holding the territory in this direction. The massacres at York and Oyster River in 1694 and the attempt to destroy Wells must have taught her rulers that the English colonies required some firmly seated support against such attempts. The effort of France was to connect Canada by a series of outposts with the Atlantic. A fort was built on the St. John, opposite Fredericton, Naxouat, and at the Jemseg to the south. The thinly-peopled northern parts of Maine and Massachusetts were thus constantly exposed to attack, and it was manifestly necessary to the protection of New England that a garrison of sufficient strength should be established in a locality where it would be available to meet an excursion from Canada, if French encroachments were to be resisted. It was thus that attention was directed to Port Royal, which had been taken in the expedition under Nicholson in 1710, and now received the name of Annapolis, from the reigning Queen. Halifax was then unknown, and the whole settlement of Nova Scotia consisted in what went under the name of Acadia, which did not contain 1,000 souls. It was resolved, however, to hold Nova Scotia permanently, and a garrison was left at Annapolis.

It was not until 1755, forty-five years after this date, that the deportation of the Acadians took place, and what follows in the history of Nova Scotia must be remembered in connection with the relentless policy of Governor Lawrence, which enforced their banishment.

Many have formed their idea of that measure by Mr. Longfellow's well known poem of "*Evangeline*," but it must be judged in a far wider view than what is suggested by those polished hexameters. Few can deny that the measure was one bringing much suffering with it, and that many innocent persons underwent tribulation, and that there is a hard, unbending purpose running through the proceeding to cause feelings of horror and pain. This cannot be denied. But what is all war but an unvarying scene of individual misery and wrong? A private execution of the most notorious malefactor makes an appeal to one's more merciful feelings. The real question to be considered is; was this step a merciless, treacherous, unnecessary brutality like the massacre of Glencoe, inflicting uncalled for suffering on a defenceless people, taken unawares, who had no chance given them to avoid such a fate; or was it an act of necessary policy entailed by most pressing circumstances, by consideration for the safety of a community, which the sufferers could have avoided, without the slightest sacrifice of principle, feeling or of individual right. The fact must be clearly stated. The Acadians, as a conquered people, obtained every consideration and kindness, and for years they were called upon earnestly to be loyal and to abstain from injury to those who were now their masters. No one ever received the slightest individual injury. They were treated with justice, with forbearance, with mercy. They were assured the practice of their religion, the maintenance of their property and their personal liberty. All they were asked to do was to give a solemn assurance to become in fact and by their lives subjects of their conquerors. Not to side with their foes, but to defend the land on which they held their property, against its enemies, and above all to abstain from encouragement of the savage Indian, whose theory of warfare was stealthy assassination. I return to the date 1710.

Port Royal was conquered, and its conquerors clearly shewed that they intended to retain it as a possession. The inhabitants never ceased from hostility in all its forms. Parties sent out to cut wood were assassinated. Travelling beyond the

fort was dangerous; for the individual it was death
The enmity of the people was kept up by the missionaries with the assurance that the fort would be attacked and retaken at the first opportunity, and that British continued possession was an impossibility. War was closed by the Treaty of Utrecht in 1713, when Nova Scotia remained a British possession. The French retained the sovereignty of the Island of Cape Breton,* which with the Port of Louisbourg, remained an eternal threat to Nova Scotia. The Acadians were pressed by the French governor, to remove to Cape Breton. By the 14th Article of the Treaty, they had one year

---

* The readers of Humphrey Clinker may recollect the astonishment of the Duke of Newcastle, the foolish Minister of George II., on hearing that Cape Breton was an island. The story as recorded is worth reproduction: "They [the Ministers] are so ignorant they scarce know a crab from a cauliflower, and then they are such dunces that there is no making them comprehend the plainest proposition. In the beginning of the war this poor, half-witted creature told me, in great fright, that thirty thousand French had marched from Acadia to Cape Breton. 'Where did they find transports?' said I. 'Transports!' cried he; 'I tell you they marched by land.' 'By land to the Island of Cape Breton?' What! is Cape Breton an island?' 'Certainly.' 'Ha! are you sure of that?' When I pointed it out in the map he examined it earnestly with his spectacles; then, taking me in his arms, 'My dear C——!' cried he, 'you always bring us good news. Egad! I'll go directly and tell the King that Cape Breton is an island.'"

in which they could leave Nova Scotia. But they would not do so. At the same time, they declared to the French of Cape Breton their intention of remaining subjects of France, and that they never would take the oath of allegiance to England under any circumstances.

In 1714 Nicholson was appointed Governor of Nova Scotia, then a recognized Province. No steps appear to have been taken for some years with regard to the Acadians. The oath had been tendered and refused. It was not enforced, and they remained in this unsatisfactory condition for thirty years, when war broke out again in 1743. It was well known that, in the event of war, every Acadian would be an enemy to British rule. Mascarene was then Governor. Descended from Huguenot French, he was a man of rare ability and power. A French force attacked the fort. The attack was to have been made in connection with a French squadron. The latter not arriving, the force retired, having shewn little enterprise. The Acadians did not join the attacking army. There was a body of Indians from the main land, friendly to the English, who were sufficient to counterbalance the Nova Scotian Micmacs, and the determined defence was a guarantee against any pronounced aid from within.

If Nova Scotia was to be retained with a population ever ready to rise at the first gleam of success of the enemies of Great Britain and its religion,

Louisbourg, it was evident could not be allowed to continue, a constant omen of danger and loss. Whoever first proposed the attack, and I think it must have been a necessity everywhere understood, it was Shirley, then Governor of Massachusetts, who prepared the organization by which the first taking of Louisbourg was effected, and whose energy and ability led to the expedition of 1745. William Pepperel was appointed its commander. Few such expeditions have been marked by such signal organization and completeness, a striking contrast to the contemptible result of Phipp's expedition against Quebec in 1690, and Walker's miserable failure in 1711. Admiral Warren commanded the naval forces. Louisbourg fell. The booty was immense, and to increase it the French flag was kept flying so that vessels from France entered the harbour to become the spoil of the conqueror. A lesson not forgotten when Boston was evacuated by the British in 1776, by the incompetent General Gage and his equally inefficient lieutenants. For the British flag, still flying on the fort, invited the English vessels unhesitatingly to sail in. if combatants, to become prisoners of war and for the stores and merchandise to be sequestrated. It is said that at Louisbourg the share of a seaman before the mast was eight hundred guineas. The efforts on the part of France to revenge this reverse were futile. The design was even to destroy Boston, but the expedition was one of the most impotent on record.

Port Royal, Annapolis seemed more easy of attainment. The commandant knowing the weakness of his garrison applied for reinforcements. On the arrival of 420 men, they were sent to Minas. A French fort was then at Chignecto. An attack was at once determined. The English troops took no precaution, as if they were in full security. Led by Acadian guides to the exact locality where the men were quartered, the French arrived at 2 o'clock in the morning on 23rd January, 1747. Snow was falling so the advance was not seen until close on the sentries. The troops, attacked in bed, made a desperate resistance, but they were defeated and capitulated. Such a result would have been impossible without the assistance of the Acadians, who led the troops precisely to the points to be attacked and withheld all knowledge of the expedition.

The disgraceful peace of Aix-la-Chapelle was made in 1748. It is hard to believe that Louisbourg and Cape Breton were given back to the French under the vague clause that no conquest since the commencement of the war should be held. England, therefore, retained Nova Scotia and France Cape Breton, for the tragedy of Louisbourg to be repeated ten years later. We all recollect the toast of Blucher that the diplomatist may not lose by the pen what the soldier has gained by the sword. On this continent we have much to remind us how a few words in a treaty, indistinct and indefinite in their purport, have ignored many years of national effort, courage and determination, at the same time sacrificing remorselessly a multiplicity of private interests.

But the time had come when the quarrel between France and England should be fought out, and both powers felt that this chronic condition of war could no longer continue. In ten years the struggle had ceased. One by one the strongholds of France passed from her hands, and in ten years her flag had ceased to be a type of power on the continent. Both countries accordingly put forth their whole strength in this period: a fact of importance when the question of the treatment of the Acadians is judged. One of the first steps was the foundation of Halifax in 1749 under Cornwallis. It was done with rare organization, with perfect success. Without delay Cornwallis called upon the Acadians to take the oath of allegiance. They declined. For six years was this request avoided with ill-concealed hostility. "In fact," said Governor Hopson in July, 1753, "what we call an Indian war is no other than a pretence for the French to commit hostilities upon His Majesty's subjects." The French, moreover, while recognizing the provisions of the Treaty of Aix-la-Chapelle, drew an arbitrary boundary of Nova Scotia: that of Missiquash River, now the boundary of New Brunswick and Nova Scotia; and La Jonquière, then Governor of Canada, sent a force under La Corne to erect a chain of forts from the Bay of Fundy to Bay Verte. They constructed Fort Beauséjour. The Governor of Nova Scotia established Fort Lawrence, near the settlement of Beausèjour. In 1755 it was resolved to drive the French from their position. As was looked for, the Acadians were there on the French side, but the fort was taken and called Fort Cumberland. It was these very encroachments of the French against Nova Scotia which led to the declaration of war in May of 1756. What followed I need but cursorily mention. Louisbourg again fell in 1758; Quebec in 1759. In 1760 Louisbourg was demolished, for no other port than Halifax was needed. In six months this monument of French power, which it had taken twenty-five years to raise, was levelled to the ground. All of value was transported to Halifax, many of the boucharded stones, even, having been taken there. In this year Montreal capitulated, and De Vaudreuil signed the capitulation which gave the continent to British rule.

All these facts require to be stated when the deportation of the Acadians has to be considered. What else could be done with them in this crisis? From the period when Cornwallis first arrived, in 1749, it was the one question: how to act with a body of men disloyal to the country as it was governed. Too weak to obtain a national standing, but constantly intriguing to injure the authority they lived under but would not recognize; refusing all efforts of conciliation; and, with the guarantee of possessing personal liberty, the free practice of their religion, the enjoyment of their property, they still declined to give the slightest assurance of good behaviour or fidelity. They refused even to furnish supplies to the British garrison, and they ranged themselves actually on the side of the French expeditions. They encouraged the savage to rob, and to plunder, and to murder. They complacently looked on while a vessel was looted under their eyes, and at the same time they were subject to no direct tax and had every privilege a loyal subject could ask. European writers who have alluded to this proceeding have dwelt much on the peaceful lives and the quiet, primitive habits of most of those who suffered. That fact has never been disputed. But poetry has endeavoured to sublimate their virtues to a height they never reached. The Acadians lived in rude plenty, unmarked by the least culture. Their prejudices were only developed among themselves. They were litigious and grasping, and French writers of that date complain that the specie which they received never left their possession, for they held it back for the hour of difficulty, which would have been in no way unwelcome if it ended in driving from their midst those who, with all the exaggeration on the subject, could not be called their oppressors. In September, 1755, a considerable number of the most troublesome were seized, arbitrarily undoubtedly, and banished from the country. What the number was which were thus scattered and shipped in transports it is hard to state. Many were left behind, as the despatches of subsequent Governors clearly establish. In Grand Pré 1,925 were collected. At Annapolis and Cumberland many took to the woods. I cannot form any other opinion than that the number 5,000 is an exaggeration. Among the papers at the Colonial Office or at Halifax the true state of the case may be found. I am quite unable, from what I can learn, to give any estimate, but the evidence leads me to think that probably less than 3,000 were so deported. A melancholy fate of suffering, sorrow and privation ; for these poor creatures were sent, homeless and destitute, to other States ; but there was no unnecessary hardship and cruelty shown, and their condition was not worse than that of the immigrant who in old days sought our shores.

Undoubtedly it is a chapter of human misery, this enforced exodus, but those who suffered by it could have avoided it by a line of conduct marked by no one act in any way unworthy or humiliating. All that was called for was the acceptance of an unavoidable condition of events, beyond their control, irremediable. They refused to become friends of those who made the offer of peace and conciliation in the hour of danger and difficulty.

They showed themselves to be avowed enemies. For upwards of forty years they destroyed the peace of the colony, and had at length to pay the penalty their conduct exacted, which was only with reluctance adopted as a necessity which self-preservation demanded.

It is not until 1714 that Nova Scotia ranks as a British Province. There were many mutations before it took this definite form, and in connection with its history there is the record common to most of the communities of this continent: that of misapprehension and a failure to understand its importance as an American possession.

For the hundred and seventy years which Nova Scotia has continued under British rule its population has steadily increased from various sources, and as a maritime people they have placed themselves in the highest rank. Nova Scotia thus possesses the distinction of being the oldest British Province of the Dominion.

CHAPTER VII.

HALIFAX TO QUEBEC.

Home in Halifax—Start for the Pacific—The Intercolonial Railway—Major Robinson—Old Companions—The Ashburton Blunder—Quebec—The Provincial Legislature—Champlain—The Iroquois.

Arrived at my Halifax home, I made the few preparations necessary for the journey before me. In the interval, I rambled through the Dingle with my children and paddled over the north-western arm, a sheet of water of much beauty. There is always unusual pleasure in such quiet occupations, exacting neither labour, nor thought, nor any great strain upon the attention. We float along or stroll idly, as it were following the bent of our inclinations, now and then considering what lies before us, or reverting in memory to that which once has happened. Then I visited my old friends, who gave me the proverbial Halifax welcome. Two vessels of the fleet were in port, the "Northampton" and the "Canada," the latter attracting some attention from the fact that Prince George, the second son of the Prince of Wales, was on board, performing the duties of a midshipman, as any other youngster in that position and as efficiently. A new Commander of the Forces had arrived, Lord Alexander Russell, formerly known in Canada as commanding one of the battalions of the Rifle Brigade, and the conversation of the garrison was the changes in discipline and general economy introduced, as is frequently the case by new administrators. All my friends were well and in good spirits. I had the additional pleasure of finding that the kindness of former days was unimpaired, and my whole visit was one of pleasantness.

I was four days in Halifax, and on the ninth of August, I started alone. Dr. Grant who accompanied me on my first trip to the Pacific eleven years ago, had accepted the invitation to accompany me across the Rocky Mountains, and it was arranged that he should join me in Winnipeg. My second son was also to be of the party. He was to meet me in Toronto.

My family went with me to the station. There was an unusual effort to say good-bye in starting on this long journey, but that matter has no interest here.

It is only on alternate nights that the Pullman car runs through from Halifax to Montreal. On this occasion I had to leave Halifax by the Pullman which went no further than Moncton Junction, and with the other western passengers I had to wait there for the train to arrive from St. John.

We reached Moncton at two o'clock in the morning, an hour not the most convenient for effecting the change. It is among the minor miseries of travelling to be obliged to turn out at such an hour for a coming train. But the fault was my own. Had I curtailed my brief sojourn in Halifax a few hours, or had my arrangements admitted of delay for another day, I would have had the advantage of a through Pullman without the inconvenience of a break at this place. Moncton is in New Brunswick, at the junction of the lines from Halifax and St. John, whence a common course is followed to the St. Lawrence.

As I was sitting on the platform in the cool summer air before dawn, I could not but recollect that the 10th of August was one of the red letter days of my life. Thirty-one years back, on that day my railway career in Canada commenced. I was appointed as an Assistant-engineer on what was then known as the Ontario, Simcoe and Huron Railway, afterwards developed into the Northern Railway of Canada, and of which I remained chief engineer for a number of years. The Montreal and Portland Railway was under construction. The Grand Trunk Railway had just been commenced, and with the exception of some small lengths of line, such as the Lachine, the La Prairie, and the Carillon Railways, it may be said that, at that date, railways had no working existence in Canada.

The station ground at Moncton was illuminated by an electric light; to escape its piercing rays, I

turned away to a seat which they did not reach.
As I was thus sitting apart, my recollection went
back over the last thirty-one years and to the many
events which the spot suggested. The night was
dark, and, excepting in the immediate neighbourhood, it seemed to be rendered darker by the light
which flickered and glared directly above me. I
cannot say that the dazzling "Brush" light is
agreeable to me at any time, or on that occasion
that my tone of thought was affected by it; but
in spite of myself my mind ran over much of the
past, and brought vividly before me many events
long forgotten. I remembered the frequent mention of Moncton by Major Robinson in his well
known report, and I felt how much I owed to his
labours and to those of his efficient assistant Captain,
now Sir Edmund Henderson. I thought of poor
Major Pipon, who was drowned in one of the
streams while gallantly striving to save the life of
an Indian boy. Prominent among the actors I
reverted to my friend Mr. Light, who constructed
the line from Moncton to St. John, whose labours
were continued on the Intercolonial Railway until
its completion, and who is still actively engaged
in his profession. Naturally, in connection with
these memories, the whole staff of engineers who
worked with me on the Intercolonial Railway
passed before me, from the first long snow-shoe
tramps through the forest and across the mountains in 1864 to the completion of the line in 1876.

Some are no more; those who remain are scattered over this continent doing their work as manfully as they did it here, wherever their field of duty.

So far as the Intercolonial Railway appears before the public to-day, those engineers who were for years engaged in its construction are as if they never existed. I was struck with the similitude between the life of the engineer and of the soldier. There is much which is identical in the two professions. In both, privations and hardships are endured. In both, self-sacrifice is called for. In both, special qualities are demanded to gain desired results; and the possessors of them for a time obtain prominence, to pass out of mind with the necessity for their service, and to be forgotten and uncared for. It is peculiarly during an hour of patient waiting in the advanced hours of night that much of the past comes vividly before us. My mind reverted to all the incidents connected with the history of this national railway. I recalled many recollections of the Railway Commissioners whom the Government appointed at that date, and I did my best to forget many an unpleasantness. Differences of view were not unfrequent. They seemed important enough at the time, but on looking back to them now, how insignificant many of them appear. Those mistakes which permanently affect the public interests are only to be deplored. The train had just passed over the scene of one of the most glaring of these departures from a wise policy.

In order to serve purely local interests, the railway was diverted many miles out of its true direction. The proper location would have cost less; the line, when completed, would have been better in an engineering point of view; the distance would have been ten miles shorter. But the local interests, in themselves insignificant, were sustained by political influence. Whatever administration was in power, there was some one prominent politician to advocate the location by the circuitous route. In this one point men on opposite sides of the House could meet on common ground, and in spite of all remonstrances * and regardless of the facts, their individual interests prevailed.

Thus the country was saddled with an unnecessary expense of construction of a needless increased length of line with its perpetual maintainance, and every person, and every ton of goods, entering or leaving Nova Scotia, has to pay a mileage charge of conveyance over ten extra unnecessary miles: a tax on the travelling public and the commerce of the country for ever! As I looked along the track into the darkness, I remembered that some fifteen years had passed since the troubles and unpleasantness of those days, and it came to my mind that the prominent actors in the events are dead. I was struck with the truth of our experience in the vanity of human wishes and the worse than folly

---

* This matter is entered into at length in the writer's published history of the Intercolonial Railway, 1876, page 102.

of sacrificing permanent public interests for matters of passing moment.

The circumstances suggested another recollection of higher historical importance and infinitely more consequence. Moncton itself, geographically, is nearly due east of Montreal, but in order to reach this point, the Intercolonial railway has to diverge northerly nearly three degrees of latitude, through the narrow limit of territory along the St. Lawrence. The extraordinary series of negotiations which led to the establishment of the Maine boundary, is a chapter in our history which the British nation equally with Canadians would willingly forget. It is with pain and humiliation that we reflect on the ignorance of the simplest facts of the case and of the deplorable inattention to every national interest which marked the conduct of the Imperial representative, Lord Ashburton, in the settlement of that question. I had occasion, some years ago, carefully to examine the whole subject, and I could never discover that the blame of the discreditable settlement of the matter at issue is in any way chargeable to the Washington Government, as many suppose, and as I myself at one time had been taught to believe. The diplomacy of the United States was perfectly straightforward throughout. Strange as it may seem, the objectionable settlement, which leaves this painful blot on the map of the Dominion, is due to the rejection of a proposition which came from the Executive at

Washington. Had the wise and just proposal made and repeated by President Jackson been accepted, there cannot be a doubt that the boundary would have been satisfactorily established, in accordance with the true spirit of the treaty of 1783. We would have been spared the bitter humiliation of the Ashburton treaty ; we would have saved ten millions of dollars in the first cost of the Intercolonial railway, and Nova Scotia would have been, for all practical purposes of trade and intercourse, two hundred miles nearer the western provinces of the Dominion.

The yearly cost of maintaining and working this unnecessary length of railway represents a large sum. The direct advantages of the shorter line would have been incalculable. The transport of coal alone, at half a cent per ton per mile, reckoned on 200 miles, would effect a saving to the consumers in the Provinces of Quebec and Ontario of one dollar per ton. Such a reduction in itself would have created great activity in the mining industries of Nova Scotia, the coal fields of which are inexhaustible, but which from their distance from market are subjected to much unfavorable competition.

The train arrives in due time ; a sleeping berth had been secured by telegraph, and I proceed onwards. The following evening, the train reaches the Chaudière Junction, opposite Quebec, having passed Rimouski and Rivière du Loup in the after noon. At the latter place, generally so quiet and free from bustle, we saw an unusual number of people assembled. It was the annual excursion of the Press Association, and the members had been listening to an address from the Premier of the Dominion.

There are three ways of reaching Montreal from Quebec. The traveller may take the steamboat up the St. Lawrence, 180 miles. He may cross the river and avail himself of the North Shore Railway, or he may remain on the south side and proceed by the Grand Trunk Railway. It is now seven in the evening and the train is about starting, so I continue on the Grand Trunk route and have a second night to pass in the Pullman car. In the morning at half past six the train enters Montreal by the famed Victoria Bridge.

To those who desire to pass a day at Quebec, the steamboat is a very pleasurable mode of travelling. The steamers on the route are well built. The accommodation is excellent, and they present a varied and animated sight during the season from the number of passengers.

I have frequently visited Quebec, and I have passed many days among its many pleasant associations. On this occasion, it was a mere point in my travels. Those who visit Canada for the first time, will certainly not hurry past this famous city as I was then doing.

Quebec will always be remarkable for its historical associations and for the exquisite beauty of its scenery. The traveller, however far he may have rambled, can not fail to recognize that the view from Durham Terrace is one of the finest he has ever seen. Some contend that it is unsurpassed. On one side is the citadel in all its strength and grandeur. On the opposite bank of the river, Point Levis stands forth with its coves and buildings and scenes of stirring life. Immediately below us the majestic river itself flows in a great, placid stream on its way to the ocean. To the north, rise the bold heights of the Laurentian range, bearing evidences of life from their base far up on the hill side. The whole scene furnishes a panorama rarely to be met. In Quebec one feels that he is on a spot where every foot of space was once of value, from the necessity of protecting the whole by works of defence. We are taken back to the European life of insecurity of two centuries ago, when every town was so protected, and yet was often ravaged and despoiled. Quebec is the one memorial of that condition of things on this continent. The city itself is built on an eminence which admits of much variety of landscape. It is a spot of great attraction which everybody visits with pleasure. The society has long been known by the genial and kindly character of its hospitality. Although its commerce is not relatively what it was in former years, it is still a centre of much activity and possesses great wealth. The commencement of a railway to the settlement at Lake

St. John, to the north, entirely by Quebec capital, is a proof that the spirit of enterprise yet remains.

The city is the seat of Provincial Government. During the sitting of its Legislature it is much frequented by men busy in political life. In summer the hotels are invariably full of tourists, chiefly from the United States, hundreds often arriving daily to go over the ground of its historic associations, to enjoy the beauty of the landscape, and to observe what remains of the life of a past, of which in their own country they are without a parallel. Much of the history of Canada centres around Quebec. Many illustrious names are associated with the ancient city. The most distinguished is its founder, Samuel Champlain.

Champlain's career in Canada dates from 1608 to 1635. He founded Quebec. He ascended the Richelieu and discovered Lake Champlain, which bears his name. He ascended from Ticonderoga to Lake George, and penetrated the valleys of the Hudson and the Mohawk. He ascended the Ottawa, passed over the height of land, and by Lake Nipissing reached Georgian Bay. He travelled the country overland from Lake Simcoe to the Trent, and by the Bay of Quinté crossed the waters of Lake Ontario to what is now the State of New York, and penetrated to one of the lakes, believed to be Lake Canandaigua. He was the first to make a map of Canada, and he published his memoirs and his travels. He, and he only, is the founder of Canada. What he effected wa wonderful. Few men have been marked by such singular honesty of character. Few men have possessed so well directed a spirit of adventure, controlled by an unusually active and penetrating mind. His fortitude, his endurance, his courage, his perseverance, his personal honour make him one of the great characters of history.

Midway between Quebec and Montreal the City of Three Rivers is situated. This place was early settled, a fort having been constructed here in 1634. Its geographical position called for this protection. It is at the foot of the St. Maurice, whose sources lie far to the north, and west of Lake St. Peter, which in those days might be called an Iroquois lake, from the frequent incursions of the Indians, who were merciless in their warfare. For forty years the early French Canadian settler never knew if he would be able to reap the harvest of the seed he had sown. Indeed, it is not an exaggeration to say that it was doubtful, when he left his home for his day's labour, if he would not be before night a scalped corpse. It was not until 1686 that Tracy passed by the Richelieu and read the Iroquois a lesson by which peace was obtained. Three Rivers was at an early day a settlement of some importance. It even obtained a preference over Quebec, but the better situation of Montreal eventually diverted the trade to that city. It has long been a pleasant enough place, but, as the saying goes, one through which everybody passes and where nobody stops.

CHAPTER VIII.

QUEBEC, MONTREAL, OTTAWA.

Montreal—Ship Channel—Hon. John Young—St. Lawrence Canals—Indifference of Quebec—Quebec Interests Sacrificed—Need of a Bridge at Quebec—Montreal Trade in Early Times—Beauty of the City—Canadian Pacific Railway—Ottawa—The Social Influence of Government House—Kingston.

It is only within the last half century that the commercial advantages, geographically, possessed by Montreal have been understood and developed. It is not possible to enter into the history of the remarkable works, extending east and west, which have secured to this city its commercial success. They may, however, be briefly mentioned. To the east a ship channel has been dredged through Lake St. Peter to a depth of twenty-five feet, to admit of the passage of ocean steamers. The original depth over the St. Peter flats was eleven feet. This gigantic work, commenced in 1840, has been continued until the present day. The excavation extends for a distance of seventeen miles, over shoals irregular in depth. At this date the sum of $3,500,000 has been expended in the work. The further deepening of this channel to admit the depth of twenty-seven feet six inches is now in progress, and to obtain this depth throughout above Quebec the shoals of the River St. Lawrence itself above and below Lake St. Peter must likewise be dredged.

There is but one parallel to this work in the world: the improvement of the Clyde, which has been continued for one hundred years. Originally only vessels drawing three feet six inches could reach Glasgow. From time to time this depth has been increased, until it may be said that at this date ocean steamers of the largest draught are found at the Broomielaw. Hence Glasgow, by artificial means, has become one of the most important ports in the United Kingdom; and similarly Montreal, although a thousand miles from the ocean, is now one of the chief seaports of the Dominion, and, judged by the standard of Customs receipts, must be held to be the first.

In connection with the improvement of the St. Lawrence, between Montreal and Quebec, indeed with regard to much which has increased the prosperity of Montreal, one name rises into marked prominence, that of the Hon. John Young, so long and so honourably known in that city, and still so well remembered, It was owing in a great degree to his energy and capacity that the deepening of Lake St. Peter was completed according to the original design. It may also be said that he was one of the first to recognize the necessity of an increased sufficiency of depth of channel above Quebec, if Montreal was to remain the unquestioned port of the ocean steamer. A project which he advocated to his death, and which until a great extent he was instrumental in placing in its present satisfactory condition, so that in no great number of years the depth will be attained

To the west of Montreal several canals have been completed to overcome the rapids of the St. Lawrence, the last of which is the renowned Falls of Niagara, and which our grandsires held to be so insuperable as to bar settlement on the upper lakes. These works are a marked feature of Canadian enterprise, and in themselves an important chapter in the history of canal construction. Nowhere in the world, on a line of navigation, are such locks to be seen. Those of the Lachine Canal are two hundred and seventy-five feet in length, forty-five feet wide, with twelve feet of water in the sills, so constructed that, without interruption to traffic, they may be increased to fourteen feet. The enlargement of the whole navigation of the St. Lawrence, now in progress, is on a similar scale. It is by the central and commanding position which these works have created for Montreal that the city has attained its present supremacy.

For a time Quebec enjoyed to the full extent

the control of the ocean shipping trade, but the day the channel was formed through the flats of Lake St. Peter for the passage of seagoing vessels the monopoly was broken and the trade diverted.

The City of Quebec has long complained that its commerce was languishing, among other causes, from the persistent efforts of Montreal to control it. The deepening of the channel between the two cities has accomplished more than was even hoped for by its far-seeing projectors, for most of the seagoing steamships steam past Quebec, to find at Montreal the point of transfer for their western freight, and the point where it is most convenient to receive a cargo. There is a recorded saying of the Hon. John Neilson, a well known public man of forty years back, that there are two advantages Montreal could not take away from Quebec: the Citadel and the tide. Evidently meaning by the former that tourists would always visit the city to see what only could there be found, and that Quebec, by constructing tidal docks, had the means of bringing to her harbour vessels which, from their draught, could not ascend the river to Montreal. The persistent, well-directed efforts of Montreal, however, have been to concede no such advantages.

What, in the meantime, has been the course of Quebec? It is well known that at this hour great efforts are being put forth by Halifax public men to establish Halifax as the winter shipping port of the Dominion. It is contended that the Intercolonial Railway is a national work, constructed with public money, and that it is precisely to meet an emergency of this character, to prevent the diversion of the winter freight to the United States ports, that one of the main causes of its construction can be found. The City of Quebec, labouring under a depression of its trade, gave its strongest support to the project of the North Shore Railway, with its prolongation to Ottawa, and even contributed $1,000,000 towards its establishment. In the eye of the Quebec merchant it is a national work, the object of which is to extend to Quebec, by railway, the same facilities for transhipment of freight which is now possessed by Montreal. The Province had a plain policy to follow. It was of paramount importance that she should retain full control of the line to Montreal and Ottawa, and that it should offer, at both points, perfect facilities for the transfer of traffic to and from the competing railway lines: the Canadian Pacific and Grand Trunk. The effect would have been to restore a share of the trade in shipping freight which Quebec had previously enjoyed. Moreover, as the navigation is confined to the summer months, it would appear to be clearly the policy of Quebec to develop and complete her railway connections to the east, so that the traffic in winter would flow in a continuous stream over the North Shore line, and be carried onward to the winter shipping port at Halifax. To carry out this theory successfully the St. Lawrence would have to be bridged as near Quebec as practicable. In the vicinity of the city, some few miles south, there is a site adapted for such a bridge. The shores of the river are high, and the deep-water channel can be crossed by a single span, lofty enough for the tallest masts of a vessel to pass beneath. Modern engineering has rendered the project not only possible but comparatively easy, for it has reduced greatly the time and the cost which some years back would have been held necessary to consummate the project. The railway connections, equally of the City and Province of Quebec, I may add of the Dominion, will always remain incomplete and unsatisfactory without such a bridge. With this structure the whole conditions of the problem would be changed. At all seasons of the year it would facilitate the arrival and increase the number of tourists. It would have the effect of augmenting traffic on both the North Shore and Intercolonial Railways. It would extend provincial as well as local advantages to commerce generally, and it would go far to establish Halifax as the winter port of the Dominion. Moreover, it would affect all this result without the sacrifice of one single Canadian interest.

There is much in the late policy of the Government of Quebec to astonish and bewilder all who study the laws of trade. It has been remarked that the City of Quebec felt its interests to be so deeply concerned in the completion of the North Shore Railway that it voted $1,000,000 to secure its establishment. Throughout the Province the railway was advocated for many years; it was fostered and cherished, and held to be the key to its future prosperity. Nevertheless the Provincial Government has deliberately sold all its interest in the work, and has passed over its control to a railway company whose interests lie in an entirely different direction. They have thus sacrificed the one chance of extending a fostering hand to local trade and regaining the prestige of the Ancient City. Indeed, the Provincial Government stands in relationship to this railway as if it had never been constructed as a public work. As I am writing I read in the newspapers that the present tariff of charges between Montreal and Quebec, a distance of one hundred and eighty miles, on certain articles of freight, is thirty-three per cent. higher than between Quebec and Halifax, a distance of six hundred and eighty miles! Possibly an extreme case; but can any fact bear stronger testimony to the sacrifice which has been made of the interests of the City of Quebec? It is long since there has been such an abandonment of a position from which so much might have been hoped, and, strange to add, the sacrifice has been made without a protest, without a remonstrance from those most interested. It would seem that there is a failure to understand the extent of the advantages which have been thrown away. If there be any truth in the adage that misery likes company, it may be some consolation to the people of Quebec to know that the shadow of this unfortunate transaction has been equally cast over the fortunes of the Intercolonial Railway and on the prosperity of the City of Halifax.

It seems to me that the error committed cannot too soon be rectified. Indeed, it is a case in which the intervention of the general government is both justifiable and necessary. The Intercolonial Railway, owned and operated by the Dominion Government, extends from Halifax to a point opposite Quebec. It connects only with the Grand Trunk Railway. The interests of the Grand Trunk Company call for the transport of freight to Portland, in the United States, rather than its transfer to Halifax. The Intercolonial was established for national purposes. Strong reasons present themselves why it should not terminate at Chaudière Junction, but that its outlet should be Ottawa. This policy of extension to the capital would involve bridging the St. Lawrence at Quebec and of obtaining control of the railway to Ottawa. Such a connection would admit of the exchange of traffic with the competing lines on equal terms at Montreal and Ottawa, and would remove from Quebec, from the Intercolonial Railway and from Halifax the serious disabilities under which they now labour.

Under French rule Montreal had simply a monopoly of trade with the Indians, and no attempt was made until a later period to overcome the natural impediments which lay in the way of its advancement. It was not until some years after the conquest, when Western Canada, now Ontario, became a field for settlement, that any improvement of the navigation of the St. Lawrence was attempted. Some rude canals, with narrow locks, were early formed to enable the Durham boats, then the only means of transit, to pass up the Cascade, Cedar and Coteau Rapids. The present canals were the impulse of a later date. In the early days of Canada commerce was not of the importance it has now attained. There was a chronic state of war, first with the red man for the possession of the country itself; secondly with the English and the southern colonies for the traffic with the Indians. The scene of the struggle was generally on the borders of the great lakes, and then, as now, the main effort was put forth to determine whether the products of the west would pass by the Mohawk to the Hudson, or whether it would follow the course of the St. Lawrence to the sea.

Montreal, at this period, was virtually the end of French settlement, and the population was small. At the present day Montreal is a city, with its suburbs, of nearly 200,000 inhabitants. Most of the old French landmarks are disappearing, one by one, and there remains little of material form to recall French rule. It may almost be said that the language, and that portion of our laws which owes its origin to France, are all that remain to remind us of her power. Her criminal and commercial law is English; the other divisions of her jurisprudence retain their early impress. There remains, however, the Roman Catholic form of worship, the most marked heirloom of those days which the French Canadian has most jealously retained. Montreal, socially, is now characterized by those features which wealth, proceeding from a long and prosperous commerce, stamps upon a community on this side of the Atlantic. On all sides you see palatial residences and highly cultivated grounds. The main business streets are marked by unusual architectural embellishments, for which the limestone quarries in the neighbourhood furnish the best of facilities. The wharves in front of the city, with the stone revetment wall, have not their equal on the continent. The canals have already been referred to, and I know nowhere else where such works are to be seen. The Canadian canal is a river, and not a small one, and the vessels which pass through it are of no ordinary size. There is much material success; and this commercial element has gathered together a busy, anxious, enterprising, pushing population, with all the accessories in connection with it which wealth gives. But I must turn to the matters which have brought me to Montreal.

I had a long and important interview with the Directors of the Canadian Pacific Railway. They desired me to proceed to British Columbia on a special professional service, and, if practicable, they wished me to pass over the line west of Winnipeg to examine the passes of the Rocky Mountains. It was agreed that I should start without delay. Some preparations are always necessary for such a journey, and to cross the mountains over an almost untrodden path I required strong, rough clothing and unexceptional protection for the feet.

I took the afternoon train for Ottawa. In Montreal the terminus of the Canadian Pacific Railway is at Dalhousie Square. It extends from Notre Dame street, at a lower level, to the quay, and it would be difficult to find a more striking site for a railway station. For upwards of a mile the line runs along the side of the harbour, and you have in view the bold landscape produced by the river and St. Helen's Island. To the west Victoria Bridge stands out in bold relief, and, in spite of its massiveness, it spans the river with the most graceful of lines. The harbour of Montreal during the season of navigation is always more or less full of shipping, among which the ocean steamer predominates. In winter it presents a totally different appearance. The river is a field of ice, often cumbered with Cyclopean masses, distorted by "shoves" into most picturesque forms, often a scene in all respects striking and rarely met. The railway, on leaving Montreal, passes through a really charming landscape. Crossing two branches of the St. Lawrence, at Sault-au-Recollet and Rivière-des-Prairies, it touches the River Ottawa, and continues generally in sight of the river till it reaches the capital. Twenty miles east the line passes directly over the falls of Le Lievre, at Buckingham, which form an object of special attraction. On approaching Ottawa we cross the long iron bridge over the river, and see the city lying before us, and the outline of the Government buildings, with their peculiar architecture, almost suggesting that you are entering some mediæval city.

At no period of the year, except during the three months when the House is in session, is there any particular animation in the Capital. Parliament meets in February, occasionally in January, and continues its sittings until April or May. From Christmas to the opening of the House the Government offices are unusually active in the preparation of documents to be laid before Parliament. Strangers arrive a week before the day of the opening. There is a constant succession of new faces in the streets. The Ministers commence their series of dinners, the intention of which is to affirm their political influence, but clothed with all the graces of social attraction. Those in the city proper who can entertain do so at this season. The Club, which for the remaining nine months can number in its rooms its visitors by tens, is then crowded, and the hotels are full of busy, bustling individuals engaged in the many schemes which await the countenance of Parliament, and the dining-room in the evening has the fullest attendance.

Few cities of the size are more lively under this aspect than Ottawa during the session. A few days after its close another story is told. Government House, which for the last ten years has been the scene of so much polished and plenteous hospitality, becomes tenantless. The two previous Governors-General, Lord Dufferin and Lord Lorne, endeavoured to bring side by side all that was estimable and prominent in the capital. There was something so cordial, so unaffectedly hearty in the welcome given to all, that no one went there without pleasure or left without regret. The invitations were not confined to a comparatively narrow clique. No hospitality could be more genial, more liberal or more unaffected. Twice a week, or so, there were skating and tobogganing parties. Once a week there were state dinners, frequently on other evenings guests were gathered around the private table. Lord Dufferin inaugurated a series of private theatricals. He was also followed by Lord Lorne in his desire to add to the common happiness, as indeed in all that was excellent which Lord Dufferin commenced. No balls ever were more pleasant than those given at Ottawa under their regime. There is a delicacy in writing all this, as both these distinguished men are in active political life, and it is not easy to speak of the actors in our Canadian drama who yet play a part in the wider Imperial life. Equally difficult to venture to allude to the Countess of Dufferin, who exercised such a healthy influence on the society in which she mixed. The more exalted position of H. R. H. the Princess Louise makes it more embarrassing to refer to her presence; but who that has, in any way, been brought within her influence can forget all the associations which it suggests, not those of rank, but the more durable impress of genius, of excellence, with the most simple and unaffected manner, blended with a consideration for others which delighted everyone.

I remained a few hours in Ottawa, and took the night train for Toronto. We start from the Canadian Pacific station, at which I had arrived, and follow the line to Brockville. Brockville is a town of importance on the St. Lawrence, at the lower end of that interesting reach of forty miles which embraces the Thousand Islands. During the night the Pullman is connected with the Grand Trunk train, and we proceed on our journey as if we were travelling on the system of lines we started on. There is no tax imposed on travellers, as at Moncton on alternate nights turning you out of your berth at three in the morning. When you awake you are still proceeding onward on the western journey. We pass Kingston at night, a town which has grown around Frontenac's fort, erected in 1672. Its site is still a barrack used for the Military College. Kingston has the advantage of a finely settled country in its rear; it has an ancient look, and is substantially built of limestone. Its position at the junction of Lake Ontario with the St. Lawrence, and the presence of many owners of craft, cause some activity during the season of navigation. Kingston is also known as the seat of Queen's College and University, in which, personally and officially, the writer has the greatest interest.

There is a restaurant car attached to the train, and one can obtain any breakfast he may require. After breakfast one generally becomes critical, for thought is turned outward. As we are moving onward it struck me that the farming between Trenton and Cobourg was not of a high character. At no season should thistles and weeds be seen in the fields, certainly not at the period when they are going to seed, and even a few slovenly farms will disfigure a whole district. The grain crop is later than usual, but is fast ripening, and in this section of the country not without promise. West of Cobourg the land is among the best in the world. Nowhere is agriculture more careful. There is scarcely any land remaining uncultivated, and no one but can be struck with the fertility of the district through which we are passing.

CHAPTER IX.

TORONTO TO LAKE SUPERIOR.

Toronto—Collingwood—Georgian Bay—The Sault St. Mary—Navigation of the Great Lakes—Manitoulin Islands—Lake Huron—Arrival at the Sault.

Arriving safely at Toronto I was welcomed by my son Sandford, who accompanies me on my journey. For the first time I am presented to a still younger descendant, who confers upon me a new claim to family respect, and whom I meet with much pleasure.

It was the civic holiday in Toronto. It has been a custom on this Continent, in the large cities and more important towns, for one day in the year to be set apart, when, by common consent, business ceases. All sorts of excursions are organized by railway and steamboat companies, and to crown the whole with additional dignity, the purport of the day is officially declared by proclamation by His Worship the Mayor. Every possible auxiliary is called in aid to give effect to the occasion. In the city there are various performances at the theatres, morning and evening. The neighbouring small towns contribute their sympathizing crowds. There are cricket matches, lacrosse matches, with other meetings of every character of pleasurable association. There is the best of good eating and drinking for all who require it and are willing to pay for it. This Toronto holiday was in no way wanting in the general characteristics which such a day brings with it. Crowds of good-looking, good-humoured, holiday-dressed personages filled the streets, and there was a gaiety of manner and an atmosphere of amusement in the main thoroughfares which even the indifferent spectators could with difficulty resist.

If Montreal may be said to be the admitted commercial capital of Canada, Toronto is battling hard to dispute its supremacy. The capital of Ontario, it is what Montreal is not. It is a political centre of great activity, where much is originated to influence both Dominion and local politics. It justly claims, too, a higher tone of intellectual life. On the whole, it may be said that there is a more assured type of culture and urban refinement by the shores of Lake Ontario than on the Island of Montreal. The city contains two Universities: one, Toronto University, without religious test, supported by the Province; the second, Trinity, supported by the Church of England. Besides which there are a Presbyterian College and Theological Halls of other denominations. The Canadian Institute also has a reputation. It numbers among its members some of the leading minds of the country, and for many years it has been distinguished as a centre for the exchange of thought on scientific and literary topics; it has greatly aided the collection of information respecting the economic resources of the Dominion and in the determination of problems which have a direct influence upon its future. There has been always a marked polish of manner, blended with a sympathy with intellectual power, which has distinguished Toronto society. The leading members of the professions have, as a rule, obtained greater social recognition, and generally the horizon of education is much more extended than in the larger eastern city.

The surrounding country is of little interest beyond what is artificially obtained, but the large sheltered sheet of water in front of the city, locally designated "the Bay," and protected from the lake by a long sandy island about a mile from the shore, will always give it value as a harbour, and afford excellent boating water for the members of the Yacht Club. The more distant environs are particularly striking. In four hours, steamboats take you to Niagara. On excursion days they are crowded with passengers. Niagara is one of those sights which the more you behold the more you are astonished. I have met those who have expressed disappointment at their first view of the

Falls. It is difficult to explain how this feeling is entertained, except by some previous extravagant misconception of their extent and appearance. Their character and beauty have deservedly included them in the wonders of the world. Necessarily they have become a show place, and to some extent one experiences the unpleasant influences which the tourist has to contend with at such resorts. The locality is the scene of many a small extortion into which the unwary occasionally stumble. There cannot be a doubt that the Falls of Niagara, with the scenery above and below them, and the masses of rushing water in all its various aspects and circumstances, present a sight to dwarf into insignificance everything of the kind generally beheld. At all seasons of the year they attract crowds of visitors to the neighbourhood, and scarcely any one visiting the Continent fails to look upon them.

I spent a pleasant day at Collingwood with my dear old mother, 83 years of age, looking fresh and hearty, without one physical ache or pain ; at the same time her mind retains its marked natural acuteness.

At four in the afternoon on Tuesday, the 14th August, with my son, I went on board the steamer " Campana " in the best of spirits. She is a staunch iron vessel, built in England and registered in London. There was an unusual crowd of passengers, but I had telegraphed and secured state-rooms, as the cabins are called, so I had not to content myself with a mattrass on the floor, the fate of many. The water was perfectly smooth. As the steamer left the dock the outline of the town of Collingwood, with the blue mountains in the background, appeared to me more picturesque than ever. What a change has taken place at this spot in the last thirty years, since the day when my men cut the first trees on the first examination of the ground on which this important town now stands. It was then in a state of nature with the primeval forest to the water's edge. It is to-day a scene of busy active life, with wharves, streets, churches, schools and many a pleasant residence. The ground on which the dry dock is constructed I recollect as the spot where I have watched for deer when I had seen their foot tracks fresh on the sand beach. Where are the men who were busy at their work in those days? Who remain of the directors, engineers, contractors, and what the newspapers called "influential personages," who, on a bright winter morning in 1851 gathered near the shore and on the ice, breaking a bottle of wine, named the future City of Collingwood. The familiar features of Sheriff Smith, Judge Orton, Captain Hancock, Messrs. Isaac Gilmour, Geo. H. Cheney, Angus Morrison, John McWatt, De Grassey and Stephens are yet kindly remembered by many, and especially by myself. There were others present whom I do not so well recollect.

How many of these voices are mute, which then joined in the cheers given as the heralds of our good wishes! Few of the actors in that scene remain but myself.

The direct course of the "Campana" was along the coast of Georgian Bay, skirting Craigleith and Thornbury. We touch at the bustling town of Meaford, where our well-filled passenger list receives additions, certainly by no means desirable. But the new-comers crowd on board, and the steamer moves off to round Cape Rich, to enter the bay of Owen Sound. It was one of those pleasant, moonlight, calm evenings so enjoyable in Canada. There was not a ripple on the water. The air was cool and pleasant, the moon three-quarters full, and its reflection seemed to dance over the whole surface of the bay. The steamer is of iron, and we move onward with little noise and without vibration. We enter the narrow harbour at Owen Sound, a town surrounded by low hills, through the gorges of which the River Sydenham penetrates, passing over some falls of great beauty a mile from the town. As we are moving up to the wharf we hear the arrival of the train from Toronto, with more passengers for the boat. The latter have come on board, the vessel has started, when all at once the cry is heard, "A man overboard!" He is soon rescued, but he has lost his hat, and the air of suffering with which he regards this misfortune would lead us almost to think that he held life of little account that it had been preserved at this serious cost. Such an event is by no means uncommon on these lakes. Generally it happens that some one is late for the steamer. Passengers have often to drive long distances; nevertheless they loiter to chat over an evening dram, and lose their time in gossip, or they fail to recollect the length of the distance they have to pass over. Be that as it may, punctuality seems to have been imperfectly learned in these latitudes. It is remembered that the steamer itself is often late, and there is ever present the good natured friend to suggest that "there is no hurry." At last the moment comes. The dawdler is made aware that there is no time to spare. The steamer's last whistle has sounded. There is a rush to get on board, under unfavourable circumstances, and sometimes the experiment is dearly paid for. It is not always the hat that is lost. Sometimes it is the fate of the unhappy wearer never again to require one.

We have recovered from this adventure. We are starting, and have actually left the wharf, but suddenly the signal is given to stop the engine, and the voice of the captain is heard shrieking out, "Sam! there is a letter left at the office by two young ladies." Sam takes no short time to find the letter, but at last we get under way, and our captain is benignity itself. Our next landing place is Sault St. Mary, which we will not reach for thirty hours.

The arrangements for the steamer leaving Collingwood to touch at Owen Sound cannot be accounted for by any doctrine of necessity. It would appear as if the owners were anxious to act with perfect impartiality to the two railway companies, which, if they cannot be called opposition lines, have few interests in common. The Northern line runs to Collingwood; the Toronto, Grey & Bruce to Owen Sound; both from Toronto. As a rule, passengers by the steamer are for the North-West. Generally Port Arthur, on Lake Superior, is their destination. But we lost some twelve hours coasting around from Collingwood, and I could not see with one single advantage. This profitless waste of time will in all probability cease when the boats of the Canadian Pacific run between Port Arthur and Algoma, on the north shore of Lake Huron, connecting at that point with the railways now under construction. The new route will give to eastern passengers what they never yet possessed: a direct connection with Lake Superior without loss of time. From Toronto, passengers will probably continue to be carried for some time as at present.

Having passed three succeeding nights on the railway train on my journey from Halifax, I willingly sought my berth. The breakfast hour is seven, but I had had some experience of the preceding evening's supper. Appetite must possess to many a somewhat tyrannical mastery, if we are to judge by the demonstrative determination to obtain seats at a steamboat table. With us there were four relays of supper, and it was an effort to find a seat at any one of them. Who has not noticed, under such circumstances, the rows of men and women who place themselves, with suppressed impatience, behind the seats, standing in the most prosaic of attitudes, in expectation for the word that the meal is ready. I was myself content to take my place at the fourth table, so that I could eat what I required with deliberation. With this experience, I was in no hurry to rise, so it was about nine o'clock when I entered the long saloon. There were a few stragglers like myself present, probably influenced by the same philosophy, who were seated here and there at a table on which lay the scattered remains of the fourth breakfast. On these lake boats the attendants are called "waiters," not "stewards," as on ocean steamers, and if there be a difference of nomenclature, there is certainly no identity of manner. The steward of the ocean steamer is the most benignant, courtly, kindly, considerate person in the world, and, as a rule, his virtues in this respect are sufficiently appreciated. On this boat I addressed one of the waiters, I thought politely enough, and gave my orders. I was met by the rugged reply, in the hardest of tones, "Ye cannot have hot breakfasts if ye lie in bed." The man's axiom was certainly borne out by fact. There was no breakfast, in the sense of the word, and what there remained was not hot. But the coffee was exceptionally good, and with a crust of bread I thought that I might have fared worse. Possibly the owners of the new steamers to be placed on the lakes next summer will introduce some improvement in the stewards' department, which the ordinary traveller, they may be assured, will duly appreciate.

We were passing through the chain of islands extending from Tobermory to the Great Manitoulin. The water is perfectly smooth. The passengers are lounging, smoking, or basking on deck. Others, proud of their prowess, are relating their adventures and experiences, enlivened with many an anecdote, to the amusement of knots of hearers. As we were running through these waters they were so beautifully smooth and the air so fresh and pleasant that my mind went back to the Adriatic as you see it near Venice, or to the western coast of Italy from Civita Vecchia to Genoa. What you miss is the deep, ultra-marine blue of the Mediterranean. Although above you to-day there is a sky not less cloudless, bright and blue than we see in Southern Europe, the hue of the water is a deep slate colour, but in no way wanting in transparency. We have a horizon only broken by the islands behind us and the Great Manitoulin, dimly lying to our right. Like the Mediterranean, this great inland sea does not always exhibit the glassy surface it presents to-day. As in the Bay of Naples, the waters of which all pictures depict in the brightest blue, the gale can sometimes produce an angry, turbid sea, so on Lake Huron, especially in the late autumn, we have many a storm, often to create the roughest of weather. Some thirty years ago, while crossing in a Mackinaw boat, those were not the days of steamers with four relays of meals, I was caught in a nor'-wester, and driven to take refuge to the windward of one of the smallest of the islands we are leaving behind us. We reached the shore before sundown by the most strenuous exertions. All of us in the boat were exhausted, and we slept soundly on the gravel beach until the following day. The island was but a few acres in extent, but we could not venture to leave it. To have done so would have been certain death, for the water rolled in on the exposed beach in giant, swelling breakers. All the subsistence the whole crew had for three days was a solitary rabbit, which we managed to snare, and a few biscuits we had in our pockets.

It seems as if the whole study of the hour on board the steamer is to provide food for the passengers. It brings to recollection the prosperous hotel manager, who related with great zest how many hundreds he had been feeding in the last few days. It certainly required some genius to feed the numerous passengers of the "Campana," with such limited accommodations. At noon dinner is provided. There are eighty seats, and four times that number of people to fill them. But dinner, like everything else, has its end. The passengers again form in knots upon the deck: the lounger, the smoker and the man who delights in euchre, the latter more within the scope of lake travel than the more classic whist, are all seen at their occupation, and the *raconteur*, with a fresh audience, is more than usually loquacious.

The moon is a day nearer the full; and when the sun sets, it does so gloriously and more brightly than last night. We arrive at a landing place and are moored to a wharf where we have to wait till morning. The Neebish Rapids lie before us. They have been improved for the purpose of navigation, but they are not yet lighted, and it is extremely hazardous to attempt to run them in the dark. Until a few years ago, when they were deepened and widened, they were positively dangerous. Eleven propeller blades were picked up by the divers during their operations. By daylight the Rapids can now be safely enough ascended, but it is not simply the Neebish Rapids which are unnavigable without daylight. An artificial channel through Lake George, made some years ago by the United States authorities, follows a circular course, and it is not possible to pass through it after dark without extraordinary precaution. It is true that it can be effected by sending two boats with lights following the course of the buoys on each side one by one, but all this was a labour our captain had no instructions to undertake, so we remained at the wharf. Had we not experienced the incident of the man overboard, and the forgotten letter of the two damsels at Owen Sound, we might have arrived in time to have ascended by daylight.

The next morning the boat left her moorings at dawn. It is a pleasant sail through Lake George and the St. Mary's River, with its Indian settlements and the quiet locality known as Garden River. We had passed all these places when I awoke. We were then moving through the canal constructed on the Michigan side to overcome the Sault St. Mary. At the "Sault" there are, on either side, the Canadian and United States town bearing its name. Neither of them has much pretension, and neither of them is deficient in picturesqueness. The United States town, on the south side, is not without a certain commercial activity, and contains some barracks, in which generally there are two or three companies of the United States regular army.

The Sault is celebrated for its white-fish, and the passer-by will frequently observe a number of Indian canoes at the foot of the rapids, paddling about, with a man in the stern to seize the fish by a hand net. The white fish is held to be a great delicacy. They appear on the table first about

Kingston, and are caught in all the lakes, but the opinion seems to be that the further north you go the better they are, those on Lake Superior being considered the best. We run out of the canal, and continue through the stretch of the River St. Mary above the Sault. There is little to attract the eye until we reach the lofty heights standing as portals to Lake Superior, the last and largest of the great sheets of water tributary to the St. Lawrence.

CHAPTER X.

LAKE SUPERIOR TO WINNIPEG.

Lake Superior—Early Discoverers—Joliet and La Salle—Hennepin—Du Luth—Port Arthur—The Far West—The North-West Company—Rat Portage—Gold Mining—Winnipeg.

The morning is dull, the sky leaden, and the temperature is not very enlivening for the most of us. But the boat moves pleasantly up the slight current until we reach Whitefish Point, then we enter the lake which lies before us in all its magnificent extent. Some idea of the size of Lake Superior may be formed when it is pointed out that from its two extremities the distance is equal to that from London to the centre of Scotland. In width it is capacious enough to take in the whole of Ireland. Its surface is 600 feet above, its bed is 300 feet below, the ocean level, the lake being 900 feet in depth. Its water is remarkably pure, with the colour of the finest crystal.

We pass a number of steamers and deeply laden vessels. We are now fairly in the lake, with its rugged, rocky hills on the north shore ascending to the height of a thousand feet. We are in the midst of a light fog. The air becomes chilly and raw, but the water continues smooth, and we sail calmly over it. Towards evening the fog has cleared away, and we find ourselves in the midst of this immense fresh water sea. The nearly full moon appears and is high up in view. Our horizon is the circumference of an unbroken circle, for there is not a trace of land in sight. Our position is near the meridian of Chicago, although six degrees of latitude further north; and we approach the longitude of that great western territory which on both sides of the International boundary is being developed with such marvellous progress.

Champlain appears to have known the existence of a northern fresh water lake of great size, but he never visited it. He showed on his map a large body of water under the title, Mer de Nor Glaciale. This was in 1632. Galinée's map of 1670 gives the River Ottawa and Lake Ontario sufficiently correctly for those days, everything considered, but Lake Michigan was unknown to him. He considered Lakes Michigan and Huron to be one body of water, and so represented them. Lake Superior he did not appear to know, although he had reached Sault St. Mary. One of the earliest works of the Jesuit Fathers in Canada is their map of Lake Superior, published in 1671, with the title of Lac Tracy-ou-Superior. It showed that the many bays and inlets had been explored, and the map is marked by great correctness, allowing for the date of its production. They also knew of the Peninsula of Michigan. Indeed by this date the general geography and coast line of the great lakes was fairly understood. In 1669 La Salle made the first of the series of discoveries which have preserved his name. He had heard of the great river to the west, and he was desirous of proceeding thither. He descended the Ohio, probably as far as Louisville, but it was not until eleven years later that he discovered the outlet of the Mississippi. Marquette and Joliet had in the meantime ascended from Green Bay, Lake Michigan, and followed the Fox River to the Mississippi. They may be held to be its discoverers, although claims antagonistic to their priority have been advanced, I believe, without sufficient proof. Hennepin, the Recollet Friar, was the first to ascend the upper waters of the Mississippi and describe the Falls of St. Anthony, where the great milling City of Minneapolis now flourishes. On his return with his captors, for he was a prisoner of the Indians, he met Du Luth some distance below the falls. Du Luth was one of those many enterprising spirits whom France sent to this Continent, a man of untiring energy and undaunted nature. He penetrated to the then utmost limit known. He was a martyr to rheumatism, but no suffering interfered with his discoveries and his devotion to the supremacy of France. At Lake Superior he had heard that there were white men on the Mississippi. The news caused him anxiety. His first thought was that English traders had penetrated from New York, and in the interest of France he felt such intrusion had summarily to be stopped. He started with four well armed Frenchmen, followed one of the streams leading southerly and passed by the St. Croix, which falls into the Mississippi below St. Paul. It was here that he met Hennepin, who proved to be the white man he had heard of. Du Luth returned by way of Lake Michigan.

Previous to this date Du Luth had established himself on the Kaministiquia, Lake Superior. In 1680 he built a fort on the site of the present Fort William on that river, for half a century the extreme point beyond which the French did not penetrate, and in itself the first settlement on the north shore. The Jesuits had established themselves on the south shore of the lake at an early date in Canadian history at La Pointe, the modern Bayfield.

It was a brilliant summer morning, Friday, 17th August, when I awoke; we were near land. Silver Islet was in sight, and Thunder Cape, a bold headland lit up by the sun, stood forth to bid us welcome. During breakfast we enter Thunder Bay, a noble expanse of water surrounded on three sides by lofty hills. The entrance is some six miles wide, protected to some extent from the storms of Lake Superior by Isle Royale, some distance to the south. We have fourteen miles to steam before we reach what was formerly called Prince Arthur's Landing, now known as Port Arthur. It has grown up of late years. It possesses an air of liveliness, and I do not think that those whose interests are centered in the town underrate the advantages of its situation or have any doubts with regard to its future. There are copper and silver mines in the neighbourhood, some of which are represented to be of value. They have been worked from time to time and discontinued, and their occasional operations have told on the progress of the town.

But Port Arthur does not possess unchallenged all the advantages claimed for it. Fort William on the Kaministiquia proffers an equal claim to become the Lake Superior terminus of the Canadian Pacific Railway to the west, and to the point of connection with the eastern bound steamers in summer. A propeller with freight, loaded in the canal basin at Montreal, can reach Thunder Bay without breaking bulk. A large movement in freight and passengers for transfer to the railway for Winnipeg may be looked for, even when the railway line on the north shore of Lake Superior shall have been completed. A trip by the lake steamers is pleasant and agreeable in the fine weather of summer, and doubtless these ports on Thunder Bay will retain their importance.

There is but one train in the twenty-four hours

from Port Arthur to Winnipeg. We were twelve hours too late for the train which had left and twelve hours too early for the one to leave. All that could be done was to accept the situation. Human nature, however, asserts its prerogative under a sense of injustice. My mind, in spite of myself, reverted to our useless journey to Meaford and Owen Sound, and to the waste of time at these places by which we lost so many hours at the Neebish. It was the old story of the nail in the horseshoe of the Cavalier. I think the experience of all travellers is that when a journey is marked by delay, little is done in the way of remedying it. Indifference succeeds the sense of misadventure or carelessness, and the chance of making up lost time becomes every hour less and less.

I had twelve hours before me, so I determined to make good use of them. I communicated by telegraph with the railway superintendent at Winnipeg and the engineer in charge of construction at Calgarry, to enlist their co-operation in our advance over the mountains. I drove with my son from Port Arthur to the River Kaministiquia, a river which assumed some importance in the early days of the construction of the railway six years back. The terminus was established three miles from its mouth. The river is upwards of three hundred feet in width, deep enough to float the largest lake craft. A bar, easily removable, extends across the entrance.

When this obstruction is removed the river will be in all respects accessible, and will extend greater capacity for shipping than the river at Chicago, which accommodates the enormous business of that city.

As it was my duty, I visited the Hudson Bay Company's post near the mouth of the river. After an existence of two centuries as a fur-trading station under varied fortunes, it is soon to disappear, the fate of all such establishments on this continent as civilization overtakes them. As Bishop Berkeley wrote a century ago, "westward the star of empire takes its way."

In my own recollection the "Far West" was on the eastern shores of Lakes Huron and Michigan, now far within the limits of civilization. Those whose fortunes were cast there looked on themselves as pioneers of an unexplored wilderness. Twenty years ago the upper waters of Lake Huron and Lake Superior were but just coming into notice, and Fort William was regarded as the chief eastern outpost of the Hudson's Bay Company, beyond which few thought of passing. This celebrated company, which has played such a part in the history of the North-West of this continent, was formed under a charter of Charles II. in 1670. It was the Treaty of Utrecht in 1713 which fully recognized the English title to the territory granted under the charter, and abandoned forever such French claims as had been preferred, for the Treaty of Ryswick with France in 1696 had left the question of sovereignty undecided.

As early as 1641 two Jesuits, Jogues and Raymbault, extended their missionary labours to the shores of Lake Superior. The main mission, La Pointe, now Bayfield, on the south shore, was established in 1670, and the Indians remained during French rule entirely under their influence. At the period of the conquest the trade of the French disappeared, for they had no longer the power to visit the country, and by degrees it fell into British hands. On the one side, the Hudson's Bay Company, from the north, pushed onwards to control it, for a period with success; on the other, parties were started from Montreal to obtain a share of the great profits which were made, the value of which was fully known.

The French trade had been carried on under admirable regulations. Liquor, so ruinous to the Indian, was withheld from him. The enterprising Montreal trader introduced it, regardless of consequences: hence the orgies, the drunkenness and the quarrels which were a scandal even to the wilderness. To intensify this condition of affairs, some Montreal merchants entered into a partnership in 1787, and formed the celebrated North-West Trading Company. It then consisted of twenty-three partners, with a staff of agents, factors, clerks, guides, interpreters, voyageurs, amounting in all to two thousand persons. If the individual trader disappeared from the field, there were two powerful companies remaining, who had to operate in the same field side by side, and there sprang up the fiercest and most embittered rivalry. I shall hereafter refer more definitely to this contention. This state of things was leading to the common ruin of the two companies, when, in 1821, after forty-three years of competition, discord and disaster, the two formed one corporation under the title of the Hudson's Bay Company.

As I looked upon the old fort on the site of its departed greatness, I thought of the many stirring scenes which it witnessed before and after the beginning of this century. The stone store houses, once so well filled with every requirement, erected around the sides of a square, are now empty, containing a few boxes of rusty flint muskets and bayonets, with chests of old papers, dating back, some of them, more than a hundred years.

The buildings will all soon be unroofed, to make way for a railway station. A year ago I saw two old cannon in the front of the courtyard. On that occasion I believe they fired their last salute. They are now removed. The old rickety flagstaff still remains, and so soon as it is known that a member of the Company of Adventurers is within the precincts the flag is run up as a salute, a service probably for the last time performed at Fort William. In a few months the whole scene will be .changed. There is still an agent of the

Hudson's Bay Company in charge, Mr. Richardson, whose complexion of bronze tells of many years of exposure; and his attendant, an Indian, who has been attached to the fort for forty years.

On leaving Mr. Richardson we called on a retired Hudson's Bay officer, Mr. John McIntyre, who lives in a comfortable house a little further up the river. He is an Argyleshire Highlander, who has the stalwartness of his race, and is as active as ever. At his suggestion we go to Point de Meuron, named after the soldiers of that regiment in Lord Selkirk's service, camped here in the memorable days of 1817. There was nothing to be seen but the farm, so we returned to the town plot, and, as the hour suggested, took dinner at the Ontario House, a place of some local reputation. There were several vessels from Ohio discharging coal at the railway wharves adjoining, showing that even the narrow cut dredged some years ago across the bar at the mouth of the river was still sufficient to admit their passage; establishing, moreover, how easily a properly excavated channel can be maintained, and plainly showing that the completion of navigation at the entrance of the Kaministiquia will eventually have an important bearing on the commerce of the North-West.

I returned to Port Arthur to prepare for the train, when some of my friends kindly gave me an invitation to a ball to take place in the evening.

I should have liked to have accepted it for several reasons, not the least of which was to see that phase of social life in this region; but it was impossible to lose the twenty-four hours, the price of my attendance.

It was dark when the train left, so all that could be done was to turn to the comfortable Pullman, and in due time retire for the night. The railway to Winnipeg is far from being completed; indeed, it has but lately been put in operation. Many of the station buildings have yet to be erected. As a consequence, the following morning the breakfast was served under a large canvas awning. There was no pretension about this breakfast, but what there was of it was good; certainly the ventilation was perfect.

The distance from Port Arthur to Winnipeg is some 430 miles, and, as the unfinished condition of a considerable portion of the line necessitated travelling at reduced speed, the journey to most of the passengers seemed very tedious. To me every mile was full of interest. We pass over that portion of the line known as "Section A," which extends to a point 230 miles from Port Arthur. Civilization and settlement have not penetrated to this district, lying, as it does, intermediate between Lake Superior and the prairie region. We have traversed a long stretch of black, boggy swamp, to which the Indian name of Muskeg has been given. One is reminded of Chatmoss, where similar difficulties in the infancy of railway construction were so triumphantly met by the elder Stephenson. Muskeg is much of the character of peat. It is here inexhaustible, and hereafter may be valuable from its capacity to be formed into fuel.

As the train moves on, nothing is to be seen but rock and forest in their most rugged forms. The falls of Waubigon and those of Eagle River, as we pass them, are the more striking by the contrast they present. We reach the far-famed "Section B," of which we have heard so much, and which is still a theme of such varied comment by politicians and newspaper writers. This section of railway passes through a country rugged in the extreme. The surface is a succession of rocky ridges, with tortuous lakes and deep muskegs intervening. The line has been carried across these depressions on temporary staging, and steam shovels and construction trains are busy converting the miles of frail looking trestlework into solid embankment. Our train moves slowly over this portion of the line; indeed, until this work is further advanced it would be hazardous to adopt a high rate of speed. Eagle Lake, with the numerous lakelets which we see from the railway, are sheets of water with beauty enough to command attention. A few rude graves on the hillside mark the violent death of the poor workmen who suffered from the careless handling of that dangerous explosive, nitro-glycerine. Although the most effective of instruments in the removal of rock, the least want of caution and care often exacts the most terrible penalty. In the fifty miles we have passed over, upwards of thirty poor fellows have lost their lives by its use. This explosive may be used with perfect safety, but in its handling it exacts prudence and attention to details; otherwise there will be no immunity from want of care. With the reckless and negligent it is a constant source of danger.

There is no great area of land suitable for profitable farming in this district. A few good townships may be laid out, but the country generally through which the railway runs is not adapted for agricultural purposes. Every acre of soil, however, is covered with timber of more or less value. Care should be taken to prevent the destruction of these forests. Stringent regulations should be made with regard to them, and no reckless waste permitted. In a few years these forests will prove sources of considerable wealth, and the ground over which we are now passing should be jealously guarded as a preserve for the supply of timber in coming years.

The passengers begin to be clamorous for the next refreshment station. We learn that it is at Rat Portage. We trust that the name does not suggest the cheer we are to receive. There is an old tradition that the Chinaman delighted in that rodent, and we all have read that during the siege of Paris it was an established article of food. Rat Portage is beginning to be an important place. It is situated where the waters of the Lake of the Woods fall into the River Winnipeg. Four large saw mills have been constructed here, and immense quantities of lumber have been despatched to Winnipeg and the country beyond. At present Rat Portage is the watering place for the City of Winnipeg. Gold mining has been commenced, but it is a pursuit on which but little calculation can be made.

For the moment there is excitement in the district, and many explorers are engaged in examining the rocky ledges which crop out on the shore and are exposed on the innumerable islands of the Lake of the Woods. It is to be seen if this is a passing spasm or an assured success. When some instance of individual good fortune in gold mining becomes known, crowds for a time push forward eagerly, many desperately, on the path which they impulsively trust is to lead them at once to fortune. Such hopes are often built on imperfect foundations. The slightest reverse depresses the sanguine gold-hunter, and the pursuit is most often abandoned with the recklessness with which it was undertaken. How many may with bitterness repeat the well known words of my countryman, John Leyden, in his ode to an Indian gold coin:

> "Slave of the mine, thy yellow light
> Gleams baleful on the tomb fire drear."

When the train came to a stand the proverbial rush for dinner was made. No regular refreshment room could be found. In fact, none had yet been erected. But there were several temporary shanties built around, whose merits were loudly proclaimed by the several touts in a great many words and the ringing of bells. We had made the acquaintance of some New Zealand travellers on their way to see two sons settled in Manitoba, and we agreed to take our dinner together. We selected one of these establishments. Our recollections of Rat Portage are not impressed by any excellence in its commissairiat. That which was set before us was execrable. I am not difficult to please, but there is a lower depth in these matters. Such a meal would scarcely have been palatable during the hunger of the siege of Paris, and a man could only have swallowed what was given at Rat Portage when suffering the pangs of starvation. There is evidently a call for improvement at this place before the line is fully opened to travellers.

Leaving Rat Portage, we pass to what is known as "Section Fifteen." It is nearly forty miles in length, and, like "Section B," runs through a district remarkable for its rugged aspect. For a long distance west of Rat Portage the country is much the same in character as the Lake of the

Woods: full of rocky, tree-covered ridges and islets, the former a labyrinth of deep, narrow, winding sheets of water, separated by tortuous granite bluffs. If the lake has within its limits hundreds of islands, the land embraces innumerable lakelets. It was this rugged and broken country, so repelling in its condition in the wilderness, which dictated the opinion of a quarter of a century back of high authorities that the country between Lake Superior and Red River was not practicable for railway construction. The difficulties have, however, been grappled with and overcome, necessarily with great labour and great cost; and, as I was passing over it, it struck my mind as no bad example of the danger of positively asserting a negative. The necessary work of placing the trestlework in good condition on "Section Fifteen" is more advanced than on "Section B." The train, therefore, runs at a higher rate of speed. As we proceed we can observe that the roadbed is fairly well ballasted, and we run at about thirty miles an hour on the finished portion of the line, over the gigantic earthworks of Cross Lake, Lake Deception and the succeeding lakes.

The distance from Lake Superior to the Red River at Selkirk is 410 miles, and notwithstanding the extreme roughness of the country through which it passes, the railway, when completed, will bear comparison with any other line on this Continent. The utmost care has been exercised to establish gradients favourable to cheap transportation. In this respect I know of no other four hundred miles of railway in the Dominion or in the United States that can be compared with the section west of Port Arthur.

We leave "Section 15" and the rugged country behind us, and enter on the prairie land of the West. We pass Selkirk, which once promised to be a centre of importance, but the City of Winnipeg, twenty miles to the south of it, has grown up, is rapidly increasing, and asserting its claim to be the first city in the North-West. As we proceed the sky becomes darkened and we are overtaken by a thunderstorm, during which the rain falls in as heavy masses of water as it has ever been my fate to see. The wind increases to a hurricane, but art triumphs over the elements. As the train continues its course on the well ballasted road, at the rate of twenty-five miles an hour, the passengers generally seemed scarcely aware of the tempest raging outside. An unusual phenomenon is presented : we pass through an electrical snowstorm, which, in a few minutes, whitens the ground over a stretch of a mile. Hail storms are in no way uncommon when the conditions of the air are disturbed, but I have never before witnessed a snowstorm under similar circumstances.

We reach the station at Winnipeg, having been twenty-four hours on our journey. A few years ago the distance from Lake Superior to this point, by the old canoe route, exacted twelve or fourteen days. When the railway is in complete working order the journey may be performed in fourteen hours. On my arrival at the station the night was black and forbidding, for the rain continued to fall in torrents. Nevertheless several old friends were there to extend me a welcome and the offer of a temporary home. Among others I grasped the hand of Dr. Grant, of Queen's College, who again is to be my companion to the Pacific Coast. Before leaving the station I made definite arrangements with the railway officials to leave in thirty-six hours for Calgary. We groped our way through the wind and rain to profit by the hospitality so kindly offered, and I was not sorry to find myself again under a roof with the best of good cheer before me.

CHAPTER XI.

WINNIPEG, HUDSON'S BAY COMPANY, LORD SELKIRK.

Early Explorers of the North-West—Du Luth—De la Verendrye—Mackenzie—Hudson's Bay Company—Treaty of Utrecht—North-West Company—Lord Selkirk—War in the North-West—Union of the Rival Companies—The North-West Annexed to Canada.

Winnipeg, with a population of 30,000 inhabitants, is the creation of the last decade. Thirteen years back there was little to distinguish its site from any other spot on the river's bank. The Red River was skirted by a single tier of holdings on the shore line, directly along its banks for a distance of fifty miles, known as the Selkirk Settlement. At the confluence of the River Assiniboine with the main stream there stood old Fort Garry, an establishment of the Hudson's Bay Company. We have in this old fort the precursor of the city. In 1859 a few buildings, including a hotel, were clustered near it as the commencement of the future Winnipeg. At an early date in the history of French Canada a great extent of the country around the western lakes was explored. Prominent among the many men eminent in these discoveries was Du Luth, who appears in connection with the North-West as having been the first to establish a fort on the River Kaministiquia, Lake Superior, about 1680, on the site of Fort William. It is not to be supposed that at this date no further explorations were undertaken westward by the French. Many of the waterways were certainly known, and to some extent they were followed. But no attempt was made to extend trade operations beyond Lake Superior; and it was only to a limited extent that discovery was pushed westward. For some years exploration was turned towards the south of the territory held by the French, to guard against the encroachment of the English from New York, which now commenced to attract more attention.

There is no proof that any change in this respect took place until the days of De la Verendrye. This remarkable man in 1731 was in charge of Fort Nepigon, Lake Superior. In that year he started westward across the height of land, passed through the chain of lakes to the Lake of the Woods and followed the River Winnipeg to Lake Winnipeg. Proceeding to the south of the Lake he ascended the Red River and reached the Assiniboine. I cannot learn that any white man, before him, ever stood on the site of the present City of Winnipeg.

A series of forts were constructed by him; one

where Rainy River flows into the Lake of the Woods, Fort St. Pierre; one on what is known as the Northwest Angle, Fort Charles; one where the River Winnipeg flows into Lake Winnipeg, Fort Maurepas, which name he also gave to the lake itself; one where the Red River flows into Lake Winnipeg, Fort Rouge; and one at the junction of the Assiniboine with the Red River, proximately on the site of the City of Winnipeg, Fort de la Reine.

De la Verendrye, himself, never saw the Rocky Mountains, but the discovery was made by his two sons in an expedition organized by him and carried out in accordance with his instructions. They started from the Fort de la Reine, followed the Assiniboine to the River Souris, which they traced to one of its sources, thence passing to the Missouri they followed that stream till they came within sight of the first range of mountains. It was therefore to the south of Canadian territory that the peaks were first seen. De la Verendrye had made a series of northern explorations, reaching the Saskatchewan by Lake Winnipeg, into which it discharges. He established Fort Bourbon at this point. He advanced along the river as far as Lake Cumberland, at the entrance to which he established Fort Poscoyac, which seems to have been the limit of his travels. He was acquainted with Lake Winnipegoosis and Lake Manitoba, and established Fort Dauphin at the northern end of the latter lake. While engaged in organizing a more extended expedition he died in 1749 at Quebec.

The succeeding ten years of French Canada were passed in the struggle for national life. The North-West obtained but little attention except for the purpose of commerce with the Indians. In spite of the difficulties of carrying it on, it had increased in extent and was now of considerable importance. With the conquest the trade almost disappeared, and it was not for some years afterwards that it was recommenced on the part of the British.

The celebrated Sir Alexander Mackenzie, the first white man who by land reached the Pacific Ocean in Northern latitudes, has left some valuable information concerning the trade of this period. We learn from him that the military posts established by the French at the confluence of the lakes had strongly in view the control of the traffic in furs. During French rule, trade had been conducted under admirable regulations. He himself tells us that a number of able and respectable men, retired from the army, had carried on their operations under license with great order and regularity. At the same time, the trade itself was fettered by many unwise restrictions Nevertheless it was taken to immense distances, and " it was a matter of surprise," he adds, " that no exertions were made from Hudson's Bay to obtain even a share of the trade," which, according to the charter of that company, belonged to it.

The Hudson's Bay Company at this date had been nearly a century in existence. Hudson's last voyage to Hudson's Bay was in 1610. In 1612 Button sailed and discovered Port Nelson, York Factory. It was not, however, until 1669 that any settlement was made, when Captain Zachariah Gillam, a New England captain, established himself at the discharge of the Nemisco and constructed a stone fort, calling it Fort Charles, the present Fort Rupert. It was after this step, on the 2nd of May, 1670, that the charter was given to the Hudson's Bay Company, a result no little owing to the influence of Prince Rupert.

The first operations of the company were marked by great energy, and their trade rapidly increased. In the first fifteen years five factories were in operation: Rupert, to the east of James' Bay, at the discharge of the River Nemisco; Hayes, at the south-western corner and at the mouth of the Moose River; Albany, on the west, some twenty miles north of Moose River; York Factory, on the Nelson River; and Churchill, north of York, the most northerly settlement on the west coast.

From 1686 to the Treaty of Utrecht there were a series of attempts on the part of French Canada to dispossess the company. No doubt the French authorities held that their supremacy was dangerously threatened by the establishment of flourishing settlements to the north, identical in nationality with the Bostonnais of Massachusetts and the English of New York. The Treaty of Ryswick itself, in 1695, even became the cause of difficulty, from the vagueness of its provisions, and it was not until the Treaty of Utrecht, in 1713, that the French claims were entirely abandoned. The English Government had determined to retain Nova Scotia, the fisheries of Newfoundland and what was called the Hudson's Bay Territory, and on that basis peace was made.

For the next half century there was no clashing of interests between the Hudson's Bay Company and the French of Canada, owing to the operations of the latter being extended in a limited degree north of Lake Superior. After the conquest, for some years, the trade was thrown entirely into the Company's hands. Indians even went to York Factory to barter their furs. During this period the profits must have been immense. It was only by degrees that the English traders from Canada penetrated into the country. They found the Indian unfriendly. The French had instilled into his mind a jealousy of the English speaking race, having represented it as the ally of the Iroquois, the long-standing enemy of the Lake Superior Indians. A rooted distrust had thus grown up which long remained. About 1766 trade somewhat recommenced, assisted by Montreal enterprise. Michillimackinac was for a long time the base of such operations, and few traders penetrated further than the Kaministiquia. Thomas Curry was the first to pass beyond this limit. He reached Fort Bourbon, where Cedar Lake discharges into Lake Winnipeg, whence he brought away so fine a cargo of furs that he was satisfied never again to return to the Indian country.

By this time the Hudson's Bay Company had pushed on their posts to Sturgeon Lake, and now commenced that antagonism between those representing the interests centered at Montreal and the members of the company, which for half a century caused difficulty, embarrassment, loss and finally bloodshed.

One of the charges made against the Montreal traders of those days was that they were the first to introduce rum into the North-West, to the ruin of the Indians.

A name of that period, preserved in the records of the law, still survives: Peter Pond, who was tried for the murder of one of his partners. He escaped by the Court determining that they had no jurisdiction in the territory. Pond was a man of much energy. Following in the steps of Frobisher, he traded north of Lake Winnipeg to the tributaries of the Churchill, and to the Westward as far as the Arthabaska and Elk Rivers. His purpose was to intercept the furs *en route* to Fort Churchill, on Hudson's Bay. The trade, in the meantime, received a severe blow from the conduct of some traders at Eagle Hills. A dose of laudanum was given to an Indian, and caused his death. In the turmoil which ensued several lives were lost, and the commerce with the Indians became much impeded.

To remedy the depressed condition of the trade and to avoid further complications, the North-West Company was formed in 1783. A rival company was started, of which the celebrated Mackenzie was a member. The two were, however, united in 1787.

At this date the North-West Company arrogated to itself full control over the country. No operations of any kind except under their authority were permitted. The company was supreme. The private trader was driven from the field, and it would seem that these extreme measures could be carried out with impunity. They were the days of the North-West Company's affluence and power. Influences even without its ranks came within their control, to make the organization irresistible. Peculiarly it was a Canadian enterprise, and as such commanded sympathy against competition from without. We can scarcely, at this day, understand the extent of its power. In our commercial world, as we find it, there are many wealthy corporations possessing social and political control. The avenues to wealth and distinction are numerous, branching out from many centres. It may be asserted that formerly the

North-West was looked upon as the one field which promised prizes in life's lottery to the youth of the country. The leading magnates, who had large incomes, indulged in princely hospitality, the memory of which has not wholly died away, and it may be conceived how, at that date, with a small population, with a limited field for enterprise, with little general wealth, the power of the company was everywhere recognized.

I have now arrived at the period when I have to record the settlement of Red River, the forerunner of the City of Winnipeg: indeed, the first step taken towards making the prairies the abode of civilized life. The task is not easy. The ashes of the fires of that day are yet warm under our feet. The sons and grandsons of the men whose names are identified with the leading events are among those who we meet daily. The story has often been told; nevertheless it is only imperfectly known. The principal actor in these events was Lord Selkirk. As his character is studied it must be conceded that few men have been marked by a higher sense of life and duty. A man of remarkable ability, his character was one of rare disinterestedness and chivalry, and I cannot but think his name will so live in our history.

As early as 1802 Lord Selkirk entered into correspondence with the English Government on the advisability of promoting emigration from the

Highlands and Ireland to Rupert's Land. The following year he arranged to carry a body of Highlanders to Prince Edward Island. We next hear of him in Canada and the United States, where he passed two years examining into the means available to carry out his purpose. During 1804 he entered into correspondence with General Hunter, then Governor of Upper Canada, now Ontario, with regard to making settlements in that Province. Those were not the days when questions such as these received much attention, nor were they even understood. The value of population to develop the resources of a country had generally to be better known before correct views could prevail as to the value of unsettled land, and the negotiations failed owing to the excessive price demanded for it.

As Canada did not offer the field sought, Lord Selkirk turned to the Hudson's Bay Company as the means by which his theories of colonization could be carried out. He and his friends took their measures accordingly. He purchased stock in the company, and thus obtained a commanding influence and the recognition necessary for the prosecution of the undertaking. This event took place in 1811.

From the commencement the North-West Company vigorously opposed his project. They looked upon Lord Selkirk as a visionary, and his scheme alike impracticable and undesirable. They might not be unwilling to divide the hunting ground of a continent with their rivals, but they did not recognise that the prairies of the west were available for support of human life. They regarded the country as a wilderness, to be reserved for the fur-bearing animals alone. Hitherto their profits had been excessive and secure, and any change threatening the discontinuance or reduction of the advantages which they possessed had to be avoided.

Evidently such a scheme as that of Lord Selkirk's was the first step towards the destruction of their trade and the diminution of their profits. The same year some ninety persons, mostly Highland cotters from Sutherlandshire, with a few additions from the West of Ireland, reached Hudson's Bay. They wintered there, and in 1812 travelled to Red River, a proceeding in itself memorable, as from it dates the settlement of the North-West. A further number was added in 1813. The two winters 1812-1813, till the spring of 1814, were passed at Pembina, at Fort Daer. The Governor was Captain Miles Macdonnell, formerly of the Queen's Rangers. In 1814 further settlers arrived under Mr. A. Macdonald, having passed the winter at Fort Churchill. Towards the end of the year the number amounted to two hundred.

It was in this year that the Governor issued the proclamation so much criticized and censured, and it has been brought forward as sufficient in itself to justify the inimical proceedings subsequently taken against the settlement. It is difficult to recognize that it was not warranted by the circumstances, and, considering the interests entrusted to the Governor, that it was not one which he had a perfect right to issue when he did so, in no way to the injury of others. He directed that no provisions should be exported from the country, as such stores were required for the arrivals expected, that money would be paid for all produce, and that those not observing these regulations would be arrested. The Governor must have known and felt the difficulties under which he was placed. The North-West Company, both in London and on this continent, had shown the strongest opposition to the settlement. Independently of the nature of the difficulties incident to the situation, there was this enmity to be met; an enmity known to be powerful and not over scrupulous. It is true that it had not taken the armed and open attitude which it ultimately assumed, but the ruin of the settlement had long been resolved upon.

A council of the officers of the North-West Company was held at Fort William in 1814, and it is in evidence that it was here that plans were formed to induce the settlers to abandon their homesteads and prejudice the Indians against them—every employé of the company was already their foe—and to buy up all the provisions so that scarcity should result and ruin to the settlement follow. It was in anticipation of such a scheme that the Governor's proclamation was issued. He had obtained information that such a policy would be followed, and he endeavoured, on his side, to meet it as best he could.

The Selkirk settlers had constructed a new fort, Fort Douglas. Its site lies within the present City of Winnipeg, not far from Fort Gibraltar, the property of the North-West Company. It was in 1814 that Duncan Cameron came to the Red River in charge of the latter. His special mission was to influence the settlers to abandon their homes. Cameron is represented to have been a man of address and plausibility, and he so well executed the duty assigned him of making those who listened to him discontented that about three-fourths of the number left the Red River for Upper Canada. Their descendants are yet to be found in the Counties of Elgin, Middlesex and Simcoe, in Ontario.

It will scarcely be believed that a notice was served on those who remained, signed by four partizans of the North-West Company, sternly requiring them to leave the settlement. It had to be entirely abandoned. The better to show their power, in the temporary absence of the Governor, they removed the cannon, implements and other property from Fort Douglas. The proceeding was doubtless calculated to show the strength of the North-West Company, side by side with the impotent character of Lord Selkirk's protection. There was no course open but compliance. The exiles took canoes and paddled down the Red River to Lake Winnipeg, and reached Norway House, to the north of the lake. They had not been long here when they were met by Collin Robertson and some twenty employés passing up Jack River on their way to join the settlement. Robertson was a man of determination, and saw that there was no good reason why the enterprise should be abandoned, and that such an outrage, with one of Selkirk's character, would only call for renewed effort. He induced the settlers to return. They found their houses burned and their property destroyed. This occurred in August, but in October an additional number came, and the settlement had regained more assured strength. We have now arrived at 1816.

In the half century which had elapsed since the conquest that which may almost be called a new race of men had sprung up: the children of the French *voyageurs* of the North-West Company, who had married or lived with Indian women in the neighbourhood of the several forts. They obtained the name of "Bois-Brulés." They were powerful in frame, disinclined to restraint, attached to a wandering life and unsettled habits, mostly without education. They were easily accessible to those who knew how to appeal to their prejudices.

They had courage, and under able leaders became a formidable foe. Their sympathies were difficult to determine. Perhaps the leading feature of their character was jealousy of their individual rights. In subsequent years their self-assertion took so threatening a form that the presence of Imperial troops more than once became necessary. Early in June, 1816, a party of them gathered at Portage-la-Prairie, on the Assiniboine. They had but one object in view. It was, in a sentence, to retain the country for themselves, and to drive out all whom they had learned to look upon as intruders. There is everything to show that they were perfectly organized. They were armed, it is said that they were painted and disguised, and every precaution taken to make their movements appear an act of the genuine Red man. The evidence, accessible to those who will examine it, shows that the Indians were in no way mixed up with the expedition. It was confined to the men whose sympathies were with the North-West Company. Their operations commenced by seizing some boats and furs at Portage-la-Prairie, belonging to the Hudson's Bay Company, and advancing to Fort Douglas, at Red River.

At the fort itself the intrigues and intentions of those hostile to the settlement were known, and in some undefined way it was felt that danger was near. What form it would take, or whence it would come, none could say, but a watch was kept night and day. It would appear that the attack came earlier than was looked for. On the evening of the 17th June the alarm was given of the approach of the Bois-Brulés. Semple was the Governor. He was a man of courage and had served. He did what little he could with the resources which at that hour were available. He collected a few men and started onwards to meet the advancing party. Seeing the numbers increase, he sent for a cannon and more force, and in the meantime continued to advance. As the opposing parties approached, each leader asked the other what he wanted. It is stated that one of the Governor's party fired a shot in the air, on which a shot from the Bois-Brulés brought down Mr. Holte, who held the rank of lieutenant in the settlement. The firing became general. Governor Semple was killed and his men fell around him. Twenty-two in all were shot. There is no report of a death on the side of the Bois-Brulés. No further resistance was attempted, and Fort Douglas was given over to the North-Westers. The settlers were compelled to take to their canoes and find a refuge where they could. The settlement was again entirely broken up.

Such was the celebrated affair of Seven Oaks on the 17th June, 1816, yet sung in the songs of the Bois-Brulés and chanted as the hymn of victory.

Lord Selkirk had heard the story of the attack

of the preceding year, and at once hurried to Canada. He passed the winter of 1815 in Montreal, the season being too late for him to go west. Governor Semple was held to be in all respects competent, and Lord Selkirk had given him his full confidence; so it was thought that until his own arrival no further difficulty would be experienced. He was, however, convinced that the attacks had not ceased, and that if the settlement had to be defended a force sufficient to meet such outrages had to be found. The deMeuron and Watteville regiments were on the eve of being disbanded, and Lord Selkirk obtained from their ranks the men he required to recruit the colony. These regiments were two of the foreign legion raised during the Peninsula war; they had been ordered to Canada in 1812. At the peace after Waterloo their disbandment was resolved on. They left the British service with the highest reputation for discipline and conduct. Early in June, 1816, the expedition started from Montreal with four officers and eighty men of the deMeuron corps. At Kingston the number was increased by seventy of the Watteville regiment. It proceeded up to Drummond's Island on Lake Huron to receive a sergeant and six men of the Imperial army, who were to be present at Red River as a proof of the countenance given to the settlement by the home authorities.

Selkirk joined the expedition at Sault St. Mary

His purpose was to have proceeded to Duluth, Fond du Lac, and to have crossed overland to Red River. They had not advanced far when they met Miles Macdonnell bringing down the news of the second destruction of the colony and of the violent death of the Governor and twenty-one of his people. Selkirk at once started for Fort William to meet the foe on his own ground. They arrived on the 12th August and encamped on the Point deMeuron, some five miles from the mouth of the Kaministiquia, a name it still retains, and which the reader may remember I alluded to when visiting that locality. A demand was at once made on the fort for the parties captured, who had been brought there as prisoners. The North-West people denied the fact of the arrest, and sent them to Point deMeuron.

Lord Selkirk had now before him the evidence of such of his people who had suffered at Seven Oaks to confirm the opinion that the trouble had been caused by the North-West Company. Fort William was unable to resist him. He arrested McGillivray, McKenzie and others of the Company who were then present, by warrant. They were allowed to remain for a time at Fort William, but as it was evident a rescue was intended, he sent them down as prisoners to York, now Toronto, under an escort. Selkirk wintered on the Kaministiquia and collected provisions. On the 1st May, 1817, he started for Red River, and arrived there the last week in June, passing over the distance in seven or eight weeks, which recently I travelled by rail in twenty-four hours. The settlement was again established.

Like all men who take a prominent part in life's drama, Lord Selkirk has his admirers and defamers. There are those who can see in his conduct only the most self-interested motives and an example of arbitrary, tyrannical self-assertion. He lived in an age when his unselfish views were rare. To-day we can better understand that his object in urging emigration as a scheme to aid the poor and struggling masses of an overcrowded country, sprang from philanthropy and a desire to relieve suffering humanity. His personal comforts and benefits lay in the opposite direction to the course he pursued. A calculation of the chances could promise only misconception of his motives and personal annoyance. He lived half a century before his time Of late years his theories have been accepted as admitted truths. Every facility has been established to carry them out. The shores of this Continent yearly bear witness in the number of immigrants who arrive, that it is the policy of all wise governments to aid the less fortunate of a people to seek a home on the unoccupied lands which are open to them. Such was Selkirk's view. Moreover, he desired to keep up the national prestige. His aim was to transplant those who were willing to struggle to better their future to a land of promise beyond the seas, where they were required to adapt themselves to no new political existence; where they changed, it is true, the scene of their lives, but still remained subjects of the mother land whence they had sprung.

In 1821 the Hudson's Bay Company and the North-West Company united their fortunes, and have since continued under the name of the Hudson's Bay Company.

Here I shall leave the subject. The events which grew out of the proceedings above described are too near the present day to suggest that any comment should be made upon them in the circumstances under which I write. For the next half century the colony passed through many difficulties. It had no assistance in the shape of emigration. The Bois-Brulés often caused trouble. After Lord Selkirk's death, which took place in Paris in 1820, the wants of the settlers were cared for by his relatives. In 1835 they gave up all control to the Hudson's Bay Company.

The events following the transfer of the Hudson's Bay Company's territory to the Government of Canada in 1870 are fresh in remembrance, and the period has not arrived to state them dispassionately. In the meantime Winnipeg has grown up to be a lively, bustling city, full of business and enterprise. One danger, however, threatens Winnipeg, that of floods; and I allude to it in the hope of directing the attention of those of her citizens who have influence, that some consideration be given to the subject, so that all possible precautions be taken to reduce the risk of danger and loss. I believe it is one of the painful experiences of humanity that where a flood has once been, there is always a probability that it may repeat itself. During the early days of the Pacific Railway this question was earnestly considered. The levels of the recorded floods of 1826, 1852 and of 1861, from which the Selkirk settlements suffered so much, showed that there was danger to be apprehended, and that it would be advisable to bridge the Red River at a point where traffic would run no risk of being impeded. The town plot of Selkirk, about twenty miles nearer Lake Winnipeg, was the point recommended. I have no desire to be an alarmist and to reproduce the accounts of these floods, written by Archbishop Taché, the Bishop of Rupert's Land, and by Mr. Alexander Ross. It is not to be said that these gentlemen were interested witnesses desirous of injuring the country in which they lived.

No one can more firmly hope than myself that no such flood may ever again happen. We have, however, before us the experience of this winter in the central United States, and the people of Winnipeg themselves have had several premonitory warnings within the past few years. Should there be a repetition of what has previously happened, damage so extensive must arise that it cannot be contemplated without dread. All but the original landowners and the speculators who have been enriched by their operations in lots will be serious sufferers, and none more than the population of Winnipeg will deplore that the city has been built within the known limits of a periodic overflow.

The time has passed for the consideration where a better location might have been obtained for the establishment of a centre of the importance which Winnipeg promises to attain. But it is necessary to endeavour to find a solution to the complicated engineering problem by which future disastrous consequences may be avoided. The responsibility is now thrown upon the Municipal Corporation, and it is their duty to care for the safety of the city, so that there will be the least cause to lament that it has not been founded on a site above all risk of injury from floods.

CHAPTER XII.

WINNIPEG TO CALGARY.

Winnipeg—Great Storm—Portage-la-Prairie—Brandon—Moose Jaw—Old Wives' Lakes—The Indians—Maple Creek—Medicine Hat—Rocky Mountains.

The rain continued to fall in torrents the whole night of our arrival in Winnipeg, and the gale increased in violence. The streets were next to impassable. Roadways, without paving or metal, in the newest of cities, formed only on the deep, black, vegetable soil of the locality, are the least fitted to undergo an ordeal such as that of the last fifteen hours. The storm increased in strength to the time when the services commenced, so on this Sunday the city clergymen preached to pews almost empty. It was not until late in the afternoon that its violence passed away. But its traces were everywhere visible. Trees recently planted had been torn up by their roots; buildings had been unroofed and many injured; frame-work in course of construction had been destroyed, and a church steeple was completely thrown down. As daylight was waning it became possible to walk on the plank sidewalk without danger of being mastered by the wind. The roads were in a terrible condition, and where no plank had been laid down, the foot sank deep into the tenacious mud.

I had arranged to start by the eight o'clock train on the Monday. Our baggage had been all collected, and we breakfasted early. The cabman anticipated the appointed hour, bearing in mind the condition of the streets through which his horses had to toil. The roads were, indeed, in a wretched state. I could only compare the thoroughly saturated, deep, black, vegetable soil to treacle, and the horses had to do their utmost to draw the load through it. The wheels were often axle deep, and the vehicle cracked, from time to time, as if it was going to pieces. The platform of the station was crowded. The last look was given to the bags, blankets and waterproofs, and to the saddles, bridles, tents and our whole outfit, to see that they were all collected and that nothing was left behind. As it would be impossible to supply a missing necessary after we had left the railway, the inspection had to be made with care.

During my stay in Winnipeg I saw the Chief Commissioner of the Hudson's Bay Company, and discussed with him the possibility of having supplies sent from the Company's establishment in British Columbia to meet us at a point east of Kamloops. It would scarcely be possible to carry with us from this side sufficient food for the whole distance. It seemed practicable, however, to make this arrangement, and he kindly undertook to telegraph and also explicitly instruct his agent in British Columbia to carry it out. Before leaving the station it was definitely agreed that such supplies should reach the Columbia River, opposite the Eagle Pass, by the 8th or 10th of September. If on our arrival at Calgary circumstances compelled us to abandon the attempt to cross the mountains, the fact would be telegraphed both to himself and to British Columbia.

The distance across from Calgary to Kamloops is possibly over 400 miles. Leaving the railway at the former place, we must carry our provisions with us, limiting our supply to the bare quantity necessary to reach the point agreed upon. To make a good start is one of the first elements of success, and it was my endeavour to avoid all ground for self-reproach whatever might hereafter happen.

As the train moved out of the station many of our old friends kindly bade us farewell. The railway company had kindly placed at my disposal a private car, attached to the rear of the four ordinary cars, which, with the baggage and post office cars, constituted the train. My small party was now joined by Dr. Grant, who had accompanied me on a similar expedition across the continent eleven years back.

There is no great extent of farming to be seen immediately in the neighbourhood of Winnipeg. The land, I believe, is generally held by speculators; probably as the "boom" has lost somewhat of its force, this fallow land may once more be considered of value to the agriculturist. During the past two years the locality has generally been regarded as given up to speculation. As we proceed, however, we come upon fields of oats and wheat, and much to the surprise of all of us the grain stands up undamaged by the recent storm.

The line runs, I will not say in the Valley of the Assiniboine, for such an expression will scarcely convey the meaning in this prairie country, but its direction follows generally the course of the river to Portage-la-Prairie, from which point the route is almost due west. Ten years ago Portage-la-Prairie had little more than the name by which it was known by the *voyageur;* it is now a thriving town with many streets and buildings extended over possibly a square mile. Two large elevators are constructed on the railway line for the storage of wheat, and there is a brisk, lively tone about the station, which, I am told, is characteristic of the place. The town is on the northern bank of the Assiniboine, directly to the south of Lake Winnipeg. A branch railway has been established north-westerly to Gladstone. The next station is Burnside, an improvement on Rat Creek, as it was once called. The new name has not unlikely been suggested by some recollection of McGill College, Montreal; the Burnside estate being the property on which that University is built, and which furnished the means of its endowment.

Eleven years ago I camped at this place, not far from the last house on the prairies, no settlers having ventured west of where we stood. The country around is now well cultivated, large fields of waving grain stretch far back from the railway on both sides; and one might easily fancy he was looking at a champagne country, developed by a century of agriculture. Archbishop Taché was on the train, and did me the favour to join us in our car. It need scarcely be said that our comfort and convenience had been much increased by the possession of this private car. Accommodation, in respect to meals, on many parts of the line is not fully completed. We had a kitchen and a cook and a well provided larder. We had bedrooms and couches, chairs and tables in perfect arrangement. Meals were served regularly whether the train was standing or moving. Our dinner with the Archbishop was very pleasant. He was in excellent spirits, and we thoroughly enjoyed his conversation. We were fortunate in respect to our cook, an artist in his way, and he did his utmost to develope the many resources kindly provided for our use.

Before reaching Brandon we passed through the luxuriant rolling prairie in the neighbourhood of

Carberry. It is diversified by groves of trees, and it is an easy effort of thought to imagine that you are in a suburban park of some large city. The soil is good and warm. Large crops of grain are visible, and in no way have they been affected by the storm of yesterday.

We arrived at Brandon, where the passengers dine. We are now 130 miles from Winnipeg. The progress at Brandon in so short a time is remarkable. The streets are well formed, and, owing to the gravelly nature of the soil, I could not but think, in a much better condition than those we had left behind in Winnipeg. The town is advantageously situated on a slope rising from the River Assiniboine, and commands a good view of the surrounding landscape. It has become a busy and important place. I was here a year ago, and then a cluster of canvas tents constituted the town. The prairie in all directions in the neighbourhood has a warm subsoil of sandy or gravelly loam, differing from the deep, black, vegetable mould of the level banks of Red River. Settlers' houses and huts are seen in all directions, and I learn that a great extent of the country has been taken up for farming. As we advance westward the prairie appears in all respects suited for settlement, and we see indications on all sides that the land is occupied.

We pass Virden, a station and village which have sprung into existence in a year. About forty good wooden houses have replaced the one tent of twelve months back. Carpenters are at work on an elevator, on the summit of which their hammers resound, and which will soon be completed. The streets of the village are also in course of formation; and one feels that there is here great promise of a prosperous future.

We have now reached the spot on the line where the reservation of the mile belt along the railway begins, so the farms cease to come within our immediate view. Stations succeed each other at every eight or ten miles. To a greater or less extent a village is springing up around each station. Passing one of these places our attention was drawn to a pile of lumber destined, we were told, for the erection of a Presbyterian Church. With some complacency we are asked to accept it as an evidence that there are farmers, not far distant, to attend the church, and that it is an evidence of their piety. It is a material proof of the confidence of those furnishing the money to build it, that there is every inducement to remain where they have settled, and that their future is one of assured confidence.

Moosomin is the place where the train halts for supper. It has a life of six months and now counts several buildings. Meals, however, are still given in a canvas tent. Broadview, twenty miles further, is a place of more importance. Here an engine stable has been constructed, and we obtain a fresh locomotive. As it is nine o'clock when we arrive, a Pullman sleeper is attached to the train. It has been raining and the night is dark; between ten and eleven the moon comes out to some extent. We can see by its light the country around us, but all of us had risen early and we were not sorry to seek our beds.

During the night we have passed fourteen or fifteen embryo towns. We even failed to see Regina, the capital of Assiniboine. I cannot, therefore, speak of its Government buildings, its terraces, its avenues and its parks. Possibly it may be described as being a place of as much importance as Winnipeg was ten or twelve years ago.

We reached Moose Jaw before breakfast, and received a copy of the *Moose Jaw News*. Amongst its advertisements we learn that pianos are offered for sale, and that these luxuries can be had side by side with buckboards, stoves, and, what is of first importance in that country, lumber. The paper, we learn, is published every Friday morning in the city of Moose Jaw. There can be no doubt of its journalistic loyalty to the interests advocated. The city is declared to be in all respects a better, larger and more promising city than its rival, Regina, and it is authoritatively claimed that the *News* has an infinitely larger list of subscribers than the *Leader*, published at the Capital. On leaving this ambitious place, four hundred miles from Winnipeg, and the editor and his readers have our best wishes for the future of their city, our cook gives us a breakfast which would satisfy the most critical *gourmet*. The line now follows Thunder Creek, gradually ascending the grand Coteau of the Missouri. It may be said that we have been passing over classic ground. According to common belief, it was this route which the sons of De la Verendrye followed when they first saw the Rocky Mountains. Leaving the Red River by the Assiniboine, they turned into its tributary, the Souris, which they traced to its source, not far to the south of us, and then passed over to the Missouri.

The herbage is light but the soil, when turned over to form the embankment, is warm, friable clay. I cannot but believe that if the rainfall be sufficient, almost any crop will thrive upon such a soil. The summers are undoubtedly dry in this section, if we may judge from the flora; all grain, it seems to me, should be sowed in the first days of spring to profit by the moisture of that season and to obtain early strength. There is an utter absence of trees on these rolling plains, and it would be well to encourage plantation for many reasons, not the least important being the improvement of the climate. It is not by spasmodic efforts at plantation that any appreciable change will be effected. It is only by constant and persevering labour that the face of the country can be changed and the climate rendered less arid.

Secretan is the name of the station on the summit and we descend westerly, passing through cuttings which expose fine beds of gravel, excellent for ballast and road work.

At some of the stations there are groups of Indians, men and women. We enter into conversation with them through an interpreter on the platform. Pie-à-Pot, the great Indian chief, we are told, has gone on a mission to the Lieutenant-Governor at Regina to complain of the smoke of the locomotive, which he considers to be an evil medicine to ruin the health of his people.

We pass a group of three salt water lakes, the "Old Wives' Lakes." Together they extend fifty miles in length and from six to ten miles broad. They abound in wild duck. Chaplin Station is in the vicinity. Buffalo skulls and bones strew the ground, telling of the past, and buffalo tracks are distinctly traceable in all directions.

We had been led to expect, from much that we have heard, that this part of the country was perfectly barren. I can entertain no such opinion. The soil is light and variable. In seasons not too dry good crops may be raised in the district we have passed over. In crossing the Coteau des Missouri we have traversed a great grassy region, the surface of which has the appearance of the ocean subsiding into a calm after a great tempest. There are countless undulations of varied extent and outline, and as the train passes along they look as if they themselves were in motion; as if they were masses of water rolling into quietness with the calm swell, so often experienced in mid-ocean after a gale has passed away.

We arrive at Swift Current, ten degrees of longitude west of Winnipeg. This station is not far from the southern bend of the South Saskatchewan, where that river makes a *détour* before proceeding northward to Carlton. A large engine house has been erected at Swift Current. Dinner is provided for the passengers and we remain an hour and a half at the station. Several Indians are lounging about. We make an effort to converse with them, but as we have no means of understanding each other the attempt is not successful. What will be the fate of the Indian as the plains are filled up? Is he to be engulphed in the common field of industry? Is he to become civilized and labour with the rest of us at the prosaic occupations of every day life? Is he to be uncared for and left to his fate, or be clothed and fed in idleness? The problem is not an easy one to unravel. I learned from one of the passengers, who seems to speak with authority, that at present some ten thousand Indians receive an allowance of rations. It may be said that the Indian territory has been appropriated in the interest of the community, and that it is a consequent duty to care for the Red man. If it be possible the course to follow is to train the coming generation to habits of industry and self-reliance. Is it possible?

As a rule we take our meals when the train is in motion, so that we can utilize the various halts to obtain information from those we may meet at the stations. There is a change to be made in the composition of the train at this point. The sleeping car goes no further, and a number of cars loaded with material for construction purposes are appended. We are really from this point half a construction train. There is only one ordinary passenger car, with the private car occupied by our party. Our speed, too, is reduced. It seemed to me somewhat churlish to retain to ourselves all the comfort and accommodation the directors had so liberally extended to me and mine, when there were others I knew on the train not so fortunately circumstanced. I was therefore glad to be of use to some of my fellow passengers. Our party became thus increased by the Baron de Longueuil, Dr. Grant the younger, of Ottawa, and other gentlemen.

We pass Gull Lake and Cypress Stations, 554 miles from Winnipeg, north of the Cypress Hills. Not a tree or shrub is to be seen; the lofty ground to the south of us is perfectly bare; the country is dry, the herbage scanty. On the other hand there are plain indications that the country is not barren and worthless. It has been described by some people as a semi-desert. So far as my memory will admit the comparison, the soil resembles in colour and character that of the Carse of Gowrie in Perthshire. Those who remember that section of Scotland will perceive the force of the comparison. The ditches and excavations expose a fine fertile clay soil, not only on the surface but to the whole depth of the cuttings. On the recently formed road-bed, in the bottoms of ditches, there are tufts of green oats growing vigorously twenty-four inches high, each plant with twelve to twenty strong stalks sticking out from a single root. This scattered growth, so luxuriant in itself, has arisen from the seed dropped from trains or the horse's feed, during construction, without any attempt at cultivation. It is true that the herbage is brown and dried up, but not more so than I have frequently seen it in Ontario at this season. I cannot speak of the country from Moose Jaw to Qu'Appelle, for it was night when we passed through it, but from what I heard at the various stations the land is good; and generally it may be affirmed that in the five hundred and fifty miles of territory between Swift Current and Winnipeg the waste and worthless land is scarcely appreciable.

We reach Maple Creek, 596 miles from Winnipeg. The country continues to be of the character I have described. I had some conversation with a Dumfries man who had passed twenty years in the County of Bruce, in Ontario. He had a comrade with him and both were fully satisfied with their new home. There is evidently nothing whatever in their experience to lead to a regret that they have left Ontario. Last November there was not a single house at Maple Creek; this evening I counted more than two dozen. The surface water is reported not to be the best. It is slightly alkaline; but good, pure water has been obtained from wells at no great depth. The snow does not appear until the end of December. Last year ploughing took place on the 11th March.* Some two inches of snow fell after this date, but it soon disappeared. This year potatoes have been obtained from the virgin soil. I was informed by these parties that all the land is fair to Medicine Hat, the country being of the character of that which we have passed through. They are decidedly of opinion that fall ploughing and early sowing will never fail to produce good crops; they consider the country is excellent for stock raising, as the winter is short and but little snow falls. The water required can be obtained from wells pumped by wind-mills, and the climate is in all respects healthy. It is men of this stamp who are of the right build to force their way in a new country. They make light of difficulties and are fertile in expedients. They know that their success depends upon their skill and labour; they have no yearning for continual holidays, nor do they affect

---

*At the same date in Ottawa the snow usually lies to a depth of two or more feet.

an exaggerated love of sport to take precedence of all duty. If they have some hardship for the moment they put aside every thought regarding it, for they feel that their reward is assured and that they are laying up a safe provision for those who are to follow them. Hence their cheerfulness is unfailing. Their romance lies in the future: numerous herds and flocks, with rich harvests of grain, and men busy gathering them in. The small wooden house they have put up is one day to give place to a more imposing building of stone or brick, with verandahs and blinds and plenty of room for occasional friends. The piano may come, too, bye and bye, from Moose Jaw or some nearer place. Crowds of settlers will succeed, with weddings and births. There will also be the churchyard, where, in future generations, some Canadian Gray may write his "Elegy" over the graves of the village Hampdens and Cromwells, whose force of character has led their memory to be handed down as the pioneers of the district they reclaimed from the wilderness.

It was dark when we left Maple Creek. Observation in the dim light was not possible. Our eyes were fatigued by reading, so recourse was had to that universal panacea when time hangs heavy, the whist table. Our rubber caused no regret on the part of the loser, for the winner had nothing to receive.

I was called early the following morning, for I

was desirous of seeing the station at Medicine Hat and of observing the course of the South Saskatchewan. We had crossed the river when I rose. I learned that the stream is spanned by a temporary structure of timber trestles on piles, some thirty feet above the water level, to be replaced by an iron bridge before next spring.

There has been a hard frost during the night, and the air is cool. I am writing on the 22nd August. We start as the sun rises and we soon experience the heat of his rays. We have, as usual, an excellent breakfast, and our cook proportionately rises in our esteem. Several people joined the train at Medicine Hat. We discuss the character of the country with them, for I desire to obtain as many independent opinions as possible. I learn that the land between Maple Creek and Medicine Hat, passed over during the night, is of the character of the country to the east and west of it, which I have described.

As we proceed we can see, undoubtedly, by the herbage, that the climate is dry, but the excavation shows the friable soil necessary to the growth and nourishment of cereals. There are probably seasons of drought when ordinary root crops will not be generally successful.

We continue through a genuine prairie without tree or shrub. Our point of vision is really and truly the centre of one vast, grassy plain, the circumference of which lies defined in the horizon.

As we look from the rear, the two lines of rails gradually come closer till they are lost, seemingly, in one line; the row of telegraph poles recedes with the distance to a point. I should estimate the horizon to be removed from us from six to eight miles. The sky, without a cloud, forms a blue vault above us; nothing around is visible but the prairie on all sides gently swelling and undulating, with the railway forming a defined diameter across the circle. Looking along the track in the distance there is a small cloud of vapour discernable, indicating that an engine is following us. The train itself is not visible. There is certainly no little monotony in a railway journey over the prairie. The landscape is unvaried: a solitude, in which the only sign of life is the motion of the train. To obtain some change in this oneness of view, I obtain permission to take a seat in the cab of the locomotive. I discover that the engine driver is from Truro in Nova Scotia, Mr. Charles Wright. I learn from him that he began his railway life under me on the Intercolonial Railway. I need not say that the look-out from the locomotive was no new sensation to me, but I was impressed with different feelings to those which affected me when looking rearward from the train. I do not think I ever was more conscious of the power of the locomotive, or in so marked a way had I ever been so capable of grasping its wonderful capacity to change the whole condition of our lives. I felt as if I was borne along on the shoulders of some gigantic winged monster, moving onward with lightning speed, skimming the surface of the ground, and setting time and distance equally at defiance.

We are now on a broad plateau between Bow River and the Red Deer River. The outline of the eroded valley of the former is visible away on the southern horizon; the latter is too far distant to be traceable. We expect soon to be able to see the Rocky Mountains. The soil improves as we advance, and the prairie has long, gentle ascents, with occasional heavy gradients. At the "Blackfoot Crossing" there is a large Indian reserve, and at the station opposite we see many red men and women still clinging to the life of their past, wrapped in the white or red blanket, with fringed leather leggings. Some of the younger men have their faces painted a brilliant scarlet, and, mounted on Indian ponies, do their utmost to keep up with the train, the women and children partaking in the excitement of the effort. They all looked so cheerful and contented that they made no appeal to our sympathies on any ground of suffering or discontent.

We gradually ascend to the summit of the rolling plain, and now for the first time the peaks of the Rocky Mountains appear in view. They are possibly one hundred miles distant; nevertheless they stand out clear and defined in the horizon, their snow-clad tops glistening in the afternoon sun. They give a marked relief to the landscape after the monotony of the prairie. They look like a huge rampart stretched from north to south to impede all progress beyond them. Their features slowly change as the sun sinks to the western ocean, but as long as daylight lasts we never tire looking upon them, and in watching the varying colours of the atmosphere reflected by their lofty summits.

Our train has become heavy by constant additions. There are now twenty loaded cars, and it is as much as the engine can do to take them up the heavy grades. We experience, therefore, some delay in the last ten miles to Calgary. It is after dark when we cross Bow River and enter the outer valley. At last we arrive at Calgary, having reached the 114th meridian, 840 miles west of Winnipeg.

When I crossed the continent eleven years ago, before Winnipeg as a city had even a name, I left Fort Garry on the 2nd August, and did not arrive in sight of the mountains until the 7th September. In that journey we did not spare ourselves or our horses, for we made over the prairies an average of over forty miles a day. On the present occasion we left Winnipeg on Monday morning, to come within sight of the mountains on Wednesday afternoon. The first journey occupied thirty-six days, and the last about fifty-six hours!

It was eleven o'clock when we stopped on a siding. We were anxious to acquire the positive information which we were to obtain here. Our further advance depended on the facts which we hoped to learn respecting the country we were desirous of passing over. For it was yet a question if it was possible to cross the Selkirk Range to the Columbia; and it was not a matter of certainty that either the Kicking Horse or the Eagle Pass could be followed. But those who could throw any light on the subject had long retired, so we could do nothing better at that late hour than follow their example.

CHAPTER XIII.

CALGARY TO THE SUMMIT.

Start for the Mountains—The Cochrane Ranche—Gradual Ascent
—Mount Cascade—Anthracite Coal—Sunday in the Rockies—
Mountain Scenery—The Divide.

We had reached the point on our journey when the accessories of modern travel ceased to be at our disposal. Before us lay the mountain zone to Kamloops, the distance across which, as the crow flies, is about three hundred miles. We had failed to obtain any reliable information of the character of the country over which we had to pass. Indeed, it was by no means a certainty that there was a practicable route through it. We had hoped to learn at Calgary all that was known of the territory, to gain such thorough information that we should know precisely what course we should take to reach British Columbia.

The problem had now to be discussed: if we could venture to advance directly westward, or if we should be driven to pass through the United States. At the worst, it was in our power to turn to the south from Calgary to Montana, and find our way by the Northern Pacific Railway through Oregon to Victoria, in British Columbia.

We had been referred to Mr. James Ross, the manager of construction of the mountain district at Calgary. He had been instructed by telegram before I left Montreal to collect the fullest information. Accordingly he had sent out Indian couriers to the exploring parties to learn all that was known, and it was in his power to acquaint us with the facts if any one could do so. I had endeavoured to ascertain by telegraph what Mr. Ross had learned; the invariable reply had been that the couriers had not returned.

Mr. Ross entered while we were at our early breakfast. The couriers he had sent to the Columbia had been detained by forest fires, but they had at last returned with letters from Major Rogers, at the mouth of the Kicking-Horse River. I learned that the journey to Kamloops through the mountains was not held to be impracticable, but undoubtedly it was marked by difficulties. There was a road which waggons could travel for some distance up the valley of the Bow River. Where the road ceased there was a rough horse-trail as far as the exploring parties had penetrated from the east, some five miles beyond the summit of the Selkirk Range. From that point the ground was perfectly unbroken. We were told that for the remainder of the distance the only way open to us was to go on foot; that the walking, at the least calculation, would occupy ten or twelve days; and that it required about ten Indians to carry supplies.

The question of supplies had specially to be considered, as there was no possibility of obtaining them by the way. The country was totally uninhabited. We could depend on no resource but our own commissariat, which should be sufficiently ample to avoid all risk of the chance of starvation. Our means of conveyance would not admit of transportation to the full extent of our requirements for the whole distance to Kamloops. Before leaving Winnipeg this contingency had been anticipated, and definite arrangements, which we thought could scarcely fail, had been made with the Hudson's Bay Company for supplies, to be sent easterly from Kamloops to the Columbia, opposite Eagle Pass. It was my calculation that we would find our stores without fail at that point on the 10th September. We therefore resolved to attempt to cross the mountains on the trail across the Selkirk Range as it had been described. To place the question of supplies beyond a peradventure, I sent a special telegram to the Chief Commissioner of the Hudson's Bay Company, which I hoped would make error impossible.*

---

*" We expect to reach Columbia River, opposite Eagle Pass, on foot from Selkirk summit about 10th September. No trail reported from that point on Columbia River to Shuswap Lake. If there is no trail the supplies must be packed through Eagle Pass. We will depend absolutely upon your agent at Kamloops sending a guide, with supplies, to meet us at Columbia River by 10th September. We leave to-day for the mountains. Good-bye."

It was the morning of the 23rd August. We all wrote some last lines home, and telegraphed some last words to our friends in the east, informing them that we were leaving Calgary to follow the mountain route. Previous to starting I called at the Hudson's Bay Company's store to learn all that was there known about the country before us, and to see the establishment itself.

We got off about eleven, meeting an unwelcome delay of an hour in crossing Bow River. The ferry was being transferred to a better site, and we had to wait until the final arrangements for stretching the wire rope were completed. Finally it is stretched and secured, and we move onwards.

Before many miles were passed our waggon broke down. To save time we take lunch during the halt for repairs. The prairie about us has good soil, but the herbage is dry. However, it affords good pasturage. We proceed onwards through the Cochrane ranche, passing along a stretch of rolling country, with hills bringing in mind many parts of the south of Scotland; well adapted for grazing. A smoky atmosphere conceals from our view the outline of the mountains. Our drivers, however, inform us that when the air is clear they stand out distinctly to view, and present a grand sight.

Our miserable waggon again causes us trouble. One of the wheels gives way. We have again to halt, and remain by a large pond bordered by willows. A fire is made to furnish some boiling water, by means of a frying pan, to Mr. David MacDougall, who has appeared on the scene. Boiling water, says this authority, repairs a wheel "slap bang, and makes it go for another hundred miles," with a few willow withes and some cod lines, which everyone should carry in the mountains, unless he has what is better, "shaginappy."* The wheel is pronounced fit for use, although it looked much less like a wheel, and we reach in safety Morley, forty miles from Calgary.

Our day's journey had been partially through rich pasture without a tree. In certain parts a few groves are seen. The general course was along a wide valley bounded by lofty hills. We had to do the best we could at Morley. What accommodation we obtained we owed to Mr. MacDougall, who gave up his own bed. But few travellers passed this way until recently, and but little provision has been made for them. We were thankful for any shelter we could obtain. It was nine o'clock and dark when we arrived, so in any case there was but time to establish ourselves as best we could. We were up at an early hour the next morning, to find that our baggage waggon had not come up. Who should we see, as we sat down to breakfast, but Senator Ogilvie, to lead us

---

*Buffalo rawhide, used for cordage, indeed for nearly every purpose, by Indians and trappers.

to think that we had still some relations with the world behind us.

I determined not to wait for the waggon, but to push on to the next stopping place and see what arrangements could be made for our further advance. The baggage was to follow. I was much struck with the view as we started. It was very fine, but its effect was marred by the cloudy atmosphere which hid the more distant peaks. For twenty-two miles to Padmore the whole route was equally striking. The valley is from three to eight miles wide, extending generally in a western direction between the foot hills of the mountains. It is marked by no sudden precipitous ascents and is usually flat, carrying the prairie character with a gentle ascent into the heart of the mountains. We are told that at one time this valley, with the country around Morley and Calgary, was the haunt of the buffalo. Mr. David Macdougall tells us that he has seen the ground black with them, and that from an eminence not far from Morley he has beheld them in herds on the plains, the number of which would not be less than a million!

The prairie diminishes in extent as we advance. We pass through park-like scenery. Groups of trees appear at intervals, and the Bow River in its windings gleams pleasantly in the sun. The heavy atmosphere is partially lifted and the outline of the mountains in the distance comes to our view. What we see is probably the outlying group; they are, nevertheless, bold bluffs, some of them defined precipices to the summit, with long slopes in one direction, and in some cases their fantastic forms look as if shaped in masonry.

The streams crossed to-day run in ravines of some depth, and the water is clear and cold. We halt at Padmore, where the valley is contracted to half a mile. Evidently we are about entering the portals of the mountains. To the north, the slopes are bare; to the south, they are wooded. The bare precipitous rock to the north is stratified and strongly contorted. The geological features are most striking and the exposure is on a grand scale. A great bluff rises nearly vertically to the height of possibly fifteen hundred feet and is about two miles in length. The lines of the strata are distinctly traceable, dipping towards the west.

Four miles west of Padmore we are completely in the mountains. On every side the sound of the hammer and drill was heard, and every turn of the road revealed new views of the grandest mountain scenery. Peaks towering behind and above each other came in sight, and the sun poured down its warmest rays, deepening the shadows and bringing out fresh beauties. As we advanced, the eye rests only on these mighty heights when they are not concealed from view by the hazy atmosphere. The smoky air, occasionally, it seemed to me, opened up, and in a way added to, the landscape by developing the aerial perspective. As we advanced the vapour disappeared, and before us stood out, clear and well defined in the horizon, bold, massive mountain heights, crowned by sharp, turreted peaks.

We pass Mount Cascade, so named from the small stream issuing from its side, said to be at the height of two thousand feet, and with one leap descending to the valley below. It is the most striking of the masses we have seen, and we learn that its summit is 5,060 feet above the plain. Discoveries of anthracite coal have been made in the flanks of this mountain, and since my visit mining operations have commenced. The road has become very rough; the wonder is how any vehicle can stand the jolting, jarring and sudden wrenches over rocks and stumps which we experience.

We are indebted to Mr. Graham, of Mount Forrest, for our dinner. He very hospitably received us at his contractor's camp, and we were in a condition to enjoy all he gave us.

About 4 o'clock we arrived at Hillsdale, named after Mr. Hill, manager of the company's store. I was glad to meet here Mr. Dunbar, the resident engineer, for I had looked forward to obtaining from him some more definite information than we had yet received, especially of our way across the Selkirk Range. A short conversation with this gentleman gave a new colour to our enterprise, and I resolved not to proceed further that day. Indeed we would have derived no advantage from doing so. One statement of Mr. Dunbar, and he was supported in it by one of his assistants who had recently come from the country in front of us, certainly surprised me. He had heard of no one having crossed the Selkirk Range. Major Rogers had made several attempts to do so, but he had only so far succeeded as to reach the summit, or one of the summits, but had not penetrated entirely through the mountains on a connected line. No one was known to have passed over from where we stood by the route before us to Kamloops; not even an Indian, and it was questionable, if it were possible, to find a route which could be followed.

I must confess that this information was unwelcome to me. I was not without experience in crossing mountains, but expected in this instance that our route would be over known ground, and that, whatever difficulties lay before us, we had only to persevere to overcome them. From what I now heard all seemed uncertain before me. It was possible that we might have to walk our toilsome way onwards for many days, suddenly to find it was impossible to proceed. I did not contemplate assuming the position of an original explorer. My knowledge of work of this kind had taught me how frequently it exacted much time and labour, often to end in failure; that a gigantic natural impedient might present itself to bar further advance, and that whatever the courage, determination and fertility of resource shown, failure to proceed onward would be the irremediable result.

I reserved, however, my opinion of our position until I had met Major Rogers, in charge of these explorations. I understood he was at the mouth of the Kicking-Horse River. In the meantime I entered into the details of our journey with Mr. George Wilson, who had been detailed to go with us in command of the pack train.

We discussed our route, estimated every day's journey, and all the possibilities and probabilities incident to our advance. George had once been a scout in the service of the Southern States during the war, and was evidently experienced in rough travelling. He appeared to me to know well the work and duty of crossing the mountains, and we formed some estimate of the pork and flour required to take us, with half a dozen packers, to Eagle Pass, at the Columbia. I went into the whole question so far as my knowledge permitted, and we talked it over until bed time.

I owed to Mr. Dunbar, on that occasion, that we had comfortable beds to sleep on, for he and his friends insisted that we should take possession of their quarters.

The weather on Sunday morning was really beautiful. Those living in cities can with difficulty understand the effect on the spirits and minds of men away from civilization of a bright, cheery Sunday. In all well ordered expeditions Sunday is a day of rest, and this view alone, denuded entirely of all religious feeling, which is to some extent dependent on early education, creates a scene of quiet and repose not always experienced to the same extent in civilized communities. To one bred like myself in the strict views of the Presbyterian Church, there is something more than this sentiment: it is as if you held it a privilege on these remote mountains to pay homage to the lessons of your youth. Not from the merely mechanical acceptance of them, but from a heartfelt sense of their truth. I have felt, on such occasions, a sense of peace and freedom from the carping cares of life I never could explain; but that the thought is not peculiar to myself many circumstances have shown. You seem, as it were, at such times, only to commune with nature, and to be free from all that is false and meretricious in our civilization. You are beyond the struggles and petty personalities of the world, and you feel how really and truly life is better and happier as it is more simple.

The sun lit up in warm colours the great mountains encircling the valley. We were surrounded by these magnificent heights. Our camp was but a few miles distant from the valley, which leaves Bow River for the Vermilion Pass. The atmosphere was not so clear as we could wish, and the distant peaks were invisible. We had, nevertheless, a remarkable view of the towering battlements to the north, in themselves so lofty and so near to us, and the details so intricate that it would be impossible to portray them within the limits of ordinary canvas. It remains to be seen what effect will be produced by photography.

Dr. Grant held a service at ten o'clock, and gave a short sermon. The congregation was composed of men engaged on the surveys and works. Some two dozen attended. There was one also of the gentler sex present, who, with her husband, came from the contractors' camp near by. We dine early. As to-morrow we have to take to the saddle, and in order to get hardened to our work, we think it prudent that we fit ourselves for the journey. We ride about twelve miles up the valley, between mountains of the grandest description. To the south two heights of great prominence present themselves. They command a view of the depression leading to the Vermilion Pass. One of the peaks is crowned with perpetual snow, and is of striking beauty. The other has a cubical form of summit. A third, at no great distance, is pyramidal, and so on in every conceivable variety these mountains tower above us. Westward we see Castle Mountain to our right. The resemblance to Cyclopean masonry has doubtless suggested the name, for it is marked by huge masses of castellated-looking work, with turreted flanks. After passing through a mile of burnt pine wood at its base, we reach Spillman's camp, where we stay for the night. The fires in the valley are extinguished, but they are still running up the mountain side, and as night comes on the flames gleam with a weird light. We soon wrapped ourselves in our blankets. Although with a certain sense of fatigue, I could not sleep. My thoughts reverted to the journey before us. Uncertainty seemed to increase as we advanced.

Next morning some of us felt a little stiff and tired from our afternoon drill, for such indeed was the object of our ride. Wilson and Kit Lawrence, his assistant, started early with the supply waggon, as our own movements are governed by those of the baggage. We did not deem it necessary immediately to follow, and hence did not hurry our start. The sun was a degree or so above Castle Mountain as we left. Our ride was very agreeable: to some extent through Banksian pine, occasionally along the bank of the Bow River, still a large stream, more considerable, for instance, than the Thames at Richmond. The current is strong, and unhappy the canoeman who has to pole up against it. Here and there we ride through burnt woods. A "brulé" is an ominous word to any one who has to make his way through the bush. The fire has recently destroyed the growth of young timber. The existence of these fires explains the frequent thick, heavy, smoky atmosphere through which we have been unable to see the outline of the mountains. Occasionally a snow-covered peak peers far above the dense smoke below, and to the south we see what the maps suggest to be Mount Lefroy; but there are several lofty summits, any one of which is sufficiently remarkable to be named after that distinguished General. One is crested like a huge camel's back; one rises to a sharp cone; a third has the appearance of an extinct volcano, and the crumbling edge of the crater reveals the glacier within.

The waggon which has brought us from Calgary has been driven by a young man named Kane. He had started early in the morning with Wilson, and at a turn in the path we came suddenly upon Wilson's horse tethered up by the bridle. Kane was lying upon the ground, suffering from a violent attack of colic. We had at once to ride and overtake the waggon for medicine. Thirty drops of chlorodine relieved him, and we left him at the nearest contractors' camp. The two waggons with which we started from Calgary have now nearly disappeared, for we have lost three wheels, and one of the drivers is left behind.

Twelve miles distant from Spillman's Camp the waggon road, bad as it had been, comes to an end, and our supplies must now be carried on pack horses. Here we met Mr. Neilson, a Kingston man, who renders us great service; and it is here also, that Dave Leigh joins our service as cook and pack man. There is always great delay in getting a pack train ready; horses, saddlery and men must be collected. Our first calculation was that three horses would suffice, as we know the weights of all the packages and our calculation had been based upon them; but from the badness of the roads we reduced the theoretical weight of the pack by increasing the number of our animals. Our whole load amounted to eleven hundred pounds, and our packers assured us that over the bad roads it could not be carried by less than six horses. Experience proved that the judgment of the men was correct; the consequence was that the pack train could not leave that night.

Our party, however, started. One of them, who left after the rest, took a wrong direction and narrowly escaped losing himself, at least for the night. George shewed wonderful judgment in hunting up the wanderer and putting him on the right track, relieving us all from great anxiety. Our course took us across two forks of the Bow River and thence along the banks of a rapid stream called Bath Creek, so named from one of the engineers having fallen into it. We ascended for a few miles, when we turned to the west by Summit Creek, a small glacier-bed stream, which we followed till we arrived at the engineer's camp at the Summit, 5,300 feet above sea level.

I had here to take leave of my friend Mr. Dunbar,

who had to return to his duties. He had been good enough to accompany us this far, and I had found his presence of great use. Sitting around the camp fire at night he was an admirable companion, for he had a fine voice. I have particularly a very pleasurable recollection of the hymns he sang on the Sunday evening in the first mountain pass. All music has a peculiar effect under such circumstances, especially when it brings back thoughts of the past and of distant friends; and there is to men of my age a peculiar feeling in listening to devotional music, the influence and power of which, however simple, are not easily forgotten.

To-night we fall asleep on the continental "Divide." Hitherto we have passed over ground draining to the east. To-morrow we follow a stream flowing into the the waters of the Pacific.

CHAPTER XIV.

DOWN KICKING-HORSE VALLEY.

The Descent—Summit Lake—The Kicking-Horse River—Singular Mountain Storms—An Engineering Party—A Beaver Meadow—A Dizzy Walk.

We were up at half-past five, and it was a cold, sharp morning. At six, Mr. Dunbar had said good bye and turned eastward. When breakfast was over the pack-train arrived, and by nine we had started for the River Columbia. It was a rugged and broken path which we entered upon. To our right two conspicuous twin summits were standing out in the range. The water of the streams which we were following was more heard than seen, for the trail exacted all our attention. Our horses were moving among sharp broken granite rocks and fallen trees. In about half an hour we passed by the side of Summit Lake. The northern mountains were now concealed from view by a forest of spruce, through which we were passing. To the south the landscape is more magnificent than ever; a bold, rocky bluff rises thousands of feet directly in front of us, while mountains of great height, in groups, tower above it to the right and left. Some of them have crater-shaped peaks filled with snow. Our progress is slow and much interfered with by the pack-horses getting continually off the trail and losing part of their load.

We pass the second mountain lake, and about four miles from our morning camp we reach the third and largest lake, about a mile in length. We cross the path of a great snow slide, an avalanche divided into two forks, one about fifty yards and the other about one hundred and fifty yards wide. Thousands of trees, two and three feet in diameter, have been broken into shreds by it, and roots, trunks and branches, in a tangled mass, have been swept away, and, with a multitude of boulders of all dimensions, hurled into the lake, to form a promontory of which three or four hundred feet still remain. To the south, beyond the lake, the eye rests upon a mighty mountain, streaked by snow-filled crevices, and reflected in the bright, glassy lake, presenting to our eyes a most striking picture. We cross the outlet by fording a stream some forty feet wide and about sixteen inches in depth. I looked upon it with no little interest for it is the stream we are to follow for some days. There is often a history lying behind the nomenclature of these waters and peaks, and in the present instance it is said that Dr. Hector, who accompanied the Palliser expedition, was kicked not far from this spot. The Indians have translated it Shawata-nowchata-wapta—Horse-Kicking River.

As we ascend the steeper and southern bank we obtain a grand view of the lofty twin mountains seen from our last camp, and it struck me that it was from the lower heights that the avalanches must have descended. A mile of bad trail brought us to Walton's camp, where we delivered the mail which had been entrusted to our care. We were now six miles from our morning's starting point. By George's account we are about entering the worst five miles of road before us, and bad enough it proved to be. Dave declared that there were places further on far more trying. We moved at a snail's pace, but our progress, if slow, was sure. The scramble on the rugged path, through the boulders, rocks and ragged surface, was a constant effort to the poor horses. In many places they had to be dragged up almost perpendicular heights. Three packs rolled off, and one of the horses fell down a side hill, accomplishing a complete somersault. No doubt the creature was saved from injury by the pack, firmly secured to his back. He was soon released by George and Dave unfastening the pack ropes and lifting him to his feet. We are seldom in the saddle, for it is safer to walk. Now and then we catch a glimpse of the stream passing along in foaming rapids, with an inclination apparently from 1 in 5 to 1 in 8. By this rapidity of current the water is churned into a liquid in colour like weak whitewash. It gathers its volume from so many side tributaries that although its source is a mere brook, yet four miles below when the water is high the stream seemingly attains a width of nearly a thousand feet. Even at the present time its volume is so great that it is only with difficulty it can be forded.

We descend the mountain side to the bed of the river and follow the gravel banks. Before we reach our night's camping ground we meet with some remarkable scenery. Looking upwards to the south at about an angle of sixty degrees, we can see high, in the clear air, a mountain peak which, lighted up by the sun, presents in its horizontal strata various colours, and assumes the form of a mural crown. Separated from this height by a great depression rises a sister peak singularly striking, both undoubtedly rising to a vertical mile above the river. A great glacier on the second mountain overhangs a precipice with a face of hundreds of feet in thickness: at the base *debris* has gathered for countless centuries to form an immense deposit sloping down the mountain. We cross its base, and accept the first place suitable for a camp which we reach. Grass for the horses is the first requirement, water we can always count upon. Our saddle horses have travelled twelve miles, the journey of the pack-horses has been seventeen. It was still early in the afternoon, but the strain upon the poor animals had been severe. The last six miles had taken four hours and a half to pass over; and then there had been no mid-day halt and feed. There cannot be a doubt that one of the secrets of driving a horse long continuous distances is to let him take his own pace and feed him regularly. Any one who has had any experience with horses well knows that the creature will by a hundred ways let you know when he looks for his food should you neglect to give it him. There is everything to show that he suffers in strength if there be great irregularity in this respect.

We learn that there is no pasture in our front for a long distance, so we camp on the gravelly beach. The ground we are on, at high water, is covered, and a few rods from us the river is winding on its rapid, rolling course. The horses are provided for in a gully near by. Close to us rise four massive, lofty mountains, and as we turn to their summits the eye is raised from forty to fifty degrees. A blue sky looks down between these heights through an atmosphere free from smoke. These high peaks rising directly from the valley form the points of a quadrilateral figure, the longest side of which does not exceed three miles. There are no foot hills, no intervening eminence between us and these mountains, rising 5,000 feet above where we stand. The sun sets behind the western heights. I have often felt the calm of evening, but I do not recollect so perfect a picture of quiet and repose as that which reigned in this amphitheatre of nature in the first twilight, when everything was marked and distinct, but with subdued colour, with no high lights, and presenting a solitude so vast that one for the time loses all consciousness of the existence of an outer world.

Two families of Stoney Indians were encamped near by. They belonged to the christianized tribe at Morley, and consisted of a father, three handsome sons, two squaws and a number of children. They had with them some of the spoils of the chase, mountain sheep and goats.

Towards night a party of the locating engineers arrived wet to the middle from fording streams. Their pack-horses had not come up, so they were without dry clothes or tents, but they made the best of the situation. They were all cheerful, and indulged in that "chaff" by which men work themselves up to make a molehill of what is often a serious hardship, accepting what is inevitable with perfect stoicism. They made a huge fire to dry their wet clothes, by which they passed the night without tents or blankets. For our part we had some days' serious work before us, and were not sorry to seek repose, and we soon were lulled to sleep by the roar of the rapid which ran within fifty yards of us.

We are now fairly up to our work. We rise about five; then breakfast, an important element at the start; then see to the packing of the animals, an operation which takes a good hour's time. We say good-bye to the Indians and to the engineering party, none of whom seem the worse for their night's experience, and we start. Often during the hour are the names of the horses shouted in those valleys, occasionally with no feeble echo; especially of the pack animals, and we soon know them one and all. There is always a wonderful link between the man and the horse, and the kinder the man the more gentle the quadruped. The names of our horses are Black, Coffee, Blue, Calgary, Coaly, Buck, Pig, Bones, Strawberry and Steamboat, and each creature knows perfectly the reproof or the cheering cry addressed to him.

We follow the bed of the river, which is of considerable width, for five miles, and leaving it we turn to a trail over low ground to return to the stream some distance down. We find it considerably increased in volume and it would be impossible to ford it fourteen miles from our morning camp. The valley has widened out, the river now flows in a well defined channel with banks six feet above the water level. We stop and take our mid-day meal; the horses, too, must have rest and be fed. The atmosphere has again become smoky, not a pleasant indication, for we may be approaching forest fires, and it is the last situation in which one desires to be placed, for when the fire is around you there is no extrication. We advanced, however, but took the wrong trail, which led to a *cul-de-sac*, where Mr. Davis was encamped, and his trail was the best defined. We made our way back and fortunately met two gentlemen, Messrs. Hogg and Shaw, connected with the engineering staff, returning from an exploration to the Selkirk Range; they spoke of the travel as of the roughest description as far as they had gone, and it was as far as it was posible to go. They held that the continuance of the route on which we were bound was impracticable; there was no path or track of any description beyond the point at which they turned back and nothing to mark the way; in fact, no one had been through to the western slope of the Selkirks. I must add that, however little I said, I had some very serious reflections on what I heard from these gentlemen.

We halted about twenty miles from the last camping ground; the horses, owing to the *detour* at Davis', had travelled about twenty-three miles and had little to eat since we first started. It was six o'clock in the evening, and on examining the grassy plain we discovered it was a beaver meadow with the beaver works in excellent condition. One beaver house was twelve feet in diameter by six feet high, formed of sticks, and each stick showed the marks of the beaver's teeth. We found a number of underground passages through which the water flowed; here and there were vertical openings twelve or fifteen inches in diameter; the passages crossed and recrossed each other like the underground passages made by moles. The dam was, generally, in good preservation, but the water had found a way for itself at some points. We pitched our camp on the edge of the beaver meadow; the horses could not have better pasture. Our beds, too, were a shade in advance of last night's quarters on the gravelly beach, for they were of hemlock boughs, and if well laid who would ask a daintier resting place. Certainly we were all asleep at half-past nine. What a sound sleep it is after a day's ride or march over a bad road!

As we started on our next day's journey a high mountain frowned down upon us; but not from its lofty summit, for its peak is hidden by rain clouds. Yesterday the smoke interfered with our landscape, for we could only dimly see the outline even when the glaciers were gleaming in the sunlight. Our last night's camp was half a mile distant from the river, but we heard the roar of the water; the heavy atmosphere, the lowering clouds and the loud echo of the rapid river warn us to prepare for rain, and we do so as best we can. We ride onward, leaving the pack animals to follow, for I am desirous of reaching Major Hurd's camp, a few miles distant, We were unfortunate on our arrival, for Major Hurd had left for the Columbia about an hour and a half before we appeared. As it was possible to overtake him we hurried forward; the trail winds through old windfalls up and down the elevations in our path. We were in hopes of meeting him at Island Camp, but on our reaching the place we found that he had stopped and fed, but that he had left before we arrived. Our horses were tired, his were fresh, and we had been told that for the next thirteen miles there was no food for the animals, so we remained there for the night. By this time it commenced to rain; we made a good fire and toasted the slices of bacon we had brought for luncheon. The pack-horses came up and there was good feed for them on the island in the river.

The clouds shortly rolled away. We could see that snow-covered mountains lay directly in our front; indeed at all points of the compass, and especially from the direction we had come, there were magnificent lofty peaks. As we sat at our early supper a cloud appeared and swept rapidly down the mountain side with a mighty rush of wind. Heavy rain commenced to fall and everything about us which we could not gather up got so drenched that we had some trouble in drying our things. We retired in good time, to prepare for an early start, for we well knew that we had a hard journey before us on the morrow.

It was cold during the night, and on rising there was a dense fog, with the prospect of a wet day. The mist hung like a thick curtain, concealing everything not directly near the camp-fire. But we start; the six pack-horses in front with their loads standing out from their backs, giving the creatures the appearance of so many dromedaries. Dave rides ahead with the bell-horse, then the pack-horses follow, and the horsemen bring up the rear to see that none stray behind. Our journey this day was over exceedingly rough ground. We have to cross gorges so narrow that a biscuit might be thrown from the last horse descending, to the bell-horse six hundred feet ahead, ascending the opposite side. The fires have been running through the wood and are still burning; many of the half-burnt trees have been blown down, probably by the gale of last night, obstructing the trail and making advance extremely difficult. The delays are frequent; ascending a long slope by a narrow path, the footing of one horse gave way and the poor animal fell, rolling over a dozen times. Our fear was that Calgary was killed, or at least seriously injured, and that he would have to be left behind. The first thought is to prepare the rifle to put him out of agony, but Dave and George unfastened the load and soon had him again on his feet at a depth of some fifty yards below the trail. After some delay the poor brute takes his place in the pack-train as if nothing had happened.

The road does not improve as we advance, and

we have many miles of burnt woods to pass through. Fortunately there was no wind. The air was still and quiet, otherwise we would have ran the risk of blackened trunks falling around us, possibly upon the animals or ourselves, even at the best seriously to have impeded our progress, if such a mischance did not make an advance impossible, until the wind should moderate. We move forward down and up gorges hundreds of feet deep, amongst rocky masses, where the poor horses had to clamber as best they could amid sharp points and deep crevices, running the constant risk of a broken leg. The trail now takes another character. A series of precipices run sheer up from the boiling current to form a contracted canyon. A path has therefore been traced along the hill side, ascending to the elevation of some seven or eight hundred feet. For a long distance not a vestige of vegetation is to be seen. On the steep acclivity our line of advance is narrow, so narrow that there is scarcely a foothold; nevertheless we have to follow for some six miles this thread of trail, which seemed to us by no means in excess of the requirements of the chamois and the mountain goat.

We cross clay, rock and gravel slides at a giddy height. To look down gives one an uncontrollable dizziness, to make the head swim and the view unsteady, even with men of tried nerve. I do not think that I can ever forget that terrible walk; it was the greatest trial I ever experienced. We are from five to eight hundred feet high on a path of from ten to fifteen inches wide and at some points almost obliterated, with slopes above and below us so steep that a stone would roll into the torrent in the abyss below. There are no trees or branches or twigs which we can grip to aid us in our advance on the narrow, precarious footing. We become more sensible to the difficulties we encounter each step as we go forward. The sun came out with unusual power; our day's effort has caused no little of a strain, and the perspiration is running from us like water. I, myself felt as if I had been dragged through a brook, for I was without a dry shred on me. About three miles from the mouth of the Kicking-Horse Valley we met Major Rogers and Major Hurd. At the same time we obtained the first uninterrupted look upon the Selkirk range. From this point to the Columbia the trail improved, but it still ran at a great height. We had not, however, got out of our difficulties, for we came upon a hornets' nest. The leading horses were stung and darted forward. To have been attacked by the whole colony on so narrow a path might have caused serious disaster, so we abandoned the trail and traced a new route for ourselves to avoid that which we were following, and thus escaped the dilemma.

The Kicking-Horse Valley turns into the valley of the Columbia River, which at the junction is some twelve miles wide from peak to peak. Our train has now travelled through the whole valley of the Kicking-Horse from its summit to the flats of the Columbia, a distance of about fifty miles, with a descent of 2,700 feet; the average fall is about fifty-seven feet to the mile, the first six miles however, give a descent of twelve hundred feet, being two hundred feet per mile; the last ten miles the river falls at an average of sixty feet per mile, leaving on the intervening thirty-two miles an average fall of thirty feet per mile.

Arrived at Major Rogers' camp, I own I was weary and foot-sore after our frightful march of many miles over rough ground high up on the mountain side, over a path every step of which was a renewed difficulty. I was somewhat indemnified by knowing that the horses had travelled without a mishap. I thought of the *Mauvais-pas* at Chamouni, which, extending only a few hundred yards, is thought to be a feat in its way, even with a special guide leading the traveller, holding his hand; but the *Mauvais-pas* of the Kicking-Horse Valley extended for miles, and they were only passed over from the very desperation of our circumstances. Having entered on the journey we could not turn back and we had to face the difficulties in our front cost what it would.

We were all tired and weary, men and horses, and all equally hungry. A sponge down with cold water, fresh, dry clothing and a good supper are always the best of comforters, so in a few hours I had been able to discuss our future progress with Major Rogers, and one of the first arrangements to which we came was that tomorrow both men and horses would take a day's rest.

CHAPTER XV.

TO THE SUMMIT OF THE SELKIRKS.

The Eagle Pass—Kicking-Horse River—Valley of the Columbia—The Selkirk Range—The Columbia River—Summit of the Selkirks—Major Rogers' Discovery.

The point which we have reached is about two and a third degrees north of the international boundary, of the forty-ninth parallel. The Columbia takes its rise ninety or a hundred miles to the south-east of us and flows in a generally direct course to a point known as the Boat Encampment, some seventy miles to the north-west. From its source for nearly this whole distance the Columbia is flanked by lofty mountains, those on the south-west side of the valley being known as the Selkirk Range. The Boat Encampment is a trifle to the north of the fifty-second parallel. At this point the Columbia completely changes its course and runs almost directly south to Washington Territory, in the United States. This section of the Columbia also flows between high mountains, the Selkirk Range being in this direction of its course on the east and the Gold Range on the west.

Near the point where the river crosses the 51st parallel there is a remarkable opening in the Gold Range, known as the Eagle Pass, which leads westerly towards Kamloops. Measured on the map, the distance, in a straight line to the second crossing of the Columbia at the Eagle Pass, is scarcely sixty miles. To reach that point is the task directly before us.

The route which we had followed to the position where we now are, is the Valley of the Kicking-Horse River, which has its source in one of the Summit lakes of the Rocky Mountains. It flows with tremendous impetuosity for the first six miles from the summit and for the last ten miles through canyons. The descent in the principal canyon is most rapid, and the water in the lower reach, now of great volume, rushes downwards with wonderful force before it falls into the Columbia. In the lower canyon this large volume of water is forced through a rocky chasm of unknown depth. At one spot which I visited, the rocks on opposite banks so over-hung the current that their summits did not seem to be more than fifteen yards apart.

The valley of the Columbia where we are now encamped is several miles in width. Although less than one hundred miles from its source the river is of considerable size, being fed by many streams, like the Kicking-Horse, having their sources in the glaciers.

It is the first of September, which we devote to the rest needed for the horses and men. The subject of discussion naturally is the chance of geting through to Kamloops. A lofty range of mountains intervenes directly before us to make our advance in that direction impracticable. We know that there is a possibility of passing round the Selkirk range by descending the Columbia to the Boat Encampment and thence continuing until we reach the Eagle Pass, and so get through the Gold Range to our destination.

We learn, however, from Major Rogers that he has found a pass through the Selkirk range which we can take, and he proposes to accompany us part of the distance and to send his nephew, Mr. Albert Rogers the entire route. We must follow the Columbia River north-westerly thirty-two miles on the way to the Boat Encampment, and then turning westerly enter the Selkirk Mountains by the valley of a stream named Beaver River to an opening in the west of the range, and crossing the summit descend the valley of a stream, the Ille-celle-waet, which, running southerly and westerly, falls into the Columbia directly opposite Eagle pass. We learn that a horse trail has been opened to the summit of the Selkirk range and a short way down the Ille-celle-waet. Beyond that point we have the wilderness in its native ruggedness, without a path for the human foot, with the river and mountain gorges only as landmarks and guides.

Such is the condition of the country to the second crossing of the Columbia. The passage through the Eagle Pass is mentioned as being of the roughest description; we have therefore to prepare for the work before us. We take a day's rest, lightening the packs as much as possible. We arrange to start the horses in the morning, while we ourselves will descend the Columbia in a canoe and overtake the animals at the end of their first day's journey.

It is again Sunday. The horses with the men leave us as arranged. We remain quietly in our camp. It is a beautiful morning; the sun lights up the whole valley of the Columbia. The great Selkirk range lies in front of us. To the west and north-west high peaks appear, forming a golden line of stern magnificence. We are at the base of the Rocky Mountains, which lie behind us to the east, and hence they form no part of the panorama. A glacier is visible to the south and huge areas of snow, possibly the accumulation of centuries, rest between the peaks. It is a prosaic fact to record, amid all this grandeur, that yesterday's halt admitted of some washing of our clothes; a homely fact but suggestive of volumes of comfort. We look forward for the rest of the day to enjoying the quiet scene in which we seek a few hours' rest, to regain our vigour and elasticity, and they have never more strength than after repose from labour.

As it is Sunday Dr. Grant holds a short service. Our congregation, gathered from the nearest engineer's camp, numbers twenty-two. The incident may hereafter be remembered as the first act of public worship in this part of the Columbia Valley. After service we walk to the river, about a mile and a half of a stroll over low ground. We find the quiet stream gently flowing in its north-western course, a strange contrast to the bold broken mountain peaks which form the border of the valley through which it runs. The evening was warm. Some of us took a plunge into the Columbia, a pleasant incident in our trip. The water was of the right temperature, and there was a certain romance in swimming in a stream in the heart of the mountains, in water as calm as the Serpentine, in the centre of a vast solitude without the slightest impress of civilization. In the cool of the evening we walked up the first gravelly terrace in rear of the camp to enjoy the view, ascending some 500 feet. We were repaid for our effort. The huge mountains in our front and the valley stretching away in the magnificence of foliage to the south-east, lit up by the warm colour of sunset, presented a noble landscape. I asked myself if this solitude would be unchanged, or whether civilization in some form of its complex requirements would ever penetrate to this region? What is the nature of the soil, what isothermal lines curve in this direction? Is there anything that can be sown and ripened? Certainly as a grazing country it must be valuable. Beef and mutton may be produced for men and women of other lands. Will the din of the loom and whirl of the spindle yet be heard in this unbroken domain of nature? It cannot be that this immense valley will remain the haunt of a few wild animals. Will the future bring some industrial development: a future which is now dawning upon us. How soon will a busy crowd of workmen take possession of these solitudes, and the steam whistle echo and re-echo where now all is silent? In the ages to come how many trains will run to and fro from sea to sea with millions of passengers. All these thoughts crowd upon me with that peaceful scene before us as the sun sinks behind the serrated Selkirk Mountains, and I do not think that I can ever forget the sight as I then gazed upon it.

The evening, like all evenings in the mountains, after sunset, became cold, and we found our camp fire comfortable. As we sat opposite it we missed our friend, Mr. Dunbar, whose cheery voice we would have all welcomed. Possibly I exaggerate my friend's powers, for it was the only human melody we heard on our travels. We retired early to prepare us for the journey. The night was cold, and sleeping in our clothes and wrapped in our blankets we could not complain of the heat. As usual we were up early. At eight we were in a canoe floating down the River Columbia. The immediate banks are low and the river winds in its course with but little current. We could now see the rocky range which we have left behind us. The terrace on which we stood at sunset lies along the foot of the hills and a second terrace is seen to follow the Kicking-Horse River, I learn, some 1,200 feet high. The ground from the canyon of the Kicking-Horse River ascends to this terrace with a slope, as far as I can judge, scarcely one to one, an angle of less than 45°, and it was along the face of this upper shelving acclivity that the narrow ledge of pathway was traced, which we followed for miles. I never wish to take such another walk. I dared not look down. It seemed as if a false step would have hurled us to the base, to certain death. There is many a joke of the strong head of the North Countryman. I shall ever listen to any wit of this character complacently, for I feel that it was because of my experience in my younger days amid hills and dales that my nerve did not fail me as we went onward. I am not ashamed to say that I still look upon the tramp in the Kicking-Horse as a serious effort. I believe that there are many who could not have passed through it in any form. The power to walk along heights is a constitutional endowment not extended to us all. For my part I have no desire to retrace my steps by the path I have followed in the descent of the Kicking-Horse Valley.

Six miles below our starting point, to-day, we

touched the shore to take note of the buildings erected by those engaged on the railway survey of twelve years back. They are five or six in number, and look as if once they offered a comfortable resting place.

We continue our journey for three miles. We feel the contrast between this comfortable advance compared to our efforts of last week. The glacier-fed river, the grand wide banks and the dim distant hills, with the snow-covered mountains far behind them, presented a panorama as striking as it is rarely seen. At noon we passed a tributary which has been called "Wait-a-bit," suggestive as the spot where travelling parties rest and adjust the loads in their canoes before passing the three miles of descending rapids which lay before them. In twenty minutes we have passed the rapids and reach the landing. We have crossed the outlet of a clear stream from the east discharging its bright blue water far into the turbid flood of the Columbia. The landing is at the upper end of a canyon through which the river passes between rocky bluffs at the foot of the mountains. At this point we have overtaken our pack train. George and Dave speedily unload the canoe and we make preparations for a twelve mile march on foot or saddle. The sun has been hot the whole day. The air is smoky and the distant mountains are not visible. The trail we follow passes up the hillside for some little distance and then descends to a lower level, and for this locality is comparatively good. It continues for six miles alongside the canyon, so called, but which, really, is no more than a series of rapid descents through the contracted portion of the river. There is nothing to prevent them being safely run by canoes and boats, as many of the rapids of the Saint Lawrence are so passed over. Indeed, I believe that a steamer could descend them, for the water is less turbulent than the rapids overcome by the Beauharnois canal. Once down, however, ascent would be impossible. As far as I can learn, the Indians of this territory do not use canoes to any extent. Generally they depend on the Indian ponies, and mounted upon them they follow known trails through the forest. We followed the flats of the river to our camping ground, some thirty miles north-westerly from the mouth of the Kicking-Horse River, opposite the mouth of the Beaver River on the Selkirk side.

We had now to ascend the eastern slope of the Selkirk range. We are up by day-break. Although only the 4th of September, as usual in these mountain valleys, the morning was raw and cold. A heavy dew had fallen during the night. Breakfast was over at six, but our horses were missing. There was little pasture for them in the neighbourhood and they had strayed in search of food. George has been absent since day-break in search of them. He shortly returns with three horses less than our number. Those he has collected have to be taken across the river, and the only way of reaching the opposite bank is to make them swim the stream. The width is about 400 feet and the water is deep for three quarters of the distance. All animals swim, especially the horse, but to land on an opposite shore is not always easy. Such was the case in this instance, and some of the poor creatures, failing to make a landing, by instinct returned to the side whence they started, the strong current sweeping them a long distance down stream. The three lost horses are found. At last man and beast are on the Selkirk side of the river.

We ourselves, and the *impedimenta* are taken across by an old leaky boat built by the Moberly surveying party in 1871. By this time it is nine o'clock. It is no use crying over spilt milk; but time is now precious, and every hour lost is a mishap. I did not look complacently on our delay; there was, however, the satisfaction that we had overcome the difficulty. We hope after crossing the mountains before us to meet the Columbia in its southern course in about a week. We follow the rough and recently cut trail by the Beaver River itself, a large stream, passing through an open canyon for four or five miles. It is quite unnavigable. There are few places where it can be forded along the whole route. We proceed through a flat well-timbered valley over half a mile in width.

There is a dense growth of cedar, spruce and cotton wood, and such magnificent cedar! Four feet and more in diameter. We have now an undergrowth which is the genuine flora of the Pacific slope. Everywhere the prickly aralia or devil's club* and ferns and skunk cabbage† are to be seen, all of the rankest growth, on the low ground. There is no pasture for horses. Having had little to eat last night the poor animals look miserable and wearily wind their way through the woods up and down the ascents, while the voices of the drivers are constantly heard encouraging them.

As we advance we come upon a flock of grouse, five of which were secured by hand without much difficulty, the birds being so tame. The packmen know them as "fool hens." We fancy that they resemble the spruce partridge of the Atlantic Provinces. A short time after the capture as we were trudging onwards a few miles beyond the spot, my friend, Dr. Grant, finds that he has lost his watch. He supposes that it dropped from the guard as he was engaged in the chase. We are three miles past the spot. Unfortunately it was a

---

*Devil's Club.........
{ Fatsia horida—Panax horridus
Echinopanax horridus—
Oplopanax horridus—
Horsfieldia horrida.

†Skunk Cabbage......
{ Symplocarpus foetidus
Pothos foetidus
Icttodes foetidus—
Lysichiton Kamtschatcensis.

gold presentation watch, highly valued, and an effort must be made to find it. Along with Mr. Albert Rogers he determines to return to make a search for it. It was not possible to halt; the pack-train moves forward and I accompany it. The smoke in the air now becomes more dense, for we were reaching a region where fires appeared to be ahead of us, the ordeal of passing through which we did not wish to experience. The forest had evidently been burning some time, and the trees had fallen in many directions, obstructing the path and causing considerable delay. With difficulty we continued our advance. The horses at one time clambered over fallen trees, still on fire, at another waded through hot ashes or burning vegetable soil. We go on with some dread. If wind arises the half burned trees may be hurled across the horses and ourselves.

We continue on wearily hour after hour in the hope of finding a spot where the horses can pasture, but none is to be seen. At last we reach an engineer's camp about six p.m., and Dr. Grant soon appears, in the best of spirits. He had found his watch, and if ever a patient search was justly rewarded it was in his case.

There is no pasture for a long way before us, and there is no alternative; we must remain for the night, even if there be no feed for the horses. The surveying party is in charge of Major Critchelow, a West Point man, with all the marks of culture which that institution extends. His assistants are equally agreeable. They give us a cordial welcome, and we have a supper of oatmeal porridge and condensed milk. I could eat only with effort when I thought that our horses were without their feed. But so it was, and nothing could be done. We have still five or six miles to ascend before we reach the summit. We have travelled eighteen miles to-day, and we are fatigued, and I do not think any of us were long wrapped in our blankets before we were fast asleep.

Our poor horses could only nibble the leaves of the devil's club in the attempt to satisfy hunger. There was nothing to be done but to proceed, and as soon as possible reach good pasture at the summit. We were now no longer by Beaver River. We had followed it for fifteen miles, and had ascended a branch named Bear Creek. We heard that a number of these creatures are to be met in this locality. The surveying party had seen as many as fifty. We pass through a tall forest until we reach a rugged mountain defile leading up to the summit, which we are to cross. The mountain peaks rise high above us, and although it is far advanced in the forenoon the sun has not yet appeared to us in the defile, for it has not yet ascended to the lofty horizon. We crossed many old avalanche slides. On the southern side of the mountains, as we wind our way, great scaurs, banked with snow, are seen two hundred or three hundred feet above the bottom of the narrow valley through which Bear Creek flows. To the north we observe a glacier, possibly fifty yards thick at its overhanging termination. It takes its origin at some remote lofty source far beyond the reach of our view. Below the glacier on the mountain side there are traces of a heavy avalanche, where trees have been broken and crushed in all directions. Judging from the age of the timber the movement must have taken place a considerable time back, and was probably caused by the breaking off of a huge mass of the glacier. What could have been more majestic than the fall of one of those great glaciers, in its descent driving everything before it as stubble in the field.

Five miles from our last night's camp we leave Bear Creek and follow a small stream to the south. Half a mile further brings us to the summit. At last there is pasture for the poor horses, so they are unloaded and unsaddled and turned out to their food. Our dinner, too, is prepared, although it is not yet noon. The horses require rest and we ourselves are now in no hurry to proceed. There is a grassy knoll in our neighbourhood which might have been placed in the most sylvan of scenes, and we recline at our full ease to enjoy the scene around us. Nothing would have been gained by leaving before the horses had satisfied themselves. I recollected that I had a package of cigars, a gift from our genial Ottawa friend, Mr. N———. They had crossed and re-crossed the Atlantic with me during the present summer, and it was little thought when they came into my possession that their aroma would mingle with the atmosphere of a summit in the Selkirk range. They are produced. We have no wine, so we can only congratulate Major Rogers over the cigars on the discovery of a pass so far practicable and on certain conditions appearing to furnish a solution of the problem of crossing over the Selkirk range instead of making a detour, following the Columbia by the Boat Encampment. We are now 4,600 feet above the sea, surrounded by mountains of all forms, pyramidal, conical and serrated. They are marked in bold relief on the lofty sky line. Between them the everlasting glaciers present the most remarkable variety of appearance. Westward there is an open valley with great peaks which stands out in the dim distance. It is by looking north in the direction whence we came that we have the grandest view. The valley is to all appearance completely enclosed by what seemed to be impenetrable mountains. The defile which we entered is not visible, although the entrance is dimly seen clothed in shadow through the smoky air. Towering high near the crest there is a series of glaciers extending for half a mile or more from north to south.

As we quietly rested, enjoying our cigars in the

midst of the remarkable scenery which surrounded us on every side, Major Rogers described to us various details connected with the discovery of the pass, and we felt that his description was as creditable to him as the discovery itself. He stated that he was indebted to the report of Mr. Walter Moberly for a suggestion which led to the examination. As far as I have any knowledge, Mr. Moberly is the first white man who ascended the Ille-celle-waet, the stream which we have now to follow on our journey. It was eighteen years ago. He was engaged in an exploration for the Government of British Columbia. In the year 1865, Mr. Moberly had discovered the Eagle pass, through the Gold Range. He then ascended the Ille-celle-waet, a distance which he estimated at forty miles, to the Forks, where it divided into two streams, one of which, the most northern, he traced some thirty miles farther. This branch terminated in a *cul-de-sac* among snowy mountains. The other branch he was unable to follow, as the season was advanced, 23rd September, and his Indian guide declined to accompany him. In his report, Mr. Moberly spoke hopefully of a route by that branch* and recommended that it "should be examined before a road is finally determined on." It was upon this hint

---

*The latter valley was evidently the one that, judging from its general bearing, would be most likely to afford a pass in the direction wished for. I therefore tried to induce the Indians I had with me by every possible persuasion to accompany me all the way across the Selkirk Range, and make for Wild-Horse

that Major Rogers acted. Three years back he traced the Ille-celle-waet to the Forks, and then followed the eastern branch. This branch also proceeded from two streams, the most southerly of which he followed. With his nephew he climbed a mountain on its northern bank, and from the summit he looked down on the meadow on which we were then resting. Major Rogers, pointing up to the height directly in front of us, said: "There Al. and I stood; we could trace through the mountains a valley, and the conclusion was established in my mind that it led to the unexplored branch of the Ille-celle-waet. We also traced a depression to the east, which we considered might lead to the upper waters of the Columbia. And so it proved." Major Rogers could go no further at that date. He was short of provisions, and he returned as he came. But next year he ascended the stream by which we have travelled for the last two days and reached this grassy plot. On this occasion also his nephew accompanied him, and recognized the meadow, the height on which they formerly stood and the peculiar features of the scenery which they beheld. All that remained was to follow the flow of water

---

Creek (The Columbia River Indians would, from the first, only engage to go as far as the head waters of the Ille-celle-waet.) All my efforts were, however, unavailing, as they affirmed that if we went on we should be caught in the snow and never get out of the mountains.—*Mr. Moberly to Chief Commissioner of Lands and Works,* 18th Dec., 1855.

westerly. They did so as far as the forks of the Ille-celle-waet. They returned by another route in the hope of finding a better pass, but this effort proved unsuccessful.

A party had been detailed to cut out a trail westward, which we are now to follow as far as it is made passable. Beyond that point our party will be the first to pass across the Selkirk Range from its eastern base on the upper Columbia to the second crossing of that river.

The horses are still feeding and we have some time at our command. As we view the landscape we feel as if some memorial should be preserved of our visit here, and we organize a Canadian Alpine Club. The writer, as a grandfather, is appointed interim president, Dr. Grant, secretary, and my son, S. Hall Fleming, treasurer. A meeting was held and we turn to one of the springs rippling down to the Ille-celle-waet and drink success to the organization. Unanimously we carry resolutions of acknowledgment to Major Rogers, the discoverer of the pass, and to his nephew for assisting him. The summit on which we stand is a dry meadow about a mile in extent, with excellent grass. On the approaches we found raspberries, blackberries, blueberries, pigeonberries and gooseberries. They were a treat to us with our hard fare. Fruit, gathered from the bush is always more pleasant to the taste, and fancy eating these delicious fruits in the heart of the Selkirk Range, nearly a vertical mile above the ocean! We are in the best of health, and have the digestion of ostriches. The air is bracing, the day is fine. We have regained our freshness and elasticity, and to show that we are all still young and unaffected by our journey we deem it proper to go through a game of leap-frog, about the only amusement at our command, an act of Olympic worship to the deities in the heart of the Selkirks! Our packers look upon our performance gravely, without a smile. It struck us that the thought passed through their minds that it would be as well for us to reserve our strength for the morrow, and that in view of the path before us our elation was somewhat premature. If such were their thoughts they were certainly justified by the following week's experience.

CHAPTER XVI.

DOWN THE ILLE-CELLE-WAET.

The Descent of the Selkirk Range—Glaciers—The Last of our Horses—Devil's Clubs—The Ille-celle-waet—A Rough Journey—A Mountain Storm—Slow Progress—A Roaring Torrent—Skunk Cabbage—Marsh—A Long Ten Miles' Journey.

Our horses having grazed on the rich pasture are evidently satisfied, some are actually rolling on the grass. So the hour has come to leave the pleasant meadow in the Rogers Pass and pursue our journey. The animals are loaded with their packs, but they are not too eager to make another start. We hear "Steamboat," "Calgary" and the other names shouted in tones of anything but gentle remonstrance, and occasionally stronger means of persuasion are employed. At last we are fairly under way. Our descent is rapid. We soon come in sight of a conical peak rising about fifteen hundred feet, as near as I can judge, above the surrounding lofty mountains. It stood out majestically among its fellows. We thought that it was a fit spot for the virgin attempt of the Alpine Club. We name it Syndicate Peak. Major Rogers declared it would be the summit of his ambition to plant on its highest point the Union Jack on the day that the first through train passed along the gorge we were now travelling. To the west there is a remarkable glacier whence issues one of the sources of the Ille-celle-waet. We descend slowly enough but with increased rapidity of actual descent, crossing a series of avalanche slides with a growth of tall alder bushes, the roots being interlaced in all directions. A line had been cut through by the surveying party, or our progress would have been exceedingly difficult. The narrow gorge occasionally widens out. The flat in the valley of the Ille-celle-waet in some parts may be a quarter of a mile in width, but it is exceedingly irregular in that respect.

We soon find ourselves five hundred feet below the summit. The adjoining mountains are steep, and tracks of avalanches are frequent. From some little distance to a point where the last pasture for the horses can be had the trail is moderately good. Later in the afternoon we came upon an encampment of two Shuswap Indians, who had left Critchelow's camp in the morning before we started. They had pack-animals with them, and had selected the spot on account of some grass growing on the line of a snow-slide. They informed us that this was the last pasture to be found on the trail, so we resolved to camp at the same place.

Our course had been westerly through a valley flanked on both sides by high mountains of all forms with interlying glaciers. We have difficulty in finding a place to pitch our tent, but finally we secure a nook with area enough on the low gravelly bank of a brook of crystal eighteen inches wide, but so small is the space available that the camp fire must be placed on the opposite side of the rivulet; the murmur of its waters at my feet was the sound by which I fall asleep.

In our encampment we had eleven men and sixteen horses, and a strange compound of nationalities we presented. We are from Massachusetts, Minnesota, Virginia, Nova Scotia, Ontario, Scotland, England, Norway and Austria, and two are Shuswap Indians of British Columbia.

The nights are now cold, and before morning we are chilled, although we wrap ourselves in our blankets without being undressed. It could hardly be otherwise in the neighbourhood of so many glaciers. The hot sun penetrates into the valley, but after sunset the cold air of the upper strata by degrees usurps its place. Breakfast and exercise make us once more ourselves, and we again start, winding along the rough and rocky edge of a rapidly descending stream on a narrow trail traced out by the surveying parties a few days previously. We continue through the valley walled in by mountains, the height of which must be counted by thousands of feet. After a progress of fourteen miles we come upon two large masses of frozen snow, one on each side of the river and fifty feet back from it. We learn that three years ago, when first seen, they were much larger and higher, forming a great natural bridge across the stream. The water, which is here of considerable volume and impetuosity, passed through the opening which it had forced in the centre. It is the remains of an avalanche from one of the glaciers, at what date no one can tell, and as I have said, it was first seen three years ago. The bridge has disappeared and only the abutments of hard frozen snow or ice are left, and they are gradually melting away. It is to be inferred that it was of no late occurrence, and that the mass must have been precipitated from a neighbouring glacier, evidently not an uncommon occurrence in this district. Mr. Moberly mentions in his journal, 26th September, 1865, having seen further up the Ille-celle-waet a snow bridge on which his party crossed the stream which flowed two hundred and fifty feet beneath without being seen.

We trudge slowly along the newly cut trail high up among the rocks, to descend again to the flats with its alders and devil's clubs until at last, we reach a surveyors' camp, twenty-four miles from the summit. Such is the measured distance but we would have estimated it as much longer by the tax upon our strength.

Our horses have now to leave us, it being impossible for them to proceed further. I feel quite sad in separating from them. In an expedition such as we are on, horses and men become identified, for they have the common object of moving onwards on the trail before them. A spirit of comradeship springs up but little known in the world of paved streets and hack-cabs. Day after day, as you see the familiar creatures obediently serving you and partaking of your fatigue, and, as in this instance, undergoing privation by your side you regard them as friends. You have always a cheery word of kindness for them, and how a horse knows a man's voice and makes an increased effort at obedience in response to it! These poor creatures had acted admirably for us. On one occasion for a spell of nearly sixty hours they had been almost without food. Yet how patiently they kept to their labours. All of us, I may say, greeted the pasture at the summit with as much delight as if our own food depended on it. But we have now to separate. They return on their way and we go onwards. I had a kind thought for the poor brutes and said to them some parting words, and I hope to-day they have a perfect paradise of pasture wherever they may be.

On reaching the surveyors' camp alluded to I find a fellow laborer of former days, one of the Intercolonial staff, and I was delighted to see him, Mr. McMillan. He commenced the active duties of his profession with me some seventeen or eighteen years back. Engineers have always a pleasure in meeting those who have been on the same work, and when there has been no unpleasantness, which, I am glad to say, does not often happen, the link having so worked together is very strong. Nothing but the best of feeling existed between Mr. McMillan and myself, so we were equally pleased at the meeting.

We spent the evening in discussing the best means of proceeding, for we required additional men to take our provisions, at least to the south flow of the Columbia.

The camping ground was not good. Between the tall cedars there was a dense growth of devil's club through which we had to pass going from tent to tent, and to avoid it we were driven to carry torches to light our way. Before the evening was over we had finally made arrangements for our further journey, and it was ten before we retired.

Last night it rained hard, with thunder and lightning. This morning everything is wet and the trees are dripping in all directions; not a pleasant prospect for those who have to travel under them. There is, however, no halting in a journey such as ours. Our horses have left us. They were driven back to find pasture last night. The men must now carry on their shoulders what we require, through an untrodden forest without path or trail of any kind. Clothing, tents, food and a few cooking utensils constitute what we have to bring with us. Fortunately we can always find water. It is a matter of some calculation and care putting these articles into proper packs, but the task is finally accomplished. We say good-bye to Major Rogers and Mr. McMillan and we start at half-past nine. In saying good-bye to them we were bidding farewell to all civilization which had forced itself into the mountains. Hitherto we had enjoyed what appliances of the great world were available. Our advance had been made as easy as it was possible to make it. We were now turning our back on civilized life and its auxiliaries, again to meet them, we trusted, at Kamloops. Our world was for a time in our little band. We knew nothing of the country before us and we had no assistance to look for from the world behind us. We were following a tributary of the Columbia to the waters of that river, and this was the one guide for our direction. One by one we march off in Indian file to the forest, and I bring up the rear. Independently of myself, the party consists of Dr. Grant, my son Sandford, Mr. Albert Rogers and five men from Mr. McMillan's party, transferred to our service to carry our necessary stores as far as the Columbia. We had also Dave, our cook. I must here say that Dave, in his way, was a man of genius; with that magnificent equanimity that is seldom unaccompanied by great powers. Dave was a plain, honest Englishman, who had spent part of his life as a sailor, and had roughed it in many parts of the world. He never shirked his duty, was of herculean frame and always shouldered the heaviest pack. With a certain roughness of manner he was, with us, one of the round formed pins set in the roundest of holes. I often think of him, and I am sure that he will be equally useful wherever he is.

The walking is dreadful, we climb over and creep under fallen trees of great size and the men soon show that they feel the weight of their burdens. Their halts for rest are frequent. It is hot work for us all. The dripping rain from the bush and branches saturate us from above. Tall ferns sometimes reaching to the shoulder and devil's clubs through which we had to crush our way make us feel as if dragged through a horse-pond and our perspiration is that of a Turkish bath. We meet with obstacles of every description. The devil's clubs may be numbered by millions and they are perpetually wounding us with their spikes against which we strike. We halt very frequently for rest. Our advance is varied by ascending rocky slopes and slippery masses, and again descending to a lower level. We wade through alder swamps and tread down skunk cabbage and the prickly aralias, and so we continue until half-past four, when the tired-out men are unable to go further. A halt becomes necessary. We camp for the night on a high bank overlooking the Ille-celle-waet.

Three of us have dry underclothing, in waterproof bags, but the poor men have no such luxury, so they make large fires by which to dry themselves. Dave, our cook, fries the pork and makes us tea in the usual way on such expeditions. We have all excellent appetites and no fear of a bad digestion; and all quite ready to sleep, literally and truly in spite of thunder, without criticizing the couch on which we lie.

The Ille-celle-waet, on whose banks we have camped, has increased from a tiny brook to a raging torrent, some fifty yards wide. The colour of the water is much as that at London Bridge; a result possibly due to the disintegration of the rock over which the stream rushes and to the grinding action of the boulders rolling down the stream. A sediment is thus formed which is visibly precipitated in any vessel where the water remains quiet.

Last night we discussed the suggestion of constructing a raft and with the current float down to the Columbia. As we look upon the water foaming past us and the numerous rocks and obstacles in the stream, we are satisfied that no raft could live long in such a torrent. The valley is narrow and is skirted by lofty mountains, wooded up their sides and of considerable elevation; but owing to the height of the trees we cannot see their summit. Occasionally during the day we have beheld snow peaks peering above the lower levels. In some parts of the valley a stray sunbeam never penetrates to the lower ground. The vegetation in consequence is peculiar, and mosses of rare variety are found. The ferns, where the soil is rich, are as high as a man's head. The aralia and skunk cabbage are as rank as possible. Here and there on rocky points, above the deeper portions of the valley, we find many berry-bearing shrubs. They enjoy but little sunshine. The fruit in consequence is acid but palatable. Darkness at an early hour enshrouds the base of the peaks, so the cook has to bake to-morrow's bread by the light of the fire. Suddenly thunder is heard and the red glare of lightning illuminates all around us. For some time we are threatened with rain and at length it falls in torrents. The thunder and lightning are now seen and heard through the valley, and our one danger is that a heavy wind may spring up, and, as often happens, root up many of the forest trees around us; but our trust is in Providence as we wrap ourselves in our blankets to sleep.

By the morning the thunder had ceased and the tall trees around us stood erect; the air is thick with mist. The mossy ground with every bush is wet with rain. Breakfast comes, with one and the same *menu* for all meals, and for us all, fried pork and bread made in a frying pan, now and then some dried apples boiled, and tea without milk, strong enough for anyone, and nothing could have been more relished. We mount our packs, for we all carry something, and start onwards for another hard day's march. Our yesterday's advance on a direct line we estimate at four miles. This day's experience was a repetition of that of yesterday, and our great business at the halting places is for each of us to extract the prickles from our hands and knees.

The scene of our midday meal of cold pork and bread was the junction of two clear streams from the mountains, the more bright and crystal like from contrast with the chocolate looking water of the Ille-celle-waet. We resolve to encamp somewhat earlier, so that the men may dry their clothes by day-light. It was fair weather when we halted by a picturesque brook, tired and weary enough. The spot we selected was at a turn of the Ille-celle-waet where the boiling, roaring torrent sweeps past with formidable fury. Coming from the south a brook falls by gentle slopes into the larger stream forming a cascade near its mouth, where we obtain a shower-bath of nature's creation. On the river side there is a forest scene of dark cedars, while here and there lie immense prostrate trunks, some of them eight or ten feet in diameter, covered with moss. Beyond the river the mountains frown down upon us as defiantly as ever. The usual routine of camp settling is gone through and after supper has been eaten the last pipe is smoked and the last lingerer leaves the camp fire for his blankets.

It is Sunday, so we venture to sleep a few five minutes longer, and as we hear the roar of the rapids which seem to shake the very ground, we wonder how we could have slept through it. It rained all night, none of the men had tents and they nestled by the trees and obtained what protection they could. Our waterproofs were divided among them as far as they would go and such as did not possess them were more or less drenched. Looking skywards through the openings in the thick overhanging branches there seems a prospect of the clouds rising. Sunday though it be, with our supplies limited, we are like a ship in mid-ocean: we must continue our journey without taking the usual weekly rest, which would have been welcomed by us all. Dr. Grant called us together, and after the simple form of worship which the Church of Scotland enjoins under such circumstances, we start onwards. The walking is wretchedly bad. We make little headway, and every tree, every leaf, is wet and casts off the rain. In a short time we are as drenched as the foliage. We have many fallen trees to climb over, and it is no slight matter to struggle over trees ten feet and upwards in diameter. We have rocks to ascend and descend; we have a marsh to cross in which we sink often to the middle. For half a mile we have waded, I will not say picked, our way to the opposite side, through a channel filled with stagnant water, having an odour long to be remembered.

Skunk cabbage is here indigenous and is found in acres of stinking perfection. We clamber to the higher ground, hoping to find an easier advance, and we come upon the trail of a cariboo, but it leadsto the mountains. We try another course, only to become entangled in a windfall of prostrate trees. The rain continues falling incessantly: the men, with heavy loads on their heads, made heavier by the water which has soaked into them, become completely disheartened, and at half-past two o'clock we decide to camp. Our travelling to-day extended only over three hours, we have not advanced above a mile and a half of actual distance and we all suffer greatly from fatigue. I question if our three days' march has carried us further than ten miles.

We build huge bonfires and dry our clothes and are just beginning to feel comfortable, under the circumstances, when we discover that an old hollow cedar of some height, near us, has caught fire and leans towards our camp threatening to fall across it. I have heard unpleasant stories about camps in such situations, so we move to another place. In the morning this very tree lay on the ground directly along the site where we were first encamped. In the meantime the rain falls more and more heavily. Our blankets, kept in their water-proof bags, are the only parts of our baggage which are dry. Under the circumstances it was a blessing we possessed this luxury.

CHAPTER XVII.

DOWN THE ILLE-CELLE-WAET.—Continued.

A Difficult March—Cariboo Path—Organization of Advance—Passing Through the Canyon—Timber Jam—A Gun-shot Heard—The Columbia Again—Indians—Disappointment—The Question of Supplies becomes Urgent—No Relief Party Found—Suspense.

It rained when we awoke at five on the Monday. Dave, our cook, had had one of those nights of misery which many have now and then to undergo, but his excellencies are more appreciable as difficulties increase. Soaking wet to the skin he performs the duty of preparing breakfast as cheerfully as if he were in the Royal Kitchen, and in such a situation good humour is the first of virtues. Some time is exacted in drying, even partially, our wet blankets and clothing, so as to lighten the loads, already heavy enough; we cannot, therefore, start as early as we wish.

In the first hours of our journey we make fair progress. We are now far up the mountain side, and here and there we come upon the path of the bear and the cariboo. Generally these trails do not run in the direction we wish to take, but if they incline in the least towards the West we gladly turn to them. They are gone over with so much more ease than the tangled forest, that however much they prolong the distance it is a saving to follow their windings. The cariboo paths, however, too frequently lead to recesses in the mountains or to alder swamps near the river. An attempt to systematize our travelling was made to-day. Hitherto our rests had been irregular. Our halts were long and we were drenched with perspiration ; we got chilled, so we laid down the rule to walk for twenty minutes and rest for five. Dr. Grant is appointed the quartermaster-general for the occasion, with absolute authority to time our halts and our marches by the sound of a whistle, and when he sees fit to call special halts after extraordinary efforts. Our period of progress for twenty minutes often seems very long, and we wearily struggle through the broken ground and clamber over obstacles, eagerly listening for the joyful sound to halt proclaimed by the whistle. It was a system of forced marches and answered admirably, for we made more progress in this way than on any previous occasion. We have another experience of an alder swamp, possibly not quite so formidable as that of yesterday, for we did not sink deeper than the knee. But we had another phase of experience. We reached the lower canyon of the Ille-celle-waet and climbed from rock to rock, grasping roots and branches, scrambling up almost perpendicular ascents, swinging ourselves occasionally like experienced acrobats and feeling like the clown in the pantomime as he tells the children, "here I am again." At some places the loads had to be unpacked and the men had to draw each other up, by clinched hands, from one ledge to another. Then we had another chapter of the Kicking-Horse Valley experience: passing cautiously along a steep slope, where a false step was certain disaster; creeping under a cascade, over a point of precipitous rock and surmounting obstacles, which, unless we had to go forward or to starve, would have been held to be insurmountable. But we persevere and overcome them, and reach our camping ground for the night, all of us showing traces of our day's work. We select for our camp a small *plateau* of about half an acre, overlooking the river, which passes in a foaming torrent through a deep canyon with perpendicular rocky sides, which twists in gigantic irregularities. Such places are only seen in these mountains. The packmen give them the name of "box canyons." A dead tree furnishes us with fuel, and we obtain water by letting a man down with a sling half way to the river's edge to a spot where there is an excellent spring. The water of the river was objectionable, being impregnated with dark sand held in solution.

As we were preparing to rest for the night a bright glare of lightning and a sharp peal of thunder warn us to protect our clothes as best we can against rain. We saw but one flash and heard its accompanying loud crash, to remind us that each night of our descent by the Ille-celle-waet we have been saluted after dark by heaven's artillery.

Our relief is great in the morning to find that it does not rain, that the sky is clear and that there is promise of a fine day. We have all slept well and are refreshed and hope to make the Columbia early in the day. We start off cheerfully, but we are not out of the canyon. We again climb through the rocky defile, and about half a mile from our starting point we reach a jam of trunks of trees, not far from its lower end. Tree after tree has been piled here by the current for many a year. Who can tell the period? For the space of some hundreds of yards up and down the stream a mass has been heaped up thirty or forty feet above the level of the water. There is an accumulation of material at this spot which would be a fortune to its possessor if he had it in London or any European city. We cautiously clamber from log to log over this jam and reach the opposite side of the canyon. We proceed onward soon to find the ground cumbered by many fallen trees, with masses of rocks and the invariable ferns and devil's clubs in all their luxuriance. We continue our march, making our halts by rule, and on the whole make decent progress.

We halt at mid-day sufficiently long to eat our

bread and cold bacon, and we thought we ought to be within hearing of a gunshot from the Columbia. We expect the party from Kamloops with supplies to meet us there. It is the eleventh of the month. I had named the 8th of September as the date at the latest when we should reach the place appointed. Accordingly I direct my son rapidly to fire two rifle shots. We listen attentively and in a short time we hear the welcome report of a gunshot. We answer with three shots in quick succession, and again we hear a gun-shot. We count almost with breathless excitement. It is repeated and again repeated,—it is the three shots! Thank God! We have established our connection. Our friends are in front of us with the provisions on which we rely. All anxiety for the future is past, and the promised waters of the Columbia cannot be far from us.

By the nature of the ground over which we have to pass some time is exacted for us to overcome the obstacles before us, but not a moment is lost. We are all alive with excitement, and move forward as rapidly as it is possible to do. At our first rest we fire another shot, and we hear two shots more distinctly than on the first occasion. We are much elated to feel that our combinations have been so successful, and that we were on the eve of having to welcome new faces from the outer world, and possibly receive letters from home. We strike a bee line in the direction of the sound and strive to follow it. Soon we are out of the green woods and are in sight of the Columbia. We observe the smoke of a camp a mile from us on the opposite shore. Impulsively we give a series of hurrahs, for it seems to us we can see our friends from Kamloops. Two canoes cross the river. We are standing upon the high sandy bank in full view of the Eagle pass, directly opposite to us. We soon observe that our expectations have deceived us. The canoes contain Indians only. We meet them at the water's edge. They can speak no English, but with the help of a little "Chinook," we learn, to our great disappointment, that no one has arrived from Kamloops! It was the Indians who had replied to our shots. They were Fort Colville Indians, and had come by the Columbia some time ago as a small hunting party, and they had been on this spot for at least four weeks. However, we decided to cross the river in their canoes and send back the men to Mr. McMillan, as we had promised him.

We divided our little store of provisions with the fine fellows who had carried our *impedimenta* down the Ille-celle-waet, so that they would have enough to take them back to McMillan's camp. I added a letter of approval to their chief. No men ever more deserved thanks than they did. Our lives had been passed side by side for many an hour, so I could judge and estimate their good-will and the cheerfulness with which they performed their duties. I never knew men with better pluck or endurance. I could easily see that my friend, McMillan, had specially picked them out for the arduous service they had to perform. They were all made of the truest and best of stuff, and let me here make my acknowledgments to them for their admirable conduct. We had Campbell, Currie and McDougall, from Ontario; McMillan, from New Brunswick, and Scoly, an Englishman, from Lancashire. These men had been put to the test, and showed of what material their manhood was made. They could not have behaved better, and they carry with them my best wishes for their future welfare.

Our canoes shot out from the shore and those we leave behind give us three hearty cheers, which we as cordially acknowledge. The Columbia at the junction of the Ille-celle-waet, is a noble stream, broad and deep. We landed at the gravelly bank of the Indian encampment, where we found three Indian families, with four canoes. We pitched our tent four hundred yards down stream, where the current was much stronger. The width here is about twelve hundred feet, and the whole river brought to my mind the South-west Miramichi, where the Intercolonial Railway crosses it.

It was early in the afternoon and the stream furnished us the luxury of a good bath. We made a fire on the beach and had dinner, after which we seriously considered our situation. We were fatigued beyond measure and every joint ached. The skin of all of us in a few places was somewhat lacerated, our hands were festering from the pricks of the devil's club, and we had not yet come to the end of our work. I was well aware that we would yet have difficulties to meet in reaching Kamloops. Our supply of food was nearly exhausted, and what was left we had to carry ourselves. I certainly felt grievously disappointed that the men from Kamloops were not present. We were three days later than the appointed day of meeting. We ought to have found the party on the spot to receive us, and their absence had a most depressing effect on us. Neither men nor provisions were on the ground. I distinctly remembered the arrangements made at Winnipeg. I read over and over copies of the directions left behind, also the telegrams sent from Calgary, and I knew that if any one could carry out the arrangement it was the agents of the Hudson's Bay Company. I had been careful in impressing upon the Chief Commissioner that we depended on him solely and absolutely for our supplies of food at this point. We were on the spot where they should have been delivered, and the time had passed when the relief party should be on the ground. We thought of all sorts of mishaps that might have befallen them. We knew there was no trail through the Eagle Pass; indeed I myself had telegraphed that fact from Calgary. Major

Rogers and his nephew had traversed it three years ago, and we were aware that the ground to be passed over was of the most trying description: that there were several lakes to be crossed. The thought came upon us that the supply party might have met with an accident in crossing one of these lakes, or they might have been overtaken by forest fires, or some other misadventure might have happened which we knew nothing of.

There was one alternative open to us. Fortunately the band of Indians were on the spot, and if the worst came to the worst we might induce them to paddle us down the Columbia to Fort Colville, in the United States, and thence find our way through Washington Territory and Oregon to our destination. But we had started to go through the mountains to reach Kamloops on a direct line, and the idea of abandoning the attempt and making a flank movement was the last we could entertain.

Our decision as to the course we are to take cannot be long delayed, as our slender stock of provisions will last but a few days. In this painful embarrassment, and it was painful, we asked ourselves the question: Would it be prudent to go on risking the chance of meeting the party from Kamloops, or do the circumstances compel us to give up the idea of crossing the Gold Range and force us to enlist the services of the Indians to take us down the Columbia, some two hundred miles to their own village, from which point we can find our way to Portland in Oregon in twelve days, and then by Puget's Sound reach our destination in British Columbia? This mode of procedure was most repugnant to us; but however desirous we were to cross the Gold Range of mountains, we had seriously to consider the situation. I may seem to exaggerate the doubt and misgiving which thus crossed my mind. But the facts of the case must be borne in mind that our dependence rested entirely upon receiving the supplies from Kamloops; this source failing, none was open to us. Had our stock of provisions been exhausted and no Indians been present on the Columbia, I do not see that our fate would have been different to that of many an explorer: starvation. There was only one deduction to be drawn from the absence of the Kamloops party: that there had been misapprehension or misfortune, and that we could not look for assistance where we stood.

The responsibility of determining the course to be taken under such circumstances was serious and depressing. It was evident that we had to act independently of others, and viewing the state of our provisions we had at once to do so. Our united feeling was strong that we should not abandon the Eagle Pass. We all recognized that after a night's rest immediate action was imperative, that we ought in no way to delay but to proceed onward, leaving behind us tent, blankets, baggage and everything not absolutely required, carrying only the remnant of food we still had, with a small frying pan, and so work our way westward as best we could. With this feeling uppermost in our minds we try to consider the prospect before us with equanimity.

We had at least accomplished an important part of the journey, and our advance had so far been without mishap. We had crossed through the Rocky Mountain Range and the Selkirk Range, and had arrived at the second crossing of the Columbia by the time estimated. We are no longer in the wet and clammy recesses which we passed through along the course of the turbulent river recently followed. We are on the banks of a noble stream in the wide open valley of the Columbia. The landscape which met our view was of great beauty. It was mellowed with autumnal tints and confined within countless lofty peaks. To the east lay the valley of the Ille-celle-waet, surrounded by towering heights gradually fading in the distance, while in front of us the Columbia swept along through its various windings, made more glittering by the contrast of the dark masses of foliage on the low ground.

Evening came on to throw a more sombre tint of colour over the scene. All that was to be heard was the peculiar sound of the rapidly flowing stream and the distant roar of the Falls of the Ille-celle-waet.

CHAPTER XVIII.

THROUGH THE EAGLE PASS.

The Kamloops Men at Last—No Supplies—On Short Allowance—An Indian Guide—Bog-wading—The Summit of the Pass—Bluff Lake—Victoria Bluff—Three Valley Lake—Eagle River—Shooting Salmon—The *Cached* Provisions—Pack-horses Again—Road Making—The South Thompson—Indian Ranches.

Our anxiety passed away when five men appeared coming from the woods on the flats of the Columbia, a short distance from our camp. We saw them approach with more than usual satisfaction, for we felt certain that they were the men we were looking for, and we hastened to meet them as they came towards us.

McLean was in charge, with four Shuswap Indians, and without delay he gave me letters from the Hudson's Bay Company's agent. And among them was a sheet of foolscap setting forth a list of the provisions sent us, which, in the condition of our own stores was peculiarly acceptable. On inquiry we learn that the sheet of paper alone represented the provisions, for it was all that the party had brought with them. The stores entrusted to them to bring to the Columbia had been *cached* at a point five days distant from us, and they had brought with them barely enough food to supply their own wants. It was neither welcome nor looked for intelligence with our slender stock of pork and flour. We had already put ourselves on short allowance, and in view of our resources we had not a moment to lose in making a start.

The non-appearance of the Kamloops party at an earlier day was accounted for by the well-meant but ill-advised attempt to bring horses with them to the Columbia, and by the exceedingly rough character of the ground through the Eagle pass itself, even for foot travel. Many parts of the valley were blocked up by fallen trees of gigantic size; and the obstructions, owing to masses of rock, the lakes, swamps and a general ruggedness, had proved to be formidable. No attempt had been made to bring on any of the provisions beyond the point which the horses could not pass. At that spot the whole was *cached*, and one of the Indians had been detailed to remain behind in charge of the animals. The main object of their mission had, therefore, not been fulfilled: that of being at the Columbia on the 8th of September with provisions. They had neither observed the date of meeting, nor had they brought with them the food which we looked for at their hands. Fidelity to an engagement of this character is indispensable in the wilderness. It ought to be felt that failure might lead to privation and suffering. Had any one of us or our party slipped on the rocks or trees, had forest fires impeded our progress, had we lost our way, or had we, through any other unforeseen cause, been delayed, our stock of supplies would have been exhausted when we reached the Columbia. Fortunately we had met with no misadventure. We had been exceedingly careful with our provisions, and hence we had a small reserve of pork and flour, which, with careful management, could be made to serve for a couple of days longer. There was nothing left for us but to make an effort to extricate ourselves from the false position in which we found ourselves.

We discovered that the Fort Colville Indians encamped near us were well acquainted with the country for some distance back of the Columbia. It had been their hunting ground; accordingly we engaged one of their party, old Baptiste, as a guide, to take us on our way by the least difficult route, to the extent of his knowledge of the country.

After the usual delay incident to a start with a new set of men we march off in Indian file, headed by old Baptiste. None of us had been impressed either by the knowledge of the country which the Kamloops party possessed or by their skill in combinations. The Indian knew the route well as far as Three Valley Lake, and we felt safer under his pilotage, and assigned him the advanced post of our party.

We imagined that we were making the best of starts. We all started forward in Indian file with that springy gait which marks men having confidence in themselves. The guide, however, led us to his own camp. He did so without explanations or remark. He entered his wigwam and we remained outside. The proceeding was inexplicable until we learned that he had to repair his moccasins before he could start. We halted three quarters of an hour, while the squaw deliberately plied her awl and leather thong, the Indian in the meanwhile sitting motionless, smoking his pipe and looking into the embers of the fire. We could only imitate his patience and await the result. At length in the same silent way he re-appeared, and started without comment on the trail. We submissively followed. The thought crossed my mind that in this case knowledge was power.

Our guide took us by a circuitous route round the shore of the "big eddy," avoiding a mile of exceedingly painful walking, which the Kamloops men had passed over last night.

We find our way over ground almost clear of trees. Some years back the country had been ravaged by one of the great forest fires, often extending over immense distances. The trees had not again grown, and we rapidly reach the green wood in the pass, where we take our mid-day meal.

We start again, skirting a large marsh. It seemed to us at first to be a beaver meadow. It was full of water holes, skunk cabbage and deep black muck. McLean and his men had waded through this bog up to their middle for the greater part of the way. It was the one part of their return they most dreaded to encounter. Do any of my readers know what it is to wade through a marsh of deep oozy mud, covered with stinking water? It is not an experience they may long for. The path we pass along is the one taken by the Indians for carrying cariboo and game over the mountains. The various wild berries we saw on the route were unusually large. They more resembled small grapes in size than the ordinary berry, and were pleasant to the taste. There was an abundance of black huckleberries and blackberries. Is not this presence of a luxurious growth of wild growing fruit an indication that garden fruits might find their home in these sheltered valleys?

We are fast ascending towards the summit. The valley leading to the Eagle pass is about a quarter of a mile wide, walled in by parallel mountains generally wooded to the top. We pass through a vast grove of fine timber, mostly hemlock, fit for purposes of railway construction. We cross several times the stream we are following, and about five o'clock encamp on its eastern side. The site we select is the freest we could find from the formidable devil's clubs. Cedars, four feet in diameter, rise up around us like the columns of a lofty temple. We counted some forty or fifty in a circle of a radius of a hundred feet, and a striking appearance they presented.

We have travelled seven miles and have reached the summit of the Pass. Our journey has been in every way satisfactory. We thoroughly recognize all we owe to our guide. He has saved us labour, time and much painful experience, and we are proportionately satisfied with our own forethought that his services could be utilized.

As night came on we lit up a hollow cedar. It is some distance from us, and when it falls it will be away from us, as it inclines in the opposite direction to our camp ground. It burns rapidly, and illuminates the scene around us for the whole evening. It was moonlight also, but the dense forest intervened, so the camp remained in shadow. The vegetation around us was rank, with a green, luxurious growth of mosses. Indeed the mosses extended in all directions, the surface of the lower branches of the lofty trees not excepted. Some of the ferns we saw were striking, and the abominable devil's club was in profusion all around us.

It rained during the night; we were comfortable in our tents, but the men were exposed to the rain, having brought with them no protection against it. Before starting their blankets had to be dried, so it was nearly eight o'clock before we got off.

In less than two-thirds of a mile we gain Bluff Lake on the summit; the steep rocky sides have given it its name, and the walking is so difficult that we deem it expedient to form a raft on which we can float to its further end.

We have now entered into the third range of mountains and have passed beyond the waters flowing into the Columbia. We have reached the waters of the Eagle River, which find their way to the Fraser. Our raft carried the tent and baggage, but was not large enough for all to find a place upon it. Accordingly some had to clamber over the rocks as best they could, and a difficult walk they had. We reached the end of the Lake and continued on our journey. Another three-quarters of a mile brings us to a second Victor Lake. We did not construct a raft to navigate it. Baptiste took us by what he called an easy route. We had, however, to clamber over rocky precipices the whole of the way, and it is the afternoon before we sat down to take our meal at its western end. The Lake is about three-quarters of a mile in length; the water is like a mirror, in which the lofty peaks are reflected in every variety of shade. Directly in our front there is a magnificent bluff rising vertically sheer from the water seven hundred feet. Its image appears in the mirror-like lake as well defined as in the atmosphere. On behalf of the Canadian Alpine Club we name the bluff after Her Majesty, and give three cheers for the Queen in honour of the occasion. We all feel in good spirits, for we are satisfied with the progress we are making. Our advance, however, was not without its difficulties. We had a seemingly endless number of prostrate trunks of trees and rocks to surmount, and on the lower ground we had from time to time to wade through troublesome marshes.

Three and a half miles from Victor Lake we arrived at Three Valley Lake. Our Kamloops men, on their way to meet us, had constructed a raft at this point, which is again available. It is large enough to take the whole party. So we embarked upon it. Baptiste followed in a small, birch-bark canoe, which he had taken from its *cache*. We move slowly through this beautiful lake, nestling in the mountains, where three valleys meet. Its shape is somewhat that of a three-corner staff officer's hat. It has lofty, wide banks, with bold rocky bluffs standing out from the spruce and birch wood, here and there visible. It is a beautiful sheet of water, dark in color and exceedingly deep. It has been said that it is fathomless. Few Swiss lakes, which I have seen in my limited wanderings, rise in my mind as superior to it in wild, natural beauty. This sheet of water has a character of its own. We reach the outlet in about an hour, somewhat chilled by sitting immovably in one position on the raft. We soon are ourselves again as we arrange our camping ground. Every spot is bright green, but there is not a blade of grass. Possibly, owing to the excessive moisture of the locality, the ground is brilliant with rich mosses of the thickness of three or four inches, and you walk on them as on a Turkish carpet.

We encamped on a small tree-covered promontory at the outlet of the lake. Eagle River has now become a good sized stream of clear water flowing over a rocky bottom. The scenery is striking in all directions. The central of the Three Valleys branches into four subordinate valleys, between each of which high peaks, covered with snow, are to be seen. To the north and west the peaks are less lofty. Baptiste tells us that much game abounds, and that from the lake large fish are taken, as we infer, salmon. The evening was very pleasant; we were all in good humour, not by any means the worst resource to the wanderer in his travels.

It did not rain last night. I do not hold my own experience as sufficient for any generalization, but from all I can learn, at this season of the year, it is seldom that such is the case in the mountains. Certainly the nights during which we have escaped rain since entering the Selkirk Range have been few.

We had now to part with our Indian guide, who had fulfilled his contract, so we settled with him and found he had a cool way of his own in reckoning the value of his services, whatever he might know of arithmetic. As a "lucky penny" we supplied him with enough matches to last him a month, a mine of wealth to him ; and he paddled away to the east to find his way back to the Grand Eddy.

The Kamloops Indians, now on their own ground, are unusually active this morning. A tree is felled on which we can cross the river, and we get off by eight o'clock, trudging through the woods, passing over alder swamps and dry rocky ground, encountering prostrate trees of giant growth until we reach Griffin's Lake, a mile in length, with rough and rugged sides. We constructed a raft of light timber and formed our paddles of split cedar. It took an hour and three-quarters to make the raft, but by paddling through the lake we made up the time and reserved our strength for further efforts. We had an excellent opportunity of seeing the country from the middle of the lake. Snow covered peaks were here and there visible, but I question if this snow be permanent; it struck me that it was only the deposit of the late storms which we had experienced. We took our mid-day meal, it was now bread and water, on the raft, so there was no delay in our starting westward when we landed. The ground was smooth for some distance, but we soon reached a part of the valley where it was entirely swamp to the base of the hills. We had, therefore, to clamber along its side, which was encumbered with large fallen trees and huge stones. Our progress was as slow as in the valley of the Ille-celle-waet; and soon, from sheer fatigue, we were forced to accept the first available camping ground which offered: a small plateau near a mountain stream.

As arranged, Albert and McLean started next morning at day-break towards the point where the horses and supplies had been left, to get everything in order, so that when we came up no time would be lost and we could at once proceed. We shall not reach the spot a minute too soon, for we are out of everything in the shape of food. McLean and the four Indians, despatched from Kamloops with supplies, have helped to finish the remnant of stores which we have carried across three mountain summits from the Bow River. Without our forced marches our provisions would certainly have been insufficient, and but for the accident of meeting a guide we might have been in an unenviable situation. Yet the failure of our plan was in itself so ridiculous that I cannot look back upon it without a smile. We were in the heart of a desert and asked for bread. We did not even get a stone, but we met five hungry Indians ready to devour the little store we had brought with us.

We started soon after seven, every member of the party carrying his own pack, except Albert and McLean, who had been already despatched without loads. Our advance had much of the character of that of yesterday, along a steep hill side, among fallen trees from four to six feet in diameter. Our progress was exceedingly slow through these difficulties; at length we reached the *cached* provisions at eleven o'clock. The hour of short commons was passed, and at our mid-day meal we had a sumptuous fare. We found tinned oysters, potatoes, coffee, bacon, flour, onions and such delicacies; we also had an example of the saying that "it never rains but it pours," for my son fortunately shot a salmon in the Eagle River. We were thus in the very lap of luxury; but our business was to do more than revel on good fare. We had to be up and moving. The Indians expressed great astonishment when the order was given to march. They expected we should remain here for a few days to feast on the good things till they were done: as they term it in British Columbia, to have a regular "potlatch."

We continued our journey, having horses to carry the loads. Occasionally we ourselves mount, but the trail is so rough that for the best part of the distance it was easier made on foot. The horses were fresh after a week's rest, and for an hour they bounded over the logs and rocks with ease, but they soon settled down into their ordinary pack-horse walk.

Two miles from our dinner camp we crossed a stream of bright blue water from the north, nearly equal in volume to the Eagle River. Four miles further we met Mr. Joseph Hunter on his way to find us. He gave us the welcome news that tomorrow we would be on a waggon road, now being constructed over the western end of Eagle Pass, and that at Schuswap Lake we would find a steamer to take us to Kamloops.

Our trail did not improve. It continued on the hill side over rocky ground, partially through a *brulé*. Our march was tedious, for we were more on foot than in the saddle.

Eight miles from our noon camp we reached the north fork of the Eagle River, a stream about eighty feet in width. The water was turbid, indicative of a glacial scource. We found some difficulty in fording it, owing to the rapidity of the current and the bed of the stream being full of large boulders. A mile further on we camped on the hill side among the charred remains of a forest fire, and had an excellent supper. The moon rose, nearly at the full, lighting the lofty hills in our front, and as we sat by the fire Mr. Hunter told us all he knew of the doings of the outer world, of which we had lost all trace for nearly four weeks. We learned that our camp is but four or five miles in a direct course from a working party constructing a waggon road in our direction.

As the morrow will be Sunday, Dr. Grant suggests that we should start as usual, and that he should hold a service when we arrive. Accordingly the following morning Mr. Hunter and he start off on foot in advance. We were so eager to reach the waggon road that all were up and at breakfast before sunrise and were under way as its early rays were peering over the mountains where, last night, the full moon came up. The sky was without a cloud. The trail was so imperfect and circuitous that, although the distance was given as from four to five miles, it took us from six until about twelve to reach the encampment of Mr. G. B. Wright, the road contractor. It was a tented village. Our hostess, Mrs. Wright, received us under a large tent, appearing to us with an additional charm as being the first white woman we had seen since we left Morley on the eastern slope of the Rocky Mountains. One of our first luxuries was the use of soap and hot water, and certainly we all required it. After we had partaken of the bounteous hospitality of Mrs. Wright, Dr. Grant held a service, at which about forty men attended, together with the only woman of our race within a long distance—our hostess. The men wore the usual long beard, bearing no signs of the scissors, and their dress was rough, but they all listened with marked attention and reverence.

In the afternoon we left this canvass town, which comprised some sixty tents of all sizes. We were accommodated with a spring waggon and were driven some sixteen miles over an excellent road. The whippletree gave way more than once, but was speedily repaired by the help of a short stick and some cod line. At half-past five we reached Shuswap Lake, where a steamer was waiting for us, Albert having ridden ahead to detain it. We were soon on board and steamed through the Sicamouse Narrows, about three hundred feet wide with about six to eight feet of water, as the last rays of the sun were lighting the lake. The moon rose and we could see the country around us with the water channels from every point of view. The shore is still in a state of nature, without a settlement. There is not even a house at the steamboat landing, and the supplies for the waggon road construction parties find shelter from the rain under canvas. The steamer is about a hundred feet in length, with a stern wheel for navigating shallow waters. It was eleven o'clock before we turned in, and I could not but contrast our present mode of travel with that of a few days back, and it seemed almost like a dream as I thought of our advance from the first summit.

We had still, however, a most unpleasant recollection of our wearing journey through the mountains; the prickles of the devil's club in their poisonous effects had become a great annoyance to many of us. Indeed, our swollen hands had to be wrapped in oatmeal poultices. In one case the swelling and pain were really serious, and as a consequence at least one of our party suffered from loss of sleep.

At eight next morning we were on deck. The steamer was sailing down the South Thompson. We stopped frequently at Indian ranches for passengers and freight. The effort of getting some pigs on board at one of the landings created some amusement; a scene in its way suggestive of our having entered again the realm of civilization. Breakfast had been delayed until our arrival at a spot where we were to obtain fresh milk and some butter. When we reached the place, a ranche by the river side, the fresh butter was not ready, so we waited until the churning had been completed. Affairs seemed to us rather primitive west of Kamloops Lake. Our cook is a Chinaman, comely looking enough, and the breakfast that he put before us was certainly a respectable proof of his skill.

We were now gliding through a country entirely different from that east of Shuswap Lake. We had left the lofty peaks behind us, and were surrounded by high hills covered with bunch grass, with groves of trees and sometimes with single massive trunks of spruce or Douglas pine. The landscape has a park-like character, and is highly picturesque. The hills are high and varied in outline. Some portions of the River Thompson recall the scenery on the upper portions of the Arno and the Tiber on the journey from Florence to Rome. No rocky bluffs are visible; the hills are smooth and rounded, but nevertheless of such variety as to take away any monotony in the landscape as we move down the river. About nine o'clock we arrive at Kamloops, some ninety miles distant from Shuswap Lake, our starting place of the previous night, where we had embarked.

CHAPTER XIX.

KAMLOOPS TO THE COAST.

Lake Kamloops—Savona's Ferry—Irrigation—Chinese Navvies —Chinese Servants—Lytton—The Fraser River Canyon—Old Engineering Friends—Sunday at Yale—Paddling Down the Fraser—An English Fog at New Westminster.

The district into which we have entered, in its physical character, is directly the opposite of that which we have traversed. We have no mosses to tell the story of excessive humidity. We are now in a country where the leading feature is extreme aridity. I can compare the dark powdered earth to nothing to which it bears more resmblance than ground pepper. On all sides the indications show that this condition of soil and climate extends over a wide district. The surface is covered by a tufted vegetation known as bunch grass. There is only one remedy to make it productive of farm crops: a system of irrigation on an extensive scale. As yet no steps have been taken for its introduction in this neighbourhood. Nowhere is the eye relieved by a flower garden or by the familiar charm of cultivated ground. The small town of Kamloops at present can boast of no such advantages, but there is nothing to lead to the belief that they are not attainable.

We are indebted for a temporary home to the hospitable factor of the Hudson's Bay Company. Naturally one of our first acts is to report our arrival to our friends in the east. Unfortunately the telegraph line is down and the operator absent repairing it. Deeming it of importance that no time should be lost we despatch an Indian courier with messages to the next station, Savona's Ferry, thirty miles distant.

We all feel that after our tramp we are entitled to a few hours' additional rest. It is true that for the most part we have slept soundly every night of our journey; indeed, if men could not sleep after serious work like ours, it would be hard to say when they could do so. But we had not indulged in the luxury of late hours. We were always up at day-break, and I never heard the complaint that any of us had slept too long. One satisfaction we had, we can thankfully say that we were generally spared the penalty of loss of sleep. Last night, however, was an exception. In my own case the wounds on my hands, swollen by the poison of the devil's club, made sleep impossible. We resolved accordingly to pass the afternoon quietly at the Hudson's Bay post, and retire early to bed; in this case not a figure of speech, for under this roof we had all the comforts of civilization.

We were up in good time next morning. I paid what bills we owed, bade farewell to our Kamloops friends, said good-bye to Mr. McLean and his Indians, and prepared to proceed westward. A steamer had been engaged to take us to Savona's Ferry. We started about nine o'clock, skirting along the north shore of Lake Kamloops by Battle Bluff. We returned by the south side, examining the ground adjoining Cherry Bluff. The day was fine, so the trip was pleasant. The sky was as clear and the air as pure and balmy as on an Italian lake. The steamer touched at a place called Tranquille, where the land has been irrigated. In this instance the experiment has been in all respects satisfactory. The result is shown in a good garden with excellent fruit and vegetables.

At Savona's Ferry I received messages by telegraph, and I was reminded of being once more within the circle of artificial wants and requirements. For the last thirty days we have been out of the world, knowing nothing beyond the experience of our daily life. Our leading thoughts were of the difficulties which lay in our path and of the labour necessary to overcome them. There was nothing vicarious in our position; there was no transfer of care or labour to others. Each one had to accept what lay before him, and our world for the time was in our little circle. Now we are reminded that we are again in another condition of being. There is scarcely anything more powerful to recall the attention to this change than the receipt of a telegram sent across a continent to remove anxieties as to home and family.

I had much pleasure in meeting Mr. Hamlin, an old Intercolonial friend, the Resident Engineer of the section under contract west of Savona's Ferry. I had telegraphed to him the previous evening, and he had taken the trouble to come seventeen miles to meet me. We took dinner at Savona; and the fact recalled to my mind that eleven years ago I had stopped at this same place. Mrs. Whorn was then our hostess, whom I perfectly recollected, but the poor lady had been dead for twelve months, and is buried not far distant.

Dr. Grant and my son started in a waggon for Cache Creek. I had professional business with Mr. Hamlin. We proceeded by the banks of the River Thompson, and reached his quarters about sunset, to receive from his wife and mother the most kindly of Irish welcomes. We passed a pleasant evening and spoke much of old days, going back to the time when we were working in the valley of the Metapedia, in Quebec.

I had another excellent night's sleep and was up early. At six Mr. Hamlin and myself started. The morning air was cold. We arrived at Cache Creek about half-past seven, and found Dr. Grant and my son under canvas. The hotel was so unpromising that they preferred their tent to the cheerless entertainment it suggested. Albert and

Mr. Hunter soon join us, and the four took the stage to Spence's bridge. Mr. Hamlin was good enough to drive me there with his own horses. We took some refreshment at Ashcroft, seven miles from Cache Creek. The country residence of the Lieutenant-Governor of British Columbia is at Ashcroft, and I felt it my duty to pay him my respects. Mr. Cornwall, himself, was absent; the ladies, however, received us with much kindness, and our conversation turned to a previous occasion when I passed an evening in their society under the same roof, some years back, of which I retained the most pleasing recollection. In fact, I may remark that, as they say in Paris, this was my *visite de digestion* after the pleasant dinner which I then had with the family.

As we proceed the sun shines upon us with unusual heat for the time of year. Small fields of irrigated land are seen here and there and present a promising appearance. The ground generally is dry, for there is little rainfall in this district. From the indications I fear no crop can thrive without irrigation, and it appears to me it is the main consideration for the residents to entertain.

We descend by the westerly bank of the River Thompson, and obtain a good view of the railway work on the opposite bank. We reached Spence's Bridge about three o'clock, where Mr. H. F. Macleod greeted me with a warm welcome and invited the whole party to his house. Mr. Hamlin returned to his own place. Dr. Grant, my son and myself availed ourselves of Mr. Macleod's hospitality. Mr. Macleod is another old friend and fellow worker on the Intercolonial Railway. Spence's Bridge has a canvas town of about one thousand Chinamen, engaged on the railway works. I presume the Chinese population will disappear as the railway is completed. The place contains a good hotel, with a garden of some size, producing apples, grapes and excellent vegetables; in itself showing what can be be accomplished with irrigation, effort and skill. No fact is more patent than that irrigation is indispensable in this district.

Mr. Macleod kindly drove us over the works. We follow the deep gorge through which the Thompson forces its way. Mr. Macleod's house is situated at Drynoch, so called from his relationship to the Macleods of Skye. It is scarcely necessary to say that at Drynoch we received a cordial and graceful Highland welcome. We were particularly struck with the appearance of the Chinaman waiting at table. His loose dress was of spotless white, and with his thick soft-soled shoes he moved so quietly as to be scarcely audible. He had always a smile on his face, and his mistress gave him the best of characters for intelligence, industry and good manners. We passed a delightful evening in this oasis in the mountains.

In the morning Mr. Macleod accompanied us to Lytton, where the Thompson falls into the Fraser.

Lytton has not greatly improved since I saw it last year. It is still a wretchedly dilapidated place. The dingy wooden buildings were marked by a striking absence of paint, and evidently the summary course applied at Truro, in Nova Scotia, on the occasion of the Prince of Wales' visit, could with benefit be introduced here. At Lytton I said good-bye to Mr. Macleod, heartily thanking him for his hospitality. Mr. Hannington, another of my old assistants, from Ottawa, now received me.

Mr. Hannington drove me to his place, three miles beyond Lytton, and we proceeded eight miles further to the site of the railway bridge to cross the River Fraser. The bridge, a massive structure of stone and iron, is in progress. Here we met Mr. George Keefer, the Engineer in charge of this section, another of my old staff. Mr. Keefer took me to his quarters, seventeen miles below Lytton, being thirty-three miles from Drynoch. Mr. Keefer's house is on the railway line on the western bank of the Fraser. So we crossed the river in a canoe and floated down the boiling, seething current to a convenient landing place. Ascending the bank about two hundred feet nearly vertically, we reached Mr. Keefer's present house, where we remained for the night. Mrs. Keefer and her children were absent on a visit at Victoria, but he himself left no effort untried to entertain us. I was delighted again to see my old friend so pleasantly circumstanced, and we were all indebted to him for his hospitality.

I was awakened in the morning by a Chinaman appearing with a bath, a luxury more appreciated after my late experience, and one among the first benefits of civilization, which we hasten to enjoy. We are forty miles from Yale, in that huge cleft in the Cascade Range through which the Fraser impetuously continues its course. The rails are laid from Yale to a point two miles above where we now are. We can accordingly reach Yale by a locomotive in little more than an hour, but it is my desire to pass leisurely over the line, in order somewhat to examine it. It has therefore been arranged that we proceed on our journey by handcar. A dense fog fills up the valley but the sun soon comes out and the fog is dispelled. As we approached Mr. Keefer's quarters last night we had to pass over the long ascent of Jackass mountain, a name familiar to British Columbians from the day of the discovery of gold in Cariboo. The road leading to the gold mines passes over it. The frame of a house on a small terrace some nine hundred feet above the river, was pointed out as the resting place for the night of Lord and Lady Dufferin when in British Columbia. It affords a magnificent view of Fraser river and the great mountains which flank the valley on both sides.

The hand-car came, bringing with it my old friend Mr. H. J. Cambie. He had left his home this morning at Spuzzem, twenty miles distant. We again start. To Dr. Grant the hand-car was almost a revelation; it was certainly a new mode of travelling which he was about to experience. Mr. Keefer follows on a railway velocipede. This machine has its two main wheels on one rail, with a third wheel to steady it, gauged to the opposite rail. It is kept in motion by a crank, worked by the rider's feet. I am sorry to say that on this expedition Mr. Keefer's velocipede was crushed by a gravel train backing, owing to a mistake of orders, and Mr. Keefer had only just time enough to extricate himself to avoid a similar fate.

Our course followed the railway down the western bank of the great canyon of the Fraser. The Cariboo waggon road runs on the opposite bank as far as the Alexandria Bridge. We had an opportunity of observing the lofty cliffs and the precipitous ledges it passes over, and from the really slight character and dangerous appearance of the staging upon which man and horse have so long risked their lives, I could not but think that the railway would not be open for traffic an hour too soon. I presume that when that result comes to pass the waggon road will fall into disuse. The construction of the railway has been exceedingly difficult and costly within the twenty-eight mile section in charge of Mr. Cambie. The work is extremely heavy, including thirteen tunnels. We reach Spuzzem in the afternoon, having travelled leisurely. We proposed making another start, but Mr. Cambie would not hear of our passing his house, and despatched the hand-car to Yale for our letters, the place where they had been ordered to be addressed. In a couple of hours I had received the bag containing my month's correspondence, including letters from home of the latest date.

I was under no apprehension of any bad news, for the telegram which I had sent from Savona's Ferry had been answered to the effect that all was well; but with what delight, when we have been for weeks cut off from those dear to us, do we read in their own words that everything is precisely as it should be.

Every onward step, every hour, was bringing us more into the world's usages. I had not been long at Spuzzem when I was invited to attend a telephone conference. On taking my place, at once I recognized the voice addressing me, although at twelve miles distance, and I had not heard it for two years. It was that of Mr. Onderdonk, giving the party a cordial invitation to make his house our home during our stay in Yale.

Under Mr. Cambie's roof we had another delightful evening, as might be supposed from my many years pleasant intercourse with him. It is twenty years since he entered my staff on the first explorations on the Intercolonial Railway in 1863, and I am glad to say our relations have been untinged by the least unpleasantness. I cannot but express the satisfaction I felt in meeting so many of my old associates in my journey from Kamloops. I was no longer the Chief Engineer of the Railway: I was simply a wayfarer. Nevertheless I felt no little satisfaction to find the works originally planned by me so well advanced and in such good hands. Nothing could have given me more pleasure than the cordial way in which the members of my old staff received me. There is always a perfunctory mode of paying a civility which it is somewhat embarrassing not to offer, and it is generally well understood on both sides what such attentions amount to. But in the case of my old friends I was received by a hearty, natural, unmistakeable kindness, and I feel confident that it will not be unwelcome to them to learn that I was much affected by it.

It was nearly ten the next morning before we started, continuing our journey on the hand-car. The works we pass still continue very heavy. We are in the heart of the Cascades, and many of the rocky masses which rise up perpendicularly from the foaming torrent must be pierced by tunnels as the only means of passage through them.

We make our halt at Mr. Onderdonk's gate at Yale, to meet with a hearty welcome from his family. I continue my journey some twenty miles further, but I return to Mr. Onderdonk's house before dark, for it is Saturday night and I had accepted his kind invitation to pass the Sunday with him. We now sleep in beds in the true meaning of the word, and how we enjoy our night's rest! We learn that there is but one church in Yale, a small wooden building of the Church of England, and we readily accept the offer to attend the service. *En route* Mr. and Mrs. Cambie joined us, increasing our number to nine. When we entered the building we really formed the major part of the congregation. As the service proceeded other parties arrived at irregular intervals There were twenty-four in all, including five children. Two clergymen officiated, evidently educated men, but with "advanced" views. To me even the Lessons, the only part of the service not chanted, were far from being read in a natural tone of voice. Intoning the service may be proper enough in some circumstances, but it certainly seemed out of place in Yale. There are possibly at this time eight hundred or a thousand people, white people, Christians statistically at least, within half a mile of the spot where the church was situated, nevertheless the congregation was little more than half as large as the number assembled for worship the previous Sunday, at the invitation of Dr. Grant, in the Eagle Pass. As we walked home we saw not a few loitering about the streets, and especially around the taverns. One would think that with all the teaching which the Church of England has received since the days of Wesley, the wants of those to whom the clergy have to minister would be better understood. I asked myself could these clergymen know the character and habits of the men who have been brought together to perform the work of the railway. No class of men are so peculiar. They are not perfect in many respects. Some are sensual, brutal and self-indulgent. But they are not all of this character. If the mass of them have any trait which is at all in prominence, it is their respect for straightforward dealing and regard of what is natural. They can understand what is plain and free from pretension and affectation, but the least shade of what is artificial and strained repels them. This very conclusion was again forced upon me from the appearance of the congregation. I doubt if a single man of the six or eight hundred workmen in Yale on that Sunday were present in the Anglican Chapel, the only church open for worship. If the workmen were not attracted by the service, the merest handful of ordinary citizens were present. It was painful to observe so small an attendance. The character of the service may not have been the wholly repelling cause which existed; but I venture the remark that in my humble judgment in circumstances of this character the simpler the worship the more consideration it will obtain. What is wanted on railway works is the active, simple effort of the missionary who will seek men out in their houses and penetrate within their daily lives and conduct. Such ministers of religion bring men within their influence by the genuineness of the sympathy which they show and by an appeal to the best feelings of their listeners. Ritualism on the Fraser was obviously not a success. I am strongly of the opinion that such men as the army chaplain whom we had on board the "Polynesian" would have found a fine field in Yale, and would have attracted crowds of willing worshippers to his services.

We pass a quiet afternoon in Mr. Onderdonk's shady verandah, around which the hop vines luxuriantly grew. In the evening, as the lights appeared in the windows, Yale had a pleasant and picturesque appearance. It is built on a bend of the river at the head of steamboat navigation, and at night, with the reflected lights in the stream, it assumes an importance which by day one would not concede to it. As a landscape the mountains are too lofty, too near, too precipitous and crowded to be remarkable for beauty. There is a total absence of all distance in the picture. One sees only a maze of rugged, towering rocks, for the most part covered with a stunted vegetation.

Monday came and with it our determination to start by the steamer for New Westminster. We gratefully said good-bye to our polished host and hostess, whose kindness reminded me of what I had heard of the hospitality of the old Knickerbocker families. During our stay at Yale it was hard to believe that we were not in some hospitable mansion on the banks of the Hudson. We take with us a dug-out canoe and a crew of Indians to paddle us on our journey when we deem it advisable to leave the boat. My purpose is to proceed by steamer to the point which on Saturday night I reached by hand car and then take to the canoe. I will thus be enabled fully to examine the whole line in the valley of the Fraser. The steamer is by no means of little account on these waters, to judge by the passengers that she carries and the places she stops at. Our landings are frequent, to receive or discharge freight, cattle and passengers.

We reach the spot where, with my son, I go on board the canoe. We arrive at Harrison River at half-past three. I was met at this point by Mr. Brophy, also an old Intercolonial friend. Mr. Wilmot, who has hitherto kindly accompanied us, goes on shore. We ourselves continue our descent of the Fraser. The three Indians paddle at a good pace down the Nicomen Slough to a point off Sumas. It is after six and twilight is coming on, so we find our way through a cross channel to the main river. We believe that any other course would be hazardous, so we follow the stream to the point where Dr. Grant was to leave the steamer and where we expect to meet him. The Fraser is wide at this spot and the current swift but we keep the centre of the river. The Indians continue to paddle briskly. We float down the current very rapidly. The air is much warmer than we have yet experienced it, both when we were in the mountains and since we reached Kamloops. Night comes on, and although there is no moon the sky is without a cloud and the stars shine brightly, giving us enough light to guide our canoe. We still keep to the middle of the river where the stream is the strongest. About eight o'clock we see a light on the shore towards which we paddle, and as we approach we hear the well known voice of Dr. Grant.

We find supper waiting for us for which we are indebted to Mrs. Perkins, who keeps a workman's boarding house. But we had a mile further to paddle to the engineers' camp, where we are to find beds. They receive us as hospitably as engineers always receive men accredited to them. They insist on me taking the one stretcher they have; the rest of the party find rest on the floor.

We were up early, for although we had come sixty miles yesterday we were anxious to continue our journey. A heavy fog made it impossible to leave before nine. We paddle for an hour and a half until we reach Stave River, where we land. There is a fine view of Mount Baker, forty miles distant, when the weather is clear, but there is too much mist in the air to-day for us to see it.

We again land three miles above Maple ridge, and walk that distance over the half-constructed railway, crossing Kanaka bridge. We owed our dinner at Maple Ridge to Mrs. Sinclair's culinary art.

We come to the site of the land slide of four years back. A surface of twenty-four acres was carried into the river, bearing along with it the forest trees with which it was covered. A large extent of the mass was thrown across the River Fraser, fully a quarter of a mile on to the opposite shore, uprooting many acres of forest and for a time damming back the stream. Its traces are still visible, to show what the consequences are of these minor convulsions of nature which on a great scale effect such wonderful changes.

We are again in the canoe. The water of this great river is as calm as a canal in Venice, and our quiet progress partakes no little of the motion of the gondola. The air conveys the idea that it is full of smoke, while the temperature recalls the season of Indian summer. The banks of the river, even at a short distance, are scarcely discernible.

We now reach the tidal waters of the Pacific. There is no great rise where we now are, and the water is still fresh for some distance, but at flood there is no current and the surface looks like a placid lake. The air is pleasant. The three Indians keep paddling with marvellous regularity. Two sit in front, side by side, and the third is at the stern steering as he paddles. The men work as if they were pieces of mechanism, in perfect silence; not a word is spoken.

We leave the main stream at the mouth of Pitt River, where we paddle up to the new railway bridge, spanning 1850 feet of a deep inlet, at one spot sixty feet below high water. We return to the Fraser, where we were about thirty-four miles from the starting point of the morning. We pass on our right the mouth of the River Coquitlum and on the left is the salmon cannery of that name, consisting of a large number of scattered buildings, the centre of one of the chief industries of the Province. We meet a number of boats manned by Indians, drawing in or laying down salmon nets. The river is nearly half a mile wide with deep water. The Fraser is a noble stream, but it is only at intervals, as the fog lifts, that you can see the opposite shore. So thick is the fog that the sun itself is obscured, and it was in weather of this character, bringing back to my mind the November fogs of the world's emporium on the banks of the Thames, that we made our landing at New Westminster, on the Pacific ocean.

CHAPTER XX.

ON PACIFIC WATERS.

New Westminster—Enormous Forest Trees—English Broom—Port Moody—Down Burrard Inlet—Sea Fog—Navigation by Echo—Straits of Georgia—The St. Juan Archipelago—Seamanship—Victoria.

We had reached the most important town on the Mainland of British Columbia. Although New Westminster is of modern date the town has had its mutations and disappointments, the last and not the least of which is to have seen the Railway terminus diverted northward to Burrard Inlet, a proceeding which her own citizens must admit to have been unavoidable.

In the morning we found the fog even thicker than last night. I had finished breakfast and was considering what course I would take when Mr. Marcus Smith did me the the favour to call upon me, and kindly offered to drive me to Port Moody, first calling at old Government House, now the Railway Engineer's office. Government House was, I believe, last occupied by Governor Seymour and, from all I have heard, many pleasant hours have been passed within its walls. It has fallen upon the evil days of ceasing to be the home of official life. Victoria, on Vancouver's Island, is the seat of government, and is the present centre of political movement. The capacious dining and ball rooms are much out of repair, but they still retain a trace of former grandeur. The grounds are well laid out with shade trees and rich green lawns, but unfortunately the fog conceals everything but the objects almost within reach, and prevents any extended examination.

New Westminster is not remarkable either for its extent or population. Two thousand five hundred is the estimated number of its present inhabitants. It possesses, however, a four peal of bells, the gift of Baroness Burdett-Coutts, the only peal on the whole Pacific coast, and indeed a rare possession on this continent. The residence of the Anglican Bishop is in the neighbourhood of Government House; and at no great distance the Lunatic Asylum and the Penitentiary are to be found.

About half-past ten, under the escort of Mr. Smith, we started in an open carriage for Port Moody, on Burrard Inlet. My attention was attracted by the forest trees of enormous size. Within the limits cleared for the roadway, blackened stumps of many of them, ten feet in diameter, still remain, on which the record of their age is traceable. Some of these trunks show a life of six centuries, and hence must have attained the rank of good sized trees before the recorded discovery of the American continent. The ground is covered with a luxuriant flora, indicating a rich soil and a moist climate. Along the road side English broom was growing wild, in great luxuriance, the first I have met in such circumstances on this continent. A drive of six miles over a hilly road brought us to Burrard Inlet, at Bronson's tavern, a recent erection, where the road terminates. At this point we had recourse to a boat and rowed about a mile to Port Moody, the terminus of the railway.

Port Moody is something more than a village, but at the present moment it is a strained recognition of its importance, even as a railway terminus, to call it a town. The number of inhabitants when I was there could not exceed two score of souls. Whatever its future, at the present time it has certainly no claim to civic rank. A wharf of good size has been constructed. At this time it was covered with piles of steel rails. A freight shed is attached. Near it stands the small house occupied by Mr. A. J. Hill, Resident Engineer. Two sailing vessels were lying at the wharf. The rail track has been laid a few miles westward. In the neighbourhood are half a dozen scattered frame buildings, some of them scarcely finished, erected by speculators to promote the selling of town lots. Several square miles of land have been so laid out. At this moment the greater part of the city of the future is covered with a dense growth of primeval forest, the age of some portions of which carries us back to the century in which the Magna Charta became law. I was told on the spot that the lots so projected would accommodate tenfold the present white population of British Columbia.

I have to acknowledge the kindness and hospitality of Mr. and Mrs. Hill. I derived no little pleasure from looking at the water-colour drawings of the wild flowers of British Columbia, which Mrs. Hill had executed. They promise to be a valuable contribution to science. I trust they may be published at some future date, when they shall have been sufficiently completed to admit of this proceeding.

The steamer on which we had to embark at Burrard Inlet had not arrived, so we obtained a small boat and descended the inlet to meet her in order to have sufficient daylight to continue our trip through the entrance. The fog, which had partly cleared away by this time, soon re-appeared, and accordingly we kept near the shore so as not to lose our reckoning. We had rowed a distance of three miles when we met the small tug sent in search of us. We got on board without delay. The fog necessitated caution in our progress. It became thicker and thicker, until it was impossible to see a ship's length ahead. Night came on and we did not know where we were. The head of the tug was turned in the supposed direction of the settlement, near Hasting's saw-mill. All that we had to steer by was a pocket compass, which on more than one occasion has done good service. Some of us fancied that we heard the squealing of a pig; important in the double sense that we were not far from land and also near a settlement. Our whistle was almost continually sounded and the sharpest look-out kept. The pig replied unmistakably. We continued cautiously to approach in the direction of the sound, and were enabled to land at almost the only settlement on the south side of Burrard Inlet, west of Port Moody.

On landing we obtained intelligence of the steamer "Alexandria," detailed to take the party to Victoria. The vessel was lying at the Saw Mill wharf, at no great distance, so we found our way to it. Supper was gone through; but the fog still continued. The captain therefore concluded that it was better not to start, but wait until morning; he on his part being prepared to leave the moment the fog lifted. The "Alexandria" is a large, powerful tug, which the owner had kindly placed at our disposal to cross the Straits of Georgia. She came expressly from Nanaimo to Burrard Inlet to meet us. We slept on board, and when we awoke found that we were still moored to the wharf. It was early, half-past five, but the fog continued heavy and damp. Capt. Urquhart, however, determined to start and to feel his way through the thick mist. About half-past seven he took his bearings, and directed the steamer towards the entrance of the Inlet. We steamed slowly on through the fog, and in a few minutes nothing was visible from the deck. The whistle was sounded continually, and the lead was cast without ceasing. We several times stopped, backed, and again proceeded slowly, till we reached the Narrows at the entrance. Here the current is rapid and the channel narrow, not having above two hundred and fifty yards of sea-room. Fortunately we got a glimpse of the shore through the haze. The captain, however, saw enough to satisfy himself, and with a fresh departure put the boat at full speed down English Bay; at least so we concluded by reference to the chart, for we could see nothing through the fog by which we are surrounded.

We proceeded down the Straits of Georgia towards the San Juan Islands, our whistle continually blowing. Mr. Joseph Hunter is the only passenger not directly connected with the party.

At Victoria I am to part with Dave Leigh, the last of the men who had been with us in the mountains. He joined us at Bow River, and had determined to see us to the end of our journey. From the day when we commenced with packhorses to cross the range of mountains, Dave has stood by us and has gallantly helped in many a difficulty. He is a powerful Cheshire man, such as one would fancy a northern Englishman to be: honest, self-reliant, plain-spoken and staunch, with a peculiar habit of calling a spade a spade. He has cooked for us in all circumstances, there is no other word for it, heroically. He did his share of the packing, and if there was a load a shade heavier it was caught up by Dave with some saying of his own, and off he trudged as if it were a plaything. He had done everything for us that a man could do with unfailing cheerfulness. and has followed our fortunes for many a mile. He has driven pack-horses, paddled canoes, rowed boats, built rafts, stretched our tent, driven hand-cars, cooked our food and indulged in many a hearty objurgation at Skunk Cabbage and Devil's Club. He crosses the Straits of Georgia, and then at Victoria we have to say good-bye, he to seek other employment. I wish him all happiness and success, but I have no fear of his future. Whatever his sphere he will do his duty, and always be found from the beginning to the end a true man.

We approached the San Juan Archipelago and made our way from the soundings read from the line and by the echo of the whistle, as its tone was affected by the nearness or distance of the land. I stood on the bridge with Capt. Urquhart, and the fidelity with which he could judge the situation was not simply the result of experience, but of a natural capacity to determine the niceties and delicacies of sound. I myself began somewhat to understand the shades of difference, but I was a very long way from possessing the ability to navigate the ship. We were approaching an island. The whistle vibrated toward it with a more muffled tone. We are warned by the echo on which side of us it lay. We came opposite to it and passed without its being visible to the eye. The echo changed as we proceeded.

The lead is unceasingly cast. We are warned that we are coming near land. The current is carrying us towards it. We see plainly before us a precipitous rock, and with difficulty we change our course, for we have to back against the current and give the ship's head another bearing; so we grope our way, stealing along to avoid mischance, without the least guide beyond the echo of the whistle, as it is affected by the nearness or distance of the shore.

The fog continued all day; it appeared, however, to have little influence upon Captain Urquhart more than to bring out his phonetic genius. Familiar with the intricate channels, currents and tidal influences of the San Juan Islands, the lead constantly going, he keeps on his course slowly and cautiously, but perfectly undismayed and without a moment of doubt. The whistle, with its echo, pilots him through the archipelago; and to this day it is a wonder to me how we found our way. I was by his side and had the benefit of his shrewd deductions and theories. Even with a bright sun, skill and knowledge of the landmarks are called for in the passage through these waters.

Our difficulties and the skill displayed in overcoming them may well be imagined. Fortunately for us there was no wind; frequently we found ourselves amongst kelp, with its rank leaves floating on the surface. At one point we passed by rocks not seventy yards distant from us on the starboard side, the land appeared through the fog a ship's length ahead. We immediately stop. The engine is backed. We are so near that we can hear the voices of children playing on the elevated shore directly ahead. No one is visible, but in reply to the question from the look-out at the bow we learn that we have passed Victoria Harbour and are near the entrance to Esquimalt.

The course of the steamer is changed and we shortly enter Victoria Harbour in as dense a fog as can be seen in any part of the world. It was dark when we reached the wharf. I do not think that any of us were sorry that the experience of the last thirteen hours had been brought to a close. It was entirely new to me, and with all its success somewhat bold and enterprising. Capt. Urquhart undoubtedly displayed great qualities, sagacity, caution, coolness and skill to track his way as he did. He achieved wonders in seamanship, but to men wanting in the qualification he possesses, the attempt to imitate it is not to be commended.

It was three o'clock in the afternoon of the following day when the regular steamer from New Westminster arrived. She left twenty-four hours before we started for Burrard Inlet, and took fifty-six hours to cross the Strait through the fog. We found our way in thirteen hours. In clear weather the trip is made in about half that time.

We went directly to the Driard house, an hotel which the Victorians never tire praising. We were late but had a special dinner, and Mr. Hunter with Captain Urquhart did us the favour to join us, when, as in duty bound, we did due homage to the captain and ship which carried us over; and we had especial cause to do so as we were indebted to Mr. Dunsmuir, the owner, who, hearing of my desire to pass to Vancouver Island, with great courtesy placed the vessel at my disposal. I did not fail next day to call and thank him for his kindness, and I feel it my duty again to acknowledge my obligations to him. The dinner was excellent and after it was over we strolled out into the gaslight of Fort street and walked a few miles into the country before we retired. I looked upon the gaslight as an old friend whose acquaintance I was glad to make again, and a pleasant duty it is to recognize all we owe to a well lighted city.

We obtained our portmanteaus, which had been sent from Winnipeg by the way of San Francisco, and we were by no means unwilling to fall back on the garb of every-day city life. Moreover we also had the happiness to receive letters from home.

Saturday was a comparatively idle day. We walked through nearly every street of Victoria.

We made some calls, and I recollected that eleven years ago on Saturday, September 29th—to-day is the 28th—I reached Kamloops after a hard journey across the mountains by the Yellowhead Pass.

My task was now accomplished. We were on the shores of the Pacific, having passed through the mainland of British Columbia and crossed the waters to Vancouver Island. Our next thought is the direction we must follow homewards. But for the moment, as birds of passage, we have to wait for the fog to lift.

CHAPTER XXI.

BRITISH COLUMBIA.

Sir Francis Drake—Mears—Vancouver—Astor—Hudson's Bay Company—Gold Discoveries—Climate—Timber—Fisheries—Minerals—Mountain Scenery.

The western Province of the Dominion cannot lay claim to even a geographical recognition of longer date than that of a century. Drake first visited the Pacific ocean three centuries back, in 1579, but it is questionable if he ascended higher than the forty-eighth parallel when he took possession of the country now included in Oregon and Washington Territory in the royal name of Queen Elizabeth and called it New Albion.

There is also a tradition that Vancouver Island was discovered by De Fuca in 1592. From this date the northern Pacific waters remained without further notice for two centuries, until the voyage of Capt. Cook, who coasted along the shores in 1778. Ten years later these possessions were on the verge of causing war between England and Spain. In that year, 1788, some subjects of Great Britain, the most prominent among whom was a Mr. Mears, purchased from the natives the land about Friendly Cove, Nootka Sound, on the west coast of Vancouver Island. What was then held to be the transfer of the territory was gone through; buildings were erected and possession assumed. Mr. Mears shortly after left the spot to return the next season, placing the whole in charge of Maquema, an Indian chief. During his absence two Spanish ships of war arrived, took formal possession of the place and declared it to belong to the realm of Spain. An appeal was at once made to the Imperial Government for protection. Spain, on the other hand, in the first instance, seemed determined to justify the act of its officers. The proceeding attracted much attention in England. Public feeling was greatly excited. The spirit of the nation was thoroughly aroused. A fleet was fitted out, and it looked as if the dispute could only be settled by war, when Nootka Sound was surrendered by Spain.

It was in 1792, when Capt. Vancouver, of the Royal navy, was sent from England to receive the transfer, and to make a voyage of discovery to the Pacific. Those familiar with the literature of the last century will recall all that was then said of Nootka Sound. By this date the mainland had been penetrated from the east. Sir Alexander

McKenzie had discovered the river which bears his name, running to the north, and he had accomplished the difficult journey of penetrating to the shores of the Pacific overland, the first of our race to find his way through the wilderness of the Rocky Mountains. To the south, the Government of the United States had fitted out the expedition of Clark and Lewis, who in 1802-3 ascended by the sources of the Missouri and Yellowstone Rivers, and reached the Columbia and the Pacific Ocean. The name also of John Jacob Astor cannot be forgotten in connection with the Columbia River, at the mouth of which he established the celebrated settlement of Astoria.

In 1821 the Hudson's Bay Company obtained a license to extend their operations to New Caledonia. as British Columbia was then designated, and the country virtually passed under their control. There was indeed little to tempt the emigrant to cast his lot there and to seek an independant existence, for without aid from the organization of the Hudson's Bay Company it was impossible to cross the continent. New Caledonia could only be approached from the ocean.

Vancouver Island continued in its state of isolation. Thirty years ago its white population of all ages, chiefly employés of the Hudson's Bay Company, was four hundred and fifty. The Mainland was even less known and had fewer civilized inhabitants. Without the influences which caused the rush of population to the Fraser, New Caledonia might have remained undisturbed for half a century. It is difficult to see how it could cease to be other than a wilderness, and its gigantic forests unpenetrated except by Indian tribes, with a few trappers of wild animals. In 1856 the discovery of gold inaugurated a total change in its character. The Fraser was then the scene of the gold excitement. This, the chief river of British Columbia, flows in a course seven hundred miles, and is marked by rare grandeur of scenery, with frequent rapids dashing through gorges almost impassable. Mr. Douglas was at that time chief factor of the Hudson's Bay Company and Governor of Vancouver Island. In April of this year, 1856, he reported to the Home Government the discovery of gold, the miners being chiefly retired servants of the Company. In 1857 the number was increased by arrivals from the United States. In a short time the report of the richness of the deposit was spread among the miners of California. The result was that by July, 1858, some twenty thousand persons left California for British Columbia. The parties who engaged in the new venture are described as being of all ages and conditions; men advanced in life, those still on its threshold, many with ample means, doubtless the greater part extremely needy; all crowded to the Fraser, it was said, some to steal, unquestionably some to die. They arrived too early in the season, and the majority experienced disappointment. The river was swollen and the bars containing the deposits covered with water. Those who failed in patience or endurance through deficiency in resources, returned to California, to share in the abuse of the district and of the country in general. Those who remained received the reward of their patience. The water ceased to cover the bars, and the miners who worked them found what was sought after in fair amount.

The political history of British Columbia goes no further back than 1840. Vancouver Island was then created a colony, with Governor Blanchard as administrator. The only inhabitants were Indians, and there was no revenue from any source. No laws were enacted, and scarcely anything was done to promote settlement. He returned to England in 1851, when Sir Francis Douglas succeeded him. In the same year a Surveyor General and assistant arrived from England, and surveys were commenced as the first step towards emigration and settlement. A Council of four was nominated to assist in passing laws. Shortly afterwards one hundred and fifty persons, farm labourers and miners, arrived from England. Mr. Labouchere was then Secretary for the Colonies, and in accordance with his instructions Governor Douglas, in June, 1856, issued a proclamation for the election of a House of Assembly, composed of seven members. The qualification of a member to be the possession of £300, that of the electors the ownership of twenty acres of land. The first House met in April, 1858.

In 1858 the discovery of gold, which had become known, led to a great increase of the population along the Fraser. The mainland, British Columbia, was, however, not declared a colony until 1859, when the license of occupation of the Hudson's Bay Company expired. It was presided over by the Governor of Vancouver Island, and possessed of itself no Legislative Council or Assembly. The Assembly of Vancouver Island, on the other hand, was increased to twelve members. There was also this further distinction: Vancouver Island was free for importation, whereas British Columbia had a revenue tariff.

In 1864 Governor Douglas retired, and Governor Kennedy was appointed to Vancouver Island, at the same time Governor Seymour was named Governor of British Columbia, with an Assembly partly nominated and partly elected.

In 1866 Vancouver Island became part of the Colony of British Columbia, with one Assembly, as above described—partly nominated and partly elected. Governor Kennedy retired. On the death of Governor Seymour, in 1869, Governor Musgrove was appointed, and it was during his rule that the incorporation of the Province in the Dominion of Canada was accomplished in 1871.

It returns to the Dominion Parliament three

Senators and six Members of the House of Commons. According to the census of 1870 the population was 8,576 whites, 472 coloured and 1,578 Chinamen.

The present population is roughly estimated at 25,000 whites, 40,000 Indians, 17,000 Chinese.

Victoria, the capital, is reported to contain 8,000 inhabitants.

The Province has been described as a sea of mountains. Within its limits, however, are considerable tracts of rolling prairie, marked by fertility. They consist of good soil, capable of abundantly producing cereals, although in some localities there is too large an admixture of gravel or of decomposed rock.

Its extent is about 200,000 square miles, extending from latitude 49° to latitude 57°. The sea coast is about 450 miles in length, indented from north to south by a succession of inlets running many miles within the coast line, in each case presenting a harbour of perfect security, of great depth of water, generally to be approached with safety and in all cases marked with the boldest scenery. In no part is the climate so severe as in the same parallel of latitude on the Atlantic. To find the eastern equivalent of the mildest sections we must descend twelve hundred miles to the south.

As a rule, throughout the Province, in the habitable portions, the climate is favourable to the conditions of human life, generally without the great extremes of heat and cold. It is marked, however, with atmospheric diversities. From the mouth of the Fraser, inland, it is moist. The rain is abundant in spring, summer and autumn, in the fall of the year continuing for days together. In winter the depth of snow is from one to two feet, in the extreme northern districts, frequently deeper. It remains on the ground, near the coast, from a fortnight to three weeks, and it disappears to be succeeded by another fall, and so continues throughout the winter. Fogs prevail in October and November, sometimes earlier, as was the case in my experience. But they do not occur every year, for on a former occasion I found the air both light and clear during my whole visit at the same season.

There is much to be learned about the climate and its variations, and it is difficult to form a close generalization of the extent of the localities where changes begin and end. We pass by insensible mutations from the one zone to the other. There is no definite arbitrary line shewing when we are in another climate. It may, however, be said that the humidity of atmosphere is found to extend from the sea coast up the Fraser, as far as Lillooet, above the junction of the Thompson, and that it is continued along the Upper Fraser to the Forks. Within this district the level land is fertile and densely wooded. In the more northern Cariboo section there are extensive tracts of forest land and of open prairie, highly fertile, fitted for farming purposes, and well watered and drained. The soil, most strongly marked by these characteristics, is found more immediately in the neighbourhood of the Fraser and of the innumerable lakes in this district. In these localities the climate is superior to that of the Lower Fraser, for it is drier. In Winter it is of a lower temperature, much like that of some parts of Ontario.

Leaving the Fraser to the east by the Valley of the Thompson, the land is elevated but the winter is less cold. Indeed whatever varieties of climatic influences may be found in different localities, it can with certainty be affirmed that Southern British Columbia is free from the extreme heat of summer and the intense cold of winter experienced in Eastern Canada and North-Eastern United States.

So far as such a statement can be made, it may be said that snow on the Upper Fraser and its tributaries does not reach the depth found in Eastern Canada. Often it is not deeper than from six to twelve inches; frequently the ground is quite bare. The authorities I have referred to assert that the larger lakes in the district do not freeze, as in Eastern Canada, nor do the Fraser and other streams become locked up in ice like the tributaries of the St. Lawrence. Stock can subsist on the bunch grass throughout the whole year. On the more lofty ranges and summits, the height to which they ascend must be taken as typical of the depth of snow..

There is, undoubtedly, east of the Fraser an extent of country where the dryness of the soil calls for irrigation, especially in the direction through which I passed; but wherever artificial moisture has been obtained by this means, the result has left nothing to be desired.

Around the more southern coast and the lower lands of Vancouver Island it is not possible to live in a more favourable climate. The winter is especially mild, the thermometer seldom falling below freezing point. The summer is temperate; the thermometer, Fahrenheit, seldom rises above 72', the lowest range being 23° 30'. Southerly winds prevail for two-thirds of the year, and summer lasts from May to September. The atmosphere is sensibly affected by the current which flows from the southern latitudes of Japan and China. The Kuro-Siwo brings the warmer temperature of the southern seas in the same way as the Gulf Stream has heightened the salubrity of the British Islands.

It has been said that the weather of Vancouver Island is milder and steadier than that of the South of England, the summer longer and finer, and the winter shorter and less rigorous; and this is saying a great deal. The climate of this Island must be almost perfection. It is its oldest inhabitant who should be the most free from disease.

There is one recorded fact to establish the salubrity of the general climate of British Columbia. I refer to the miners, who suffered great hardship and exposure, toiling in cold, rapid streams, camping on damp ground, constantly wet from the rain, wading in water of low temperature, and even suffering from insufficiency of food. Nevertheless, no sickness, no epidemic was experienced by them. It was the saying at the time that many increased in weight, and it was the boast of not a few that they were never so robust. This circumstance was brought into strong prominence by a recollection of the contrary results which had been experienced in California when the conditions of mining operations were much the same, and where there remained a painful record of broken health and shattered constitutions. To a far greater extent is this condition experienced in Vancouver Island, described as one of the gardens of the world. The residents of Victoria speak of the delight which Her Royal Highness the Princess Louise experienced in this healthy locality, the more so as she could, unrestrained and without annoyance, follow the simple habits she prefers. Many anecdotes are still told of Her Royal Highness during her residence, and twelve months have elapsed since she left.

Medical men prophesy that the lower lands of Vancouver Island will be constantly visited by many whose health exacts absence from latitudes marked by severe temperature. Such as now visit Colorado will find a more salubrious and genial retreat on the waters of the Pacific. Vancouver

Island promises not simply to furnish coal and to be a site of many a manufactory of iron, but equally, to offer to the invalid a home and a sojourn where he may hope for renewed health.

The timber of British Columbia, drawn from its majestic forests, might supply the markets of the world for years without a perceptible diminution of its extent. In many localities trees, tall and straight, stand so close together as to be a marvel. Its wealth in the pine or cone-bearing family is very great. It consists of the celebrated Douglas pine, white pine, hemlock, spruce and balsam. The cedars, I may say, are of fabulous size. I have measured them and found the diameter not less than twelve feet. At the saw-mills where the Douglas pine is manufactured, it is strange to have to relate it, no log of greater diameter than eight feet is received, for the trees of larger diameter are unmanageable.

There are localities of prairie destitute of trees, but the growth on the river flats is abundant and varied. Birch, oak, ash, yew and maple are found in some localities, and in the swamps alder, cotton wood and Balm of Gilead.

The wild fruits and berries seem inexhaustible. With fish they furnish the diet of the Indian in his native state. They consist of the wild plum, the cherry, the crab-apple, prickly pear, the raspberry, blueberry, scarlet currant, gooseberry, bearberry, and on low ground the cranberry.

The game is most varied and plentiful, as every one who has lived at Victoria can bear witness. I have counted fifteen deer hanging in a butcher's shop. The mountain sheep, when full grown, weighs several hundred pounds. It is covered with long hair resembling coarse wool, with enormous horns. There is a tradition that when escaping pursuit the animal leaps over precipices to a lower level, and it is upon these horns it throws itself. The flesh is equal to that of the domestic sheep, but they are rarely caught as they keep up in the mountains until forced down by the snow in search of food.

The fisheries have already become a prolific source of wealth and yet they are in their infancy. The British Columbia salmon is well known, even in the English market, in which it has been introduced preserved, and has been favourably received. Herrings abound around the islands, and many kinds of fish are caught off the coast. The development of the fisheries naturally will create other industries, such as are connected with their own requirements, with fish oil and isinglass.

The mineral deposits are coal, iron and copper, with the precious metals. More or less gold is found in every stream. There are immense iron ore deposits at Texada Island, in the Gulf of Georgia. Bituminous coal is found on Vancouver Island at several points; at Nanaimo the mines are profitably worked. Anthracite coal is obtainable on Queen Charlotte Island. The proximity of iron and coal cannot fail to have a large influence on the fortunes of the Province, especially as manufactured articles will find an outlet to the east by rail equally as by water in the opposite direction.

It remains only to allude to the scenery, of which it would be impossible to omit mention, for it is in every respect remarkable. It presents the most marked contrasts. Gigantic mountains, themselves overcapped by snow-covered peaks, quiet prairie, foaming cascades, striking waterfalls, the most rapid of running waters, river reaches with scarcely a ripple. Everywhere it is bold and even its occasional sylvan quietude is impressive, sometimes reaching a grandeur as majestic as it is wild. The canyons are clefts in the mountains which ascend almost perpendicularly from the rivers and in some spots incline inwards, while a torrent fiercely rushes through the fissure. On some sections of the Fraser terraces are seen to rise in regular gradations and to extend far back, each change of level shewing angles and slopes as defined as if formed by art. The peaks, in clear weather, are seen standing out in bold relief, receding by gradations until the last outline can with difficulty be traced. Among all these bewildering spectacles are seen waterfalls descending hundreds of feet of perpendicular height.

The fiords indenting the whole line of coast run into the Cascade Range. Their shores rise perpendicularly to peaks, often a perpendicular mile from the water's edge, while the water is so sheltered as to be without a ripple and lies dark and fathomless at their base.

Travellers relate how, in the solitude of the wilderness, sounds have come upon them as of muffled thunder. It is the descent of an avalanche from a glacier, miles away from them; or one of those mountain slides of earth and trees which occur in the summer heat in the lands at high elevation. These spectacles are among the most wonderful movement of the earth's forces. I have spoken of some of these phenomena as traces of them passed under my notice.

It would be difficult to find in any one of the four continents more majestic or more varied scenery, marked by more of Nature's fertility of resource in grouping together scenes of astonishing grandeur. I do not except Switzerland, with which no comparison can be made, for British Columbia has a character of its own. It must be seen to be appreciated.

CHAPTER XXII.

HOME BY THE NORTHERN PACIFIC.

Puget Sound—The Columbia—Portland—Oregon and San Juan Disputes—Arid Country—Mountain Summits—The Yellowstone—The Missouri—The Red River—Chicago—Standard Time Meeting—The British Association—Home.

The fog had become less dense on the early Monday morning we were leaving Victoria to cross to Puget Sound, to proceed thence to Portland, in Oregon. We had now entered on October. It was the first of the month. My object in taking this route was to pass over the Northern Pacific Railway. It seemed to me in every way desirable, that correct information should be obtained of the nature of the country through which that line passes, and I had already travelled over the Central Pacific line from San Francisco. The last spike had been driven when we were in the Valley of the Ille-celle-waet, and the opening ceremonies had been celebrated on an unusually large scale, three weeks back, before we had finished our journey across the Selkirk Range.

We had crossed from the Atlantic to the Pacific.

We had passed over the four ranges of mountains by a hitherto partly unsurveyed route, and I had satisfied myself as to the possibility of establishing the railway on the line we had traversed. The journey we made was the first of its kind, and no limited portion of the distance had proved exceedingly trying. In a few years the railway connection will be completed, and what a field for travel will then be opened to those who desire to visit the boldest and most majestic of Nature's scenes which the traveller will be able to visit with very little effort.

The Northern Pacific Railway extends from the western end of Lake Superior to Portland, in Oregon, where it will have a connection with a branch line to Puget's Sound. To the east it is at present connected with St. Paul and Minneapolis, and is accordingly brought into relationship with the whole railway system of the continent. Its charter dates from 1864, so it has taken twenty years to complete the line. The enterprise has passed through many vicissitudes. No real progress in its construction was made until Messrs. Jay Cooke & Co., of Philadelphia, arranged in 1870-71 to float thirty million dollars of its bonds, by which means the line was constructed from Lake Superior to Bismarck, on the Missouri. The misfortunes of that firm in 1873, involved the railway in the common ruin. The line was thrown into bankruptcy. The company was re-organized, the bonds transferred into preferred stock, and the building of the railway commenced at the western end. The Missouri division followed. Several presidents endeavoured to carry the line to completion. Finally a first mortgage loan was negotiated. At this period the credit of the company was established, money was obtained, and the track was pushed on equally from east and west and the rails finally connected.

The steamer North Pacific crossed the San Juan de Fuca Straits to Admiralty Inlet and ascended Puget's Sound. The day was wet and cloudy. Neither at Victoria nor the Straits were we able to obtain a glimpse of Mount Baker. I well remember the first view of the majestic outline of this mountain, reaching far above snow-line. I was then at sea at a point eighty or one hundred miles distant. Its appearance is as familiar to the British Columbian as the less elevated "Fujisan" to the Japanese. Nor could we see the striking Olympic Range, which in clear weather in so marked a way strikes the the eye on the southern coast of Vancouver Island. The steamer called at one or two places before reaching Seattle, the principal port of Puget's Sound, itself a place of considerable importance as the locality whence the product of the coal mines is shipped. Tacoma, however, was our destination, which we reached after dark. It has an excellent harbor. and is the terminus of the railway. It was so dark on our arrival that we proceeded to the nearest hotel, a few yards distant. In the evening, to obtain some exercise we indulged in the proverbial "sailor's walk" up and down the platform in front of the building.

We rose early next morning, for the train left at seven. The rain had ceased, but the sky was dull, and there was no view of Mount Tacoma to the east of us.

The railway line ascends rapidly from the level of the Sound, and continues through a partially settled country, much of it prairie, with here and there groves of pine. The soil is generally of gravel except in the flats of the Kalama River. The appearance of the homesteads differs little from the backwoods settlements of Ontario. I saw no example of good husbandry, nor could I trace any signs of productiveness in the country through which we passed. We arrived at Kalama about noon, striking the Columbia for the third time. First, when we descended by the Kicking-Horse pass; again, when we came by the Ille-celle-waet. From the latter point the river has flowed some six hundred and fifty miles, four hundred of which are through the United States territory on a course southerly and thence westerly. It now makes a slight deflection to the north previous to discharging into the ocean at Astoria.

At Kalama we waited for the steamer which ascends the river to Portland, that portion of the railway being yet incomplete. We also took dinner at the one hotel, near the station. The fare was bad, the charges exorbitant. It seemed to me that there was much uncalled for delay in moving on board a small quantity of lumber. Incidentally, it may be remarked that there is a tone of thought, a course of action with the people on the Pacific slope by no means in accord with eastern energy. There is no appearance of the bustle and rush you see nearer the Atlantic. The steamer is propelled by a stern wheel. She is of some size and is a regular river boat, with tiers of state-rooms above the main deck. The river is about half a mile wide and is navigable for sea-going vessels to Portland, and for some distance above that city for vessels of less draught. Our trip is limited only to the thirty miles between Kalama and Portland. We passed places with ambitious names but of little promise. The cities of St. Helen and Columbia, so called, neither of which is half so large as the new town of Brandon. Each may be described as the site of a saw-mill, with dwelling houses for the owner and workmen.

We ascended the Columbia until we reached a branch, the Williamette, which we followed to Portland. We were now thirty miles south of Kalama.

The River Columbia is the boundary between the State of Oregon and Washington Territory. Portland, on the Willamette, is in Oregon. It is a commercial centre of such territory on the Pacific slope as San Francisco has not made tributary. The construction of the Northern Pacific has exercised great influence on its growth, for in twelve years it has increased in population from 11,000 to 35,000. This city, like Montreal, is some distance from the coast, being one hundred and twenty-five miles from the ocean. But, unlike Montreal, it is not easily approachable by a very large class of ocean going vessels. The wharves, however, present some animation from the ships moored there. On this occasion there were one iron steamer and six sailing vessels. The railway accommodation for the transfer of freight is on an extensive scale, and its promise of a prosperous future seems well assured.

We went to the hotel, which we were told both at Victoria and on our way up the river, was the best. If such be the case, Portland must be one of the worst provided cities, in this respect, in the United States. Our rooms were small. One had no window to admit light. Not one of them had a fire-place to assist in ventilation, which was especially needed, for the passages were filled with a nauseating stench proceeding from the filthy offices immediately below. The beds were without clean linen; the towels seemed scarcely washed, certainly they had not been ironed nor been passed through the mangle. The supply of water was insufficient, and when more was asked for it was refused. To crown all, we were hurried off from the hotel at half-past five without breakfast, to cross the river to wait until seven, when the train started.

The night previous we secured tickets for Chicago and paid for a Pullman drawing-room, but there was no Pullman on the train on starting, nor a restaurant car where we could get breakfast. From Portland the railway runs easterly two hundred and twenty-eight miles, to Ainsworth. Our first view of the Columbia is striking. It is the locality where it flows through the Cascade Mountains The line runs along the base of bold, rocky bluffs, twisting and curving a few feet above the water line. The fog and smoky atmosphere conceal the mountains, but I should judge, when visible, that the view is picturesque.

For eighty miles from Portland the flora indicates a somewhat moist climate, but on passing east of the Cascade Range everything is as dry as at Kamloops. We are informed that no rain has fallen for four months. We see bunch grass on the hills. The rocks are balsaltic, and the indications suggest that the geology of the Thompson extends to this locality. One of the most characteristic features of the landscape are the basaltic columns which stand out prominently on both sides of the river.

Before twelve we reach the Dalles at the eighty-seventh mile. I have kindly recollections of this place, for we broke our fast here. It was dinner hour for the passengers, and what was served was very good. Our hostess was an Ontario woman from Kingston, and the landlord one of those genial, imperturbable geniuses whom our neighbours so often produce, who have been everywhere and learned much. In his wanderings he had been in Canada, whence he had carried away his wife. He had so much to tell us of the Dominion that we looked upon him as a countryman. Dalles, in Indian phraseology, we learn from him, means "swift water," or rapids.

We continue the ascent of the southern bank of the Columbia. The valley is generally from two to three miles wide, in the centre of which the stream flows in its placid course. The banks are hilly and appear broken frequently by trap and balsaltic rock. For miles not a tree is to be seen. The light, dry sand is drifted with the wind, like snow in winter, and sand is often formed during storms into mounds and banks, which are more troublesome to the company than snow itself. We were told that the trains were often seriously delayed by it. From the car windows we could see the "dunes" which have accumulated in many places. An occasional house is visible, with the sand half concealing the windows; sometimes cast up to the very eaves. Persevering efforts have been made to arrest its progress by planting trees, and to prevent the saplings from being blown away the roots have been covered with paving stones. At other places the surface is shingled with boards to hold down the sand, so that it will not be blown on the railway track. The landscape has a dreary and forlorn look, which even the river fails fully to relieve.

About one hundred and fifty miles from Portland the high river banks have disappeared. We run through a flat, level, barren country covered with sage brush, and we are probably less than three hundred feet above tide water.

Umatilla, one hundred and ninety miles from Portland, is the ghost of a once flourishing centre, which existed when gold digging in the Blue Mountains was actively followed. To-day it is a picture of desolation, with deserted streets, with dilapidated wooden buildings surrounded by a desert of sage brush. There is one marked memorial of its prosperity: a graveyard, where many a poor miner lies in his last home. The fence which encloses it is maintained, and what makes it more remarkable, it is the only fence to be seen for many a mile.

At Wallula Junction we have supper. There is at this place a branch to Walla-Walla, thirty-one miles distant. On the side track there is an excursion train full of "Oregon pioneers" travelling towards St. Paul. They left Portland seventeen hours before us and had been detained by an obstruction. As a regular train we take precedence and arrived at Snake River about seven, a little way above its junction with the Columbia at Ainsworth. Snake River is one of the chief tributaries of the Columbia; it takes its rise five hundred miles to the south-east. It is as yet unbridged, and we cross to the opposite shore by a ferry; passengers, mails and baggage being transferred to the train, attached to which, for the first time, we find the Pullman.

We have followed the valley of the River Columbia from Kalama to this point, generally on an easterly course, south of the 46th parallel, ascending its great current flowing westerly. It runs in a southerly course directly from 49° lat. to this place; and now we leave this magnificent river to see it no more on our journey.

The railway has followed the south or Oregon bank of the Columbia from Portland. As a Canadian I could not but feel a deep interest in looking across on the opposite bank to Washington Territory. I reverted to the settlement by treaty of the Oregon question in 1846. Great Britain most justly claimed the whole territory north of the 42° parallel. The claims of the United States as set forth by them were only limited by Alaska. At that date the fact is undoubted that there was not a single citizen of the United States established north of the Columbia River. The country was occupied only by the Hudson's Bay Company. The Columbia was the thoroughfare of that Company to the Boat Encampment, already alluded to, at the extreme north of the Selkirk Range. This river would have made a good natural boundary line, and in itself would have been a compromise most favourable to the United States. It would have given them Astoria and all the discoveries of Lewis and Clark, but the treaty of 1846 was simply a capitulation even more inglorious than the Ashburton Treaty of four years earlier date, and will so live in history. Six degrees of latitude by three degrees of longitude of British Territory were deliberately abandoned by the Imperial diplomatists, and what is more remarkable the settlement was so ill-defined as, some years afterwards, to cause the San Juan difficulty, which raised great trouble and much ill-feeling.

At six next morning we arrive at Spokane Falls, a well built town with a population of fifteen hundred. The soil is light and gravelly, with groves of pine. We reach Rathdrum, thirty miles distant, described in the guide book as an agricultural centre in the best portion of the valley. The train remains here twenty minutes. We learn that no rain has fallen since early in May, and that the crops are almost a failure. All the soil we have looked upon for three hundred miles is sandy and gravelly, and without rain good crops can scarcely be looked for.

At nine we reach Sand Point, four hundred and forty-five miles from Portland. From Ainsworth we have been running in a north-easterly direction and we are now fifty miles south of the Boundary Line. The mouth of the Kicking-Horse River is two hundred miles from us, nearly due north. I looked on Sand Point with some interest, for if we had been driven at the Ille-celle-waet to abandon our journey through the Eagle Pass, it was at this spot we would have reached the Northern Pacific Railway on our descent by the Columbia past Fort Colville.

We have passed the northern part of Idaho and are entering Montana. At Heron, thirty-eight miles from Sand Point, a few drops fall from the cloudy sky, we are told the only rain since spring! We are following Clark's Fork Valley towards the Rocky Mountains. We come upon open prairie with good soil and bunch grass pasture, with patches of good sized forest trees. The valley varies in width from one to five miles, and is not wanting in natural beauty. It resembles somewhat Bow River, above Calgarry; but at Bow River the mountains are higher and bolder in outline than on the Northern Pacific, and at this spot the heights are wooded to the summit and are unmarked by bold, rocky, lofty peaks.

We have rain during the afternoon. If it be acceptable to the arid soil it is equally welcome to the traveller as an accessory to comfort. Hitherto the dust has followed us like a cloud, but the rain dispels it. It is getting dark. My intention had been to stay up to observe, as best I could, the mountain "divide," but as it was hopeless to look for moonlight I turned in before twelve.

I slept an hour when I again rose. It was still dark and drizzly, but the glare from the engines working their full power up the ascent was reflected by the hanging clouds, and near objects were dimly visible. I was desirous of seeing what I could of the country, for we were approaching the divide of the water flow of the continent; the one turning to the Pacific, the other to the Atlantic and the Gulf of Mexico. As morning advanced the sky became clear and the features of the country visible. A tunnel two-thirds of a mile long, the Mullan tunnel, is in progress through the summit. At present the rails are connected over the mountain by a surface line, four miles in length, with steep grades. The train was drawn up by two engines and we crept up at a slow pace. On reaching the highest point we came to a stand to admit of an examination of the couplings and of the whole machinery of the locomotive and train.

We had now to face the serious work of descent. The heaviest grade is confined to a mile. The inclination, evidently great, was shown by the angle formed by the hanging articles in the Pullman, with the vertical lines of its panels. I extemporized a plummet and line with the silk cord of my glasses, and according to my calculation the gradients we passed over for some distance exceeded two hundred and sixty feet to the mile;

in one spot they reached nearly three hundred feet: 5.7 feet to the hundred feet.

We left the temporary line and followed the permanent track, the gradient of which I was told is one hundred and sixteen feet to the mile. In our passage over the summit no mountains were visible. The hills through which we passed were but a few hundred feet higher than the track. We crossed the "divide" by a narrow depression, as far as we can judge, of no great depth. The exact length of the completed Mullan tunnel will be 3,850 feet, its height 5,547 feet above sea level.

We have reached Helena. We are now in the valley of the Missouri. The second summit, between the Missouri and the Yellowstone Rivers, is about one hundred and forty miles distant from the main summit. Before reaching it I take the opportunity to get some sleep.

Seventy miles from Helena we come to Gallatin. At this spot the Missouri may be said to commence. It is fed by three important tributaries, the Jefferson, the Madison and the Gallatin, all rising within the periphery of a semi-circle of mountains visible to the south and east of us.

We passed through the fertile plain of Bozzeman, where we obtained a fine view of the Rocky Mountains, south of us. Their lofty peaks, tipped with snow, are probably eighty miles distant. It could not have been very far from this neighbourhood that the sons of De la Verendrye first looked upon the mountain heights as they ascended a branch of the Missouri. At Bozzeman we prepared for another ascent and pass over a temporary track until the Bozzeman tunnel is completed. It will be 4,500 feet long and 5,572 feet above tide level. There is a marked contrast in the character of the heights at Bozzeman to those of Mullan. The latter are wooded, whereas the former are bare, with only a few small bushes. The Bozzeman tunnel, although only through a spur of the Rocky Mountain chain, is a few yards more elevated than the Mullan tunnel through the main divide. At Livingstone we are in the Yellowstone Valley, eight hundred and eighty miles from Portland. We followed the Yellowstone for three hundred and forty miles. Yellowstone park is sixty miles to the south, and a railway leads to it from this point. We can see the mountains of the National park in the distance, grand, lofty and striking, recalling some portion of the Selkirk range. I saw nothing on the Northern Pacific Railway except this distant view, to equal the mountains on our Canadian line.

We cross the Yellowstone River, about one hundred and fifty feet wide, and which takes its rise in Yellowstone Lake, one hundred miles south of us.

At Livingstone we enter a prairie country which we follow in our journey eastward for twenty degrees of longitude. As we pass over the two water sheds, between five and six thousand feet above the sea, we form the impression that there is abundance of moisture at this elevation. We are now, however in comparatively low ground, and the district generally is evidently dry, if not to some extent rainless. Possibly the mountains intercept the vapour-bearing clouds, or drive them into the higher regions. The maps show that there are spurs of the Rocky Mountains continuing to the north and south of the Yellowstone Valley for a long distance east of the main range, but all of them are too distant from our point of vision or too low to appear above the horizon.

The railway follows the general direction of the river, sometimes along its banks, and at no place at any great distance from it. The soil on the bottom lands is loam or clay with a gravelly sub-soil. The grass is dry and thin, but preparations for irrigation on a considerable scale have been undertaken west of Billings' station, one hundred and fifteen miles east of Livingstone. By this means the lowlands adjacent to the river will be brought under cultivation. Beyond the immediate valley itself, in which irrigation is practicable the ground must remain much as it now is. East of Billings we meet the same arid country, with scanty herbage and a few scattered trees of small size along the river's edge.

We are now in the territory which for so many years was the scene of frequent Indian wars. Fort

Custer is to the south of us, and to the east Fort Keogh. At Custer station an officer entered the train on his way to Fort Keogh. Like most officers of the United States army, he was agreeable and full of conversation. He had had fifteen years' experience of the country, and consequently had many anecdotes to tell of the wars. He showed us a rusty revolver which, a few days previously, he had picked up from the field where Custer's whole command was destroyed in the last successful effort of the Red man on a large scale. We can recollect the extraordinary excitement the news caused on this continent. I must frankly say that, making all allowance for Custer's known gallantry, my sympathies have always been with the men who rode after him, rather than with their leader. Custer himself, it is true, paid the penalty of his rashness. The record is simple. He, with his command, some six hundred sabres, rode up the valley of the Rosebud. Not one returned to tell the tale of their extermination. The criticism of the day was not favorable to Custer's generalship. He had turned into an attack what was intended as a reconnaisance. His critics accuse him of endeavoring to attract public attention by some bold dashing movement, the one justification of which would have been its success. Every reader of the Indian wars knows that the strategy of the Red man is that of surprise and ambuscade, and that failure in observing caution in an advance, incurs the danger of defeat and loss. The snare into which Custer fell is one of the most remarkable in its results that not a man escaped. Its parallel in misfortune, however, was not long after witnessed at Isandula, when not one man of the two hundred in the ranks of the Imperial second 24th regiment survived the Zulu attack on the unfortified camp.

During the night we left the Yellowstone at Glendive. We have passed over the *Mauvaise Terre* which I had wished to see; but it was not possible, as it was dark when we came through it. Our restaurant car no longer accompanies us. The fact is brought to our mind by a bad and expensive breakfast at Richardson, in Dacota. Between Glendive and Bismarck the soil is good; the grass, however, is brown, but of better growth than to the West. At Sims, coal mining has been commenced with some success.

This place is scarcely a year old, but it contains a number of brick buildings. The site of the town is on an eminence, and altogether it looks more promising than any spot we have seen since we left Portland. We are now in the hundred and second meridian of longitude.

Improvement advances as we proceed easterly; the towns are more numerous and better built, and are marked by more bustle. The land is of a higher character and better cultivated, and we see a superior class of station buildings.

We reached Mandane on the Missouri. Bismarck is on the eastern bank, opposite. These two places are the creation of a few years, and the progress they have made is marvellous. They are connected by a high level iron bridge. The three centre spans are each four hundred feet, on stone piers. The height from the bottom of the deepest foundation to the top chord is one hundred and seventy feet, the height of the truss is fifty feet. It is approached by timber trestling at one part sixty feet in height. It is a bold piece of engineering, and the cost is named at one million dollars. The bridge was finished in May of last year.

The land near Bismarck is very good. Already the country is well settled; but night came on and cut off further observation. We passed over an important but scarcely perceptible water-shed, about one hundred and fifty miles east of Bismarck. The elevation above the general level cannot be distinguished, and we have prairie around us on all sides. Near the small station of Sanbon we leave the basin of the Gulf of Mexico, and without visible signs of change pass to that of the Hudson's Bay. From the Rocky Mountains to this point the drainage has been by the Missouri. The rainfall passes now to the Red River and Lake Winnipeg to the north. We are in the upper part of the Red River Plain, an extension of that district in Canada so unequalled for fertility.

At eleven at night we reach Fargo, where the

line crosses the Red River. Fargo, like Winnipeg, is the wonderful creation of a few years. The Station is illuminated by electric lights, and even at the late hour the place has the appearance of an important commercial centre. Moorhead is on the eastern bank of the river, opposite Fargo. Glyndon, ten miles further east, is 1,626 from Portland and 274 miles from St. Paul. It is a place of importance, in so far that a connection is made with the railway from St. Paul for Winnipeg, but is not otherwise remarkable. I was sorry to separate from my old friend and fellow traveller, Dr. Grant, who left the train for Winnipeg. We had been together for six weeks through the adventures which I have recorded. At midnight we shook hands; Dr. Grant to go northward, and myself and my son to find ourselves at St. Paul on the next forenoon.

At St. Paul we are on known ground. Twenty-four hours brings us to Chicago and another twenty-four hours to Toronto. There are many Canadian interests in St. Paul, and this picturesque city on the banks of the Mississippi has been often visited and described. We are now thoroughly within all the influences of busy life, and the meagerest of newspaper readers turns to the journals of the day to learn what has happened and is to be looked for.

I am gratified to learn that the next meeting of the British Association will be held in Canada, and

I read that in a couple of days there is to be a gathering in Chicago of railway managers from the United States and Canada in special convention to determine what steps are to be taken to establish the standards for the regulation of time.

Twenty years ago, personally, I had felt that in connection with the railways of Canada in the future, extending over several degrees of longitude, difficulties would arise in the computation of time. To my mind it was evident that, in place of the rude mode followed, some more scientific system was called for. When I became Engineer of the Intercolonial Railway from Nova Scotia to Quebec, and of the Canadian Pacific Railway from Ontario to the far West, my views were confirmed, and, as I devoted time and study to the problem, I became more than ever impressed with the importance of the question, not only to Canada or to this continent, but to the world generally.

Reasoning on the subject *à priori* from the admitted necessity of a change of system it struck me forcibly that it could only be effected on principles which would meet every objection and generally commend themselves as well founded Moreover, the subject appeared to me of unusual interest, and as such I thought it my duty specially to bring it under the notice of the British Association for the Advancement of Science. I formed the opinion that this Association, having been established for promoting the general welfare, was the body above all others to which any proposition having so universal an application should be submitted. I was in London in 1878, and addressed the permanent officers of the Association on the subject, expressing my wish to bring it forward. I complied with all the regulations, and gave notice of my intention to introduce its consideration before the forty-eigth meeting to be held in Dublin the following August. I prepared a paper and submitted an outline of it. I was informed by letter from the Secretary that it would be brought before Section A, "Mathematics and Physical Science." I arrived in Dublin the first day of the meeting, the 14th August, and lost no time in addressing the Secretary, personally, and informing him that I was prepared to read my paper when called upon. He answered that I should receive a reply in due course. Not receiving any communication for three days, I saw the Secretary and was then informed by him that the Committee had decided that my paper should be read on the 21st. It turned out that on that day there would be no meeting. The last meeting was on the 20th. My paper was put down at the end of the list: it was the twelfth. I attended the Section until the meeting closed, but no opportunity was given me to introduce it. There was still another day, so I approached the Secretary and endeavoured to make some arrangement for its being read in the morning. I was curtly told that Section A would not meet again, as all the papers but mine had been disposed of, and he took upon himself to add that the reading of my paper was of little consequence. I deemed it my duty, without delay, to bring the circumstance under the notice of the President of the Association, but my letter did not receive the slightest attention. What could I do?

The letter of the Secretary received in London distinctly informed me that my paper would be considered, and consequently I had travelled to Dublin and waited from day to day until the last meeting, but all to no purpose. I was unknown. I was from the other side of the Atlantic, and in those days there was no High Commissioner to obtain common justice for the Canadian. I had simply experienced one of those acts of official insolence or indifference so mischievous in their influence and so offensive in their character, which I fear, in years gone by, too many from the Outer Empire experienced. I assume that the secretary represented the Committee, and that the Committee had the right to form their own opinion as to the importance of the subjects proposed to be brought before the Association, and reject such as to them seemed unworthy of attention. But they were not justified in saying one thing in London and acting as they did in Dublin. I will take upon myself to remind the officers of the British Association that since that date the subject I proposed to bring before the Dublin meeting has not been considered beneath the notice of many scientific societies on both sides of the Atlantic, that it has been earnestly discussed at International Congresses in Venice and Rome, and it has led to the House of Representatives and the Senate of the United States passing a joint resolution requesting the President to invite the attention of all civilized nations to the question.

It struck me as a singular coincidence that among the first things that I read in the Chicago newspapers was the notice of the important meeting of Railway Managers* to take definite action on the subject of regulating time, so unpleasantly disposed of in Dublin by the British Association, and that the Association itself was coming to Canada to learn that the managers of one hundred thousand miles of railway, travelled over by fifty millions of people on this continent, had taken the first important step in the scheme of Cosmopolitan Time Reckoning, which, as an Association, it officially and offensively refused to entertain; and, further, to learn that on the 1st October, after their visit to Canada, an International Conference will be held in Washington, on the invitation of the President of the United States, to take another step in its establishment, and to recommend to the

---

*This meeting was held on October 11th. As a result the Standard Hour system went into force throughout North America on the 18th November following.

world such further action regarding it as may be deemed expedient.

I venture to say that members of the British Association visiting the Dominion next summer will be received with cordiality and hospitality, and some may recross the ocean with new ideas of the busy world outside of England. Possibly their visit to Canada and the warm reception which, I am sure, they will receive, will engender new feelings; less insular, perhaps, and more kindly, more sympathetic, towards their fellow subjects whose homes are to be found in the territory of the Empire which lies beyond the four seas.

From Chicago I followed the usual route to Ottawa. I paid my respects to His Excellency Lord Lorne and Her Royal Highness, so soon to leave Canada. Lord Lorne was in a few days to proceed to Quebec to meet Lord Lansdowne. I went on my way to Halifax, where I arrived on Saturday, 13th October, exactly seventeen weeks since I left for England, on the 17th of June.

CHAPTER XXIII.

THE INDIANS.

Indian Population—The Government Policy—Indian Instincts—The Hudson's Bay Company—Fidelity and Truthfulness of Indians—Aptitude for Certain Pursuits—The Future of the Red Man.

In the foregoing chapters I have alluded more than once to the Indian population scattered over the Dominion and more especially remarkable in the North-West and British Columbia. It is a subject to command attention when the future of Canada is at all considered. Fortunately it is one concerning which little anxiety need be felt. The Government on one side recognizes its obligations to the Red man, and is desirous of doing him justice. The Indian is satisfied that there is a desire to treat him fairly. The land formerly held by them and now owned by the Dominion has not been ruthlessly seized, arbitrarily held in possession by squatters and remorseless traders. It has been obtained by treaty on principles of right and justice, and has been ceded to the commonwealth for an agreed equivalent; when the settler enters upon possession, he simply takes his holding on Government land.

The decrease of the Indian population has steadily advanced since the settlement of the east coast by the first Anglo-Saxon in the seventeenth century. The number of the native race at that date must be always a matter of conjecture. Catlin estimated it at that time to have been fourteen millions, and half a century ago he described it as reduced to two millions. All the early writers of Canada describe the populous condition of the Indian tribes. That they no longer present this character is undoubted. General Lefroy, in a paper read before the Canadian Institute, of Toronto, in 1853, estimated the total number of Indians in North America at 250,000. Even without intercourse with the white man, their desolating wars, the frequent scarcity of food and the want of knowledge of the means by which life can be preserved, all had their influence. As the country became more occupied and under the control of the European, their territory became narrowed, and hence the greater cause of quarrel arose. Then the Indians of the Mohawk and those of Lake Huron became mixed up in the wars of the English and French. During the revolutionary war with the United States and the war of 1812 the tribes took opposite sides, while there were whole races who lived in open hostility to the white man.

Except in the North-West, they have almost passed out of mind. In Ontario they are seldom thought of, but in the neighbourhood where they are seen, nevertheless their number amounts to 18,000. In Quebec they attract greater attention; their number, however is only 12,000. In the Maritime Provinces they number 4,000. At present the estimated number of Indians east of the Rocky Mountains is 51,500; in British Columbia proper there are nearly 36,500; in the more northern Hudson's Bay Territories, Labrador and the Arctic coast, 9,000. In the North-West, at no late date, there was much to unsettle confidence, in view of the rapid strides with which settlement was advancing, and in view also of the difficulty which appears inherently to attend the solution of this important problem in political economy; more especially when we consider the constant turmoil and difficulty experienced in the United States. But the solution has been found, as much else in life, by following the very simple principle of justice and honesty.

There are now in the North-West under the immediate care of the Government 10,000 Indians. The proximate cost of beef and flour furnished them is twelve cents per head per day.

It may confidently be affirmed that the present satisfactory condition of our North-West Indian relations is entirely owing to the admirable government of the Hudson's Bay Company. One principle observed was never to allow the Indian to suffer from starvation. Provisions under conditions of privation were given to those in need; but the recipients were made clearly to understand that it was an advance of goods to be repaid in the future. Those receiving assistance when in want, or to enable them to start for the hunting grounds were held to give back the value of what was then given, when the recipient was in a condition to do so. A principle was accordingly established, which the Dominion Government is endeavouring to enforce: that the Indian should never regard himself as an object of charity, specially to be provided for. He is by these means taught that to beg is discreditable, and to receive Government rations as alms is personally dishonourable to himself. He is taught self-reliance, for he is made to understand that the rations, or clothing, or powder must be repaid by work or otherwise as he can satisfy the claim.

The duty has accordingly been imposed on those able to work to make some return for what they have received. Such as these labour under the eye of the farm instructor on each reserve. If there be no work there will be no food, a principle perfectly within Indian comprehension and sense of justice. Moreover, what labour they give redounds to their own personal advantage. The strides to civilization may not be immediate, but they are perceptible, and progress is in that direction. Above all things, the Indian is satisfied, for he feels that he is treated with justice.

We must, on our side, be reasonable in our expectations. We must remember that the Indian has never been habituated to steady labour, and it should not be a matter of bewilderment if he is vacillating and irregular in accepting that condition. For countless generations his life has been nomadic. He has been lord of the soil, bred a warrior, and the white men who has been the cause of the change in his condition should bear with him and be patient, and extend him help and aid. It is not only the Indian who finds it hard to accept the life of monotonous employment, day out, day in. Many of our race who, at a somewhat advanced period in their career are set down to patient effort, find it no little of a trial. The hand of little employment hath the daintier sense, and we must look to two or three generations passing away before the Indian will take his place in the family of civilized man. He has much of his former life to unlearn; he has to struggle against the instincts of his blood; he has to accept the great truth that labour is honourable. Those human lilies of the valley who toil not, neither do they spin, do not hold the same high grade in human estimation which they obtained a century back. No doctrine is more recognized than that every right is co-existent with a duty. The Indian has to reach the condition of understanding that he can only hold his place by the side of the white man by fulfilling the obligations attendant on the position he claims.

The white man engaged in the effort to elevate the Indian, must not be discouraged if the attempt made on his part does not at once lead to little more than perceptible results. He must look forward to much patient perseverance for many years, and he must guard against discouragement. If he has difficulties to meet there is also much in the Indian character by which they are fitted for peculiar employment; as guardians of rivers, as herdsmen, as boatmen; and they have extraordinary aptitude for any calling which exacts readiness of resource and quickness of perception. Moreover, the Indian in many ways displays much artistic skill. The Indians of the Pacific coast especially are noted for their taste. This is exemplified in the really fine models of ship architecture seen in their large sea-going canoes. They are also distinguished for carving in wood and their work in metals.

They are capable of taking part in many profitable occupations. In British Columbia they are preferred as labourers to the Chinamen. The Indian has proved himself to be an excellent assistant on a farm. He is useful in a saw-mill, and in such manufactures as he can undertake. He can be relied upon as an overseer of rivers and to protect fisheries. He can be trained to look after forests and to prevent the wholesale destruction of timber, so often the result of carelessness and imprudence. As forester and guardian of the observance of the game laws he would be invaluable; and it is only by strict observance of our regulations with regard to the season in which fish and game can be hunted and killed that its preservation can be assured. Who more fit for this duty?

The Indians have already some minor industries, by which they show strong commercial instincts. They split cedar logs by means of yew wedges, which they sell to the northern tribes for seal or whale oil, blankets and dried fish. The seal fisheries which they carry on are of great extent. The annual value is named at $200,000. Speaking generally of them in British Columbia, they are in no way held in this western part of the Dominion, where they are well known, to be the unimpressible animals many assert them to be. I can myself trace many strong indications of progress, and I do not think that many years will pass before this fact has been clearly established.

Many are now receiving instruction in agriculture. They are furnished with the necessary implements and seed. Cattle have also been given them. If in some instances there have been failures, the majority of those to whom these advantages have been extended have fairly profited by them.

On many of the reserves much interest has been shewn in agriculture, with the important result that the grain raised has reduced the number of rations issued. It is proposed to introduce on their farms pigs to breed from. It is held that many will understand that they are not at once to be killed and eaten. If successful, it will prove a step of importance; on one side inculcating thrift, on the other being a provision against want. Even the Blackfeet, who a few years back were continually on the war-path, have settled down to peaceable pursuits. Most families have a small farm or garden in place of the wigwam. An attempt is to be made to establish industrial schools. But the Indians do not willingly see their children separated from them.

The Sioux, who were driven out of the United States twelve years back, came to Manitoba with the stigma of the atrocities they were charged with; into these I will not enter. They asked a home. They prayed to be allowed to be hewers of wood and drawers of water. No special privilege was claimed by them. The desire was granted; and they have never violated the hospitality extended to them. Their career has been one of patient labour.

The Hudson Bay Company obtained control over the Indian, by its inflexible regard to its obligations. They never falsified their word. The love of truth in the Indian in his natural condition is one of the marked features of his character. It is a virtue he respects in others, for he himself practices it. It has been said that such was the confidence in every officer of the Company, hence in every white man, that an Indian would accept a few pencil words which he could not understand, on a sheet of paper, from a stranger, telling him to present it as a certificate at a certain post in payment for provisions or skins or any service rendered.

The fidelity of the Indian to his engagements is best known by those who have intercourse with him. However the fact may be disputed by mere petulant abuse, it is uncontradictable. A proof of the strongest character can be adduced, even at this hour, by the agents of the Hudson's Bay Company. There are many localities where the business is not sufficient to support a resident storekeeper, where there are none but Indians. At the same time there are requirements of traffic which cannot be ignored. This condition is met by an arrangement of a simple character, but it is only possible when unvarying good faith and honesty are observed. The Hudson's Bay Company erect a store, generally a large log shanty; glass being difficult to obtain, generally the windows are made of parchment. The door is only secured against the intrusion of wild animals, that is to say, it is securely fastened from the outside by a latch or bar. So any one can enter it at any time. Here are stored such supplies as the Indian may need: blankets, clothing, arms, powder, shot and such articles as are used by the Red man. When an Indian in the district requires any article from the store, he enters and takes what he wants, leaving behind the requisite number of skins in barter, denoting by some mark the individuality of the deposit. A tariff of equivalents has been established, and the Indian knows precisely what he has to leave behind for the value of that which he takes away. This arrangement has existed for many years. I have never heard an instance of the store having been fraudulently visited, or of the least dishonesty on the part of the Indian. In the regular periodical visit to these localities, in some cases not oftener than twice a year, the agents have invariably found everything in order and satisfactory. In these visits the stock is replenished and the furs deposited taken possession of. The system still prevails, and until fraud has been learned from intercourse with the white man it will continue in the remote districts.

It is difficult amid civilized commerce to find a parallel to the confidence on one side and to the honesty shewn on the other. If all the chronicles related of the days of Alfred be true, the national honesty may then have partaken of the reliability and trustworthiness of the Indian. But no other record of this character is to be found in any page of history. It can only exist, indeed, in a simple state of society in which the dominant class is marked by the strictest honesty and fidelity to a promise made. It is this tone of personal honour which the Red man both appreciates and in his own conduct observes, until it is lost in the vices and misfortunes of a civilization which generally he has experienced to his ruin, subsequently to be developed to untiring calumny of his race. Whatever the feelings and weaknesses of the Indian in his natural condition, in other respects truth and honesty are his marked characteristics.

There is a special difficulty in British Columbia, found in no other part of Canada, the custom of holding "pot-laches": feasts spread over much time, when extravagant gifts are made. A proclamation was issued by Lord Lorne forbidding these meetings. It is now proposed to make them a misdemeanor by statute. In some parts of this Province liquor has been introduced among the Indians by the Chinese and others, and in some tribes the spirit of gambling is springing up. In one agency, however, they have been induced to burn their cards.

A more important proceeding is the introduction into the House of Commons of a measure to give some of the old tribes self-government. What is specially required is to make the Indian self-reliant and self-respecting. If he have to live by the side of whites he can only be taught a sense of equality with them by removing every remnant of patronizing protection. Even communities not Indian, not subject to effort, from whom little exertion is called for, easily drop into habits of indulgence and indolence. The true policy towards the Indian is that of extending to him protection from being robbed and abused, but at the same time teaching him to feel how much of his happiness depends on his own conduct, and that his future depends largely on himself.

There are a class of men who reason themselves into the theory that the best civilization for the Indian is to civilize him off the face of the country. Such as these seem to forget that the worst faults of the Red man are those which he has learned from our race. From the days of Columbus and Cortez until modern times, the white man has looked upon the Indians as a class of beings to whom he was bound by no tie of honour. By the wrongs he himself has committed he awakened feelings of revenge, and one policy only was known, coercion and force. In modern times, happily, one duty has been recognized, the enforced abstinence of the Indian from liquor. Throughout the Dominion, but especially in the North-West, on Canadian soil, the strongest precautions are taken against the introduction of spirituous liquors. No alcohol is admitted into Indian territory. Were the contrary course allowed, the Red man would soon degenerate into the lowest depths of misery and crime. It is not to be denied that our own race shew many examples of dishonesty and fraud; but crime with the Indian is found in its most marked form when in contact with the white man. The experience of all who know them is that they have great tenacity of purpose, and will endure hardship and privation uncomplainingly. The advance of events has changed their whole lives, and in the proportion that governments have recognized this fact and have endeavoured to adapt the tribes to the new relations in which they have to live, so are they found to be willing to accept what lies before them and to be grateful for the consideration which they receive. The Canadian Government is acting on this principle. Those who study the question hopefully look forward to the day when the Indian population of the North-West will turn to pastoral and agricultural pursuits and constant labour to obtain their bread. The present peaceable character of the Indian is sufficiently established by the fact that the mounted police, which consists of five hundred men, is sufficiently strong to exercise the neccessary control over the fifty thousand of Indian population east of the Rocky Mountains. All authorities agree in stating that they are under perfect subjection to law, and that the police are competent to keep out the mischievous whiskey trader, whose progress through the land is a blight and a curse where it passes.

It is true that the days of adventure and individual prowess have passed away, but their energy and power of almost untiring effort remain. All that is needed is a healthful, well-considered, just policy to turn these good qualities into the right direction.

CHAPTER XXIV.

THE CANADIAN PACIFIC RAILWAY.

Rapid Construction—Travelling—Old and New—Beginning of Pacific Railway—Difficulties—Party Warfare—The Line North of Lake Superior—The United States Government—Mountain Passes—Soil and Climate—National Parks—Pacific Terminus.

Any one who, with the least attention, has followed the writer in his journey cannot fail to have observed the ease with which long distances on this continent in modern times are passed over. Within the last quarter of a century the whole system of travel has changed. With efficient railway carriages, possessing sleeping accommodation and accessories to personal comfort and with a restaurant car, making allowance for time and distance, the traveller may pass over half a continent with no greater difficulty than he meets in going from London to Liverpool. The Canadian Pacific Railway Company has shewn extraordinary energy in the construction of the work. The progress seems fabulous Four hundred and fifty miles of main line, independently of collateral branches in the North-West, aggregating one hundred and forty miles, which they have completed in one summer. The railway now extends westerly from Port Arthur, Lake Superior, to the first range of the Rocky Mountain zone, thirteen hundred and ninety miles. It has practically reached the eastern boundary of British Columbia, in itself identical with the mountain crest forming the continental watershed. The Canadian Government, in accordance with the contract, retained in its hands the construction of the line from Kamloops to Port Moody, 215 miles. The intervening distance of 300 miles remains to be constructed to complete the connection between Lake Superior and the Pacific.

North of Lake Superior the line is under construction easterly. During the present winter a force of 10,000 workmen have been continually engaged in the task of establishing the line between Port Arthur and Callander, 650 miles, at which last named point connection has been made with the railway systems of Ontario and Quebec.

By degrees these gaps will be closed, and in two or three years it is estimated that trains starting on the eastern seaboard will run on an unbroken line to the Pacific waters. Literally a new continent will be opened to the traveller; the tourist of other lands will be tempted to visit Canada by the care bestowed on his comfort and convenience, and by the moderate expense at which the journey can be accomplished.

During the last century travelling was the prerogative of the wealthy alone. The spirit of enterprise which leads to the examination of the institutions and the inner life of foreign countries was not general. The journey itself was marked with so much discomfort that it required no little love of adventure to face the ordeal. There was also the insular prejudice against the continent and what is still called foreign manners. Men of ancient families and of large ancestral acres frequently, during a long life, were known not to have extended their visits beyond the county town of their shire. The grand tour of the continent, it is true, was a portion of the education of the sons of noblemen and of men of large fortune, but it was enjoyed by few others. It was not simply a matter of money which imposed a limit to the number. Leisure was equally necessary for its enjoyment, and men in busy life could not give the time required. To pass from one locality to another, separated by long distances, even in England itself, was a matter of expense; and, although in their day the mail coach and the post chaise achieved wonders in the then standard of rapid movement, it was only the possessors of assured and ample means who could use those conveyances to any extent for a pleasure tour.

The wide influences which steam applied to motion, exercised upon life in all its forms was rapidly felt. When we consider the shortness of the period within which these changes have arisen, we recognise additional ground for astonishment, that in so limited a period so much has been done to mould us to a new condition of being. All the important departures from our old theories and habits have taken place within this century. It was but a few years beyond this limit when Johnson expressed the belief that one of the happinesses of life was to be whirled rapidly along in a post chaise. Only a few years previously, in 1762, Brindley commenced his first canals which, if they did not admit of speed, permitted intercommunication along their line, until the very traffic which they created led to the establishment of railways, in one sense, to supplant them.

The success of the locomotive and the rapidity of movement which it created, with the decreased cost of travel, were early suggestive of the modifications which would arise in thought, in manners, in the form of life and the political aspirations of modern times. The opening of railways in the early stages of the system established that the new mode of conveyance was one attended with less risk and danger than the old stage and mail coach, and by the control obtained over it applicable to all our wants. Moreover, it was of common utility from the extreme lowness of the charge which it exacted from those using it. It is no exaggeration to say that with the highest class of minds profound emotion was experienced in the changes which they saw would follow in the introduction of this new awakening of thought. It was to them an entirely new departure from old traditions. The ordinary mass of men saw but little beyond the excitement of the hour. Not a few feared trouble in its democratic developments, that something portentous and inevitable had come into being, the consequences of which could not be foreseen. It was felt that life henceforth would be turned into a new track. Men traced an analogy of feeling to that experienced by their fathers when America was discovered, when printing became a power, when the Reformation established liberty of thought and made inward conscience the guide of conduct. It was felt that new relations of life, new comforts, joys and sorrows had come upon us; that the institution of the railway seemed almost a special dispensation, the ends of which were inscrutable, and that the very form and colour of our being had been changed. There are numerous passages in modern literature to prove that in no way I exaggerate the anticipations which were formed, and doubtless which many can well remember.

As we look back to 1839, when the "Rocket" ran the first trip, we have but a few years of interval beyond half a century within which every department of human life has been expanded, enlarged and widened. Much as successive additions, adaptations and developments have made the locomotive in its character, weight, power and capabilities, wonderfully in advance of the primitive machine of that date—in itself, be it said, in every respect remarkable, containing many elements of what was to follow—so our lives, by its influence have, step by step, assumed a totally distinct and different character to that which marked the early days of the century.

Few of those who are struggling in the business and pleasures of the day stop to consider that the world was ever different to what it now is. The positive results and advantages which we now enjoy have come to us gradually. They are accepted by our children as if they had always existed. It must, however, be evident to all who for a moment think, that to the creation of the railway system we owe much. If the railway has revolutionized many parts of Europe, I cannot but think that the history of the United States would have been very different but for its introduction. Certainly the lines of travel would have been by no means so extended, and what influence a restricted field of settlement might have exercised on the fortunes of the Republic no mere speculation can define. It is obvious that without the new agency the successful settlement of the great North-West of Canada would have been impossible. We have only to compare the condition of the Selkirk settlement of a few years back and the limited progress made during half a century to the sudden and extraordinary bound which it took when the first few miles of railway were put in operation.

It is now twenty years since I was first publicly called upon, as a delegate on behalf of the Selkirk settlement, to give my attention to the question of opening up British North America by the establishment of a line of communication from the Atlantic to the Pacific. I was then called upon to submit my views on the subject to the Imperial and Canadian Governments. Those views were recorded in the parliamentary documents of that year, 1863,* and since that year have frequently been referred to in debate.

British Columbia became connected with Canada in 1871, and one of the conditions of union was the construction of the Canadian Pacific Railway. I was appointed Engineer-in-chief of the undertaking. What the condition of the country was at that period may be seen in the many volumes published by the Government. I shall quote but one passage from the report for 1873, of the Department of Public Works, issued by the Hon. Alexander Mackenzie, then Premier: "It is no exaggeration to speak of the extent of territory to be explored as immense." I undertook the duty with all the zeal I could command, and moreover, I did so with a strong feeling of sympathy with the work as a great national undertaking, and as

---

* Vide Sessional Papers, Province of Canada.

one which, I believed, would in the future command more than an equivalent for all the moneys expended upon it, in its bearing on our history and the advantages it would extend.

In the tenth year of my labour in connection with this gigantic undertaking political or rather party exigencies compelled me to sever all official connection with it. I do not wish in any way, directly or indirectly, to allude to my retirement from the position I held. The subject can be of no interest to the general reader, but I may say that before I retired, in 1880, the problem of the practicability of the Railway had been grappled with and solved. The formidable natural barriers which lay before us had been penetrated. Construction had been commenced at several points between British Columbia and Lake Superior, within a range of two thousand miles; and, further, the completion of a length of railway of eight hundred miles, embracing some of the most difficult sections of the work, was assured within a very short period of time. The latter in the west piercing to the heart of British Columbia from the Pacific, and in the east opening up a way through Canadian territory for the influx of settlers to the fertile prairies of the North-West.

As I am writing, the subject of the Canadian Pacific Railway is again before Parliament. Four years ago the Ministry entrusted the construction of the railway to a Company. The measure was carried by large majorities in both Houses. If I understand the argument advanced for this policy, it was advocated on the ground that a Company could carry on the work more efficiently and more economically than a Department of the Government.

The facts disclosed in the recent discussions in the House of Commons establish that a Company cannot find money at less than double the cost at which it is obtainable by the Canadian Government. The Company has been raising capital at more than nine per cent. The Government can find money at four per cent. or less. That a Company can carry out a national undertaking more efficiently and economically than a government, if the argument be not a fallacy, most certainly implies that there is some defect in the system of government itself.

The difficulty with our present system lies in the fact that the interests of party must be consulted, whatever the cost, whatever the sacrifice. Party takes precedence of every other consideration. Party seems to cloud the judgments of men who, in many instances, are irreproachable in private life. Public men seem to act on the principle that there is one creed and language for the hustings, the press and parliament, and another for social intercourse.

The Canadian Pacific Railway has been considered a political question during three administrations, and has played an important part in party warfare. Every year, since 1871, motion after motion has been made in Parliament relating to engineering operations and the mode of conducting the work. Seldom have there been such acrimonious discussions. Frequently the whole debate was dictated by the party results supposed to be obtainable. Committee followed Committee, year after year, in the Senate and House of Commons, nominally to investigate matters, in reality to create party capital. Who now can point out the slightest result from all these efforts? Two Royal Commissions of special enquiry were appointed. The first made no report; the second prolonged its sittings for two years, at a cost of some $40,000 to the country. What remains of the labours of those Commissions beyond the items of their cost in the public accounts? The report of the second Commission was contained in two bulky volumes. The record of an attempt for party ends to blast the reputation of men who had given the best years of their lives to the performance of public duty. When this report was considered it was held to be so valueless that it has never been circulated.

In Canada we enjoy a liberal constitution, and it may be affirmed that it is the only principle of authority which, as a people, we would tolerate. It cannot, however, be said that in its present form our system of government is an unmixed blessing.

We may ask if representative government is ever to be inseparable from the defects which form the most striking feature in its application and administration, especially on this continent. Must a country constitutionally governed be inevitably ranged into two hostile camps? One side denouncing their opponents and defaming the leading public men of the other, not hesitating even to decry and misrepresent the very resources of the community and to throw obstacles in the way of its advancement. Never was partyism more abject or remorseless. Its exigencies are unblushingly proclaimed to admit the most unscrupulous tactics and the most reprehensible proceedings. Is there no escape from influences so degrading to public life and so hurtful to national honour?

It is evident that the evils which we endure are, day by day, extending a despotism totally at variance with the theory and principles of good government. Possibly Canada may be passing through a phase in the earlier stage of her political freedom. Can we cheer ourselves by the hope that institutions inherently good will clear themselves from the slough into which they unfortunately may be immersed? May not the evils of partyism at last become so intensified that their climax will produce a remedy. As by natural laws a liquid in the process of fermentation purifies itself by throwing off the scum and casting the dregs to the bottom, so may we be encouraged to believe that we are approaching the turning period in the political system we have fallen into, and that year by year Parliament will become less and less a convention of contending party men and be elevated to its true position in the machinery of representative government. Public life will then become more ennobling; it will, indeed, be an object of ambition for men of honour and character to fill places in the Councils of the Nation, when rectitude of purpose and patriotism and truth will be demanded in all and by all who aspire to positions of national trust and dignity.

From the earliest days of my connection with the Pacific Railway I felt convinced of its national necessity. If the North-West country was to become a part of the Dominion vigorous efforts for its settlement were necessary. Among the facilities to be given to the immigrant one of the most important was that of obtaining a means of ingress and a market for his produce. Taking the geographical central position of the country it was not enough to have completed a connection in one direction. If, in due time, a market was open to the Atlantic, it appeared equally essential that an outlet to the Pacific should be obtained. It was clearly foreseen that the only true principle on which the line could be constructed was to form a connection equally with the valley of the St. Lawrence and with the Pacific Ocean.

This view was not generally entertained. There

were many who readily admitted that the Railway should be carried across from Red River to Lake Superior, to find an outlet to the East by the St. Lawrence. For without such a connection no Canadian character would have been given to the line, and freight and passengers equally would have been diverted to St. Paul and Chicago, to be engulfed in the United States system of railways. But while such as these recognized the commercial and political wants of a line from the interior to Lake Superior, there were many who saw no advantage in its Eastern extension along the north shore of Lake Superior, to connect with the lines in operation to the East. It was held that the Railway should terminate at Lake Superior. It was argued that from May to the month of November navigation is open for vessels to proceed by the lakes and the St. Lawrence; and that during the remaining five months of the year it was contended that connection could be obtained by passing over the Canadian frontier to St. Paul and by following the railways eastwards. It was remembered that Montreal had been many years without a winter port, and that no practical inconvenience by that arrangement had followed. On the contrary, that every convenience had resulted, and for the five winter months the limited travel of that period had been profitably directed through the United States Railways to Portland. Very many, therefore, argued that the line should stop at Port Arthur, and that the completion of the portion on the north shore of Lake Superior should be postponed for an indefinite period. I have always held a different opinion. My theory, from the first, has been that the construction of a Pacific Railway meant the construction of the whole Railway.

If Canada had held the sovereignty of the south shore of Lake Superior or controlled the railways in operation by the South Shore, there was much plausibility in the argument that the several links should be connected by the completion of the parts wanting, and that this route should be followed for a quarter of a century or until a large increase of population called for the construction of the line along the north shore of Lake Superior. But all lines south of the lake pass through the States of Michigan and Minnesota. Any diplomatic difficulty would at once be felt in this direction. We were, by such a policy, creating for ourselves a weak spot to be felt on the least strain in our relations with our neighbours. That it is not a fanciful supposition may be found in President Grant's proposition to Congress in his annual message of 1880. In alluding to the course taken by the Canadian authorities in seeking to protect the inshore fisheries of the Dominion and to the Statute passed by Parliament in that intent, General Grant makes the following deliberate proposal to Congress : " I recommend you to confer upon the

Executive the power to suspend by proclamation the operation of the laws authorizing the transit of goods, wares and merchandize in bond across the territory of the United States to Canada; and, further, should such an extreme measure become necessary, to suspend the operation of any laws whereby the vessels of the Dominion of Canada are permitted to enter the waters of the United States."

Such language as this is a threat of no slight moment, and its record is a warning both so powerful and unmistakeable as not to allow it to pass without providing against the contingency of its future execution. With a summer route by water *via* Port Arthur and a winter railway line through the United States to Winnipeg, encouragement would be offered to the United States Government on the slightest provocation, to repeat the language of General Grant, and for Congress to carry it into effect. Without a connection on the north shore of Lake Superior we would have possessed but a shadow of a line, which an hour's declaration of unfriendliness would have nullified. Even in summer Canada would be practically cut in two, for the canal overcoming the Rapids of Sault St. Mary, at the outlet of Lake Superior, is in the State of Michigan. With the connection completed from Ottawa we are perfectly independent of any diplomatic strain on our relations. Possibly the cost of our freedom from this risk may be some millions of dollars, but it is precisely the situation when cost cannot be counted.

Some attempt has been made to cumber the problem by assertions of the bleak and barren character of the intervening distance from Callender to Port Arthur. One important industry is certainly ministered to by this line : that of the lumber trade. At a period when some of the old fields of enterprise have ceased to furnish the timber supply of former days, all the territory where the waterfall runs away from the Ottawa will be directly served by this line, and an opportunity for working it opened up. It is also confidently affirmed that the mineral wealth of the territory is great and that in no long period many important industries will arise in connection with its development.

The British Columbia terminus of the Pacific Railway involved many considerations and it could not at once be determined. At any early stage of our proceedings it was expedient to adopt a pass through the mountains which would admit of a connection with any one of the many harbours advocated. The Yellow Head Pass was the only one to meet this condition ; it was attended also with the accompanying advantage that the line from Red River to this locality passed through the heart of the best land in the North-West. It has been designated the fertile belt; a fact, I believe, indisputable On both sides of the proposed line the land was marked by great productive qualities; the soil was considered, in every respect, suitable for agricultural purposes. Moreover, the line so projected ran within easy reach of the extreme Peace River District, by some reported to be the most fertile of the North-West. It was these reasons, its low elevation and its freedom from objectionable features of climate, which led to the almost universal recognition of the excellency of the Yellow Head Pass. I have not seen it necessary to modify the views which, under the aspect in which it was selected, I then expressed concerning it. I still regard it as peculiarly favourable, and under that aspect superior to every other passage through the mountains to the south or to the north.

When the Railway Company entered into their contract with the Government and assumed the work of construction, the conditions under which the consideration of the location presented themselves were no longer the same. Port Moody, Burrard Inlet, had been definitely chosen as the terminus, and construction had commenced between Kamloops and Port Moody, that distance being the extent of line which the Government undertook to complete. To the East the line between Lakes Superior and Winnipeg was also being pushed forward with vigour by the Government. The problem which the Company had to solve was the location between Winnipeg and Kamloops. They have considered it on the principle of obtaining the shortest trans-continental route, and in these few words they explain the theory of their selection. They claim that this reason, in itself, is all powerful to determine the location by the more southern route which they follow, and one in itself sufficient to meet any objection urged against it.

In the earlier pages of this volume I described the soil of the country west of Winnipeg through which the Railway has been constructed, and I expressed my opinion as to its capability for agricultural development. It is generally conceded that for four hundred miles, to Moose Jaw, it is of great fertility. I could not learn one unfavourable view of any portion of this extent with the most trifling exception. The whole distance may be said to be entirely free from that sterile, forbidding surface soil which passes under the name of waste land.

There is by no means the same unanimity of opinion regarding the country from Moose Jaw to Calgary. Travellers and land jobbers in Winnipeg described it to me as a semi-desert. I came to a different conclusion. I was surprised, from what I heard, to find the soil such as I have described it. I am satisfied that the same land in the climate of the farming districts of England and Scotland would produce the most luxuriant crops. I will not compare it in character to the land away to the north on the route by Edmonton. In many places I found the pasture short and dried brown, as it is often to be seen in the best districts of Ontario at the end of August, the period of the year I passed through the North-West. The fears which I heard expressed respecting an insufficient rain-fall exacted more attention, for without moisture even good soil will bring only indifferent crops. This important consideration, however, will soon be brought within the domain of fact. The railway company has commenced a series of experimental operations, breaking up the land and bringing it under cultivation in the neighbourhood of the stations in those localities where any doubt has been expressed of the character of the soil.

I have crossed the continent on the four different lines now known, and to a certain extent can contrast the features of the country and its fertility as they are represented on each line by such an examination as I could make. We have, likewise, the known opinions of each separate route by those familiar with it. So some fair ground of comparison exists as to their characteristics: —

1. The Central and Union Pacific from Omaha to San Francisco;
2. The Northern Pacific from St. Paul *via* Portland, Oregon, to Puget Sound;
3. The Canadian Pacific from Lake Superior to Port Moody by the Kicking-Horse, Rogers and Eagle Passes;
4. The line originally surveyed from Lake Superior to Port Moody by the North Saskatchewan and Yellow Head Pass.

Speaking generally, the country traversed by these lines is the least valuable on the most southern and increases in value as the lines run through the more northern country.

The best land is undoubtedly to be met on the line through the valley of the North Saskatchewan, leading to the Yellow Head Pass. The most indifferent is the Central Pacific at the south. The Northern Pacific line passes through a better country than the latter, but is again greatly inferior to the land between Winnipeg and Calgary, which I cannot recognize as so good as on the more northern route.

The engineering character of the four trans-continental routes may in some respects be judged by the mountain summits passed over.

The Central and Union Pacific Railway passes over four main summits at intervals apart of from 300 to 400 miles; the lowest of which is 6,120 feet, the highest is 8,240 above sea level.

The Northern Pacific line passes over two summits 120 miles apart, reaching elevations of 5,547 and 5,572 feet.

The Canadian Pacific Railway, by the route followed on the recent journey, has the Bow River summit, 5,300 feet, and the Rogers summit, 4,600 feet above sea level. The latter summit may, however, be entirely avoided by following the River Columbia, a *detour* which would somewhat lengthen the line.

The one main summit on the line by the North Saskatchewan is at the Yellow Head Pass, 3,720 feet above tide water.

As nearly as can be ascertained, the lengths of the four lines are as follows: From Montreal to Port Moody by the Yellow Head Pass 2,940 miles, and by the route adopted 2,890 miles. From New York to Tacoma by the Northern Pacific 3,380 miles, and from New York to San Francisco by the Central Pacific 3,270 miles. It thus appears that the railway through Canada will be 380 and 490 miles shorter between ocean ports than the other lines established through the United States.

The Canadian Pacific, now in process of construction, has this remarkable peculiarity: it is unsurpassed in the variety and magnificence of its scenery. Between Calgary and Kamloops we meet a group of bold, striking combinations of rivers and mountains, not yielding in any way to the scenery of Switzerland, so often visited and described. I have not myself seen the Yosemite Valley, but, judging from the photographs which are well known, my experience suggests that there are scores of places in the mountain zone to be made accessible by the Canadian Pacific equally as striking and marked by as much beauty. They only require to be known to obtain a world-wide fame. There are also some localities near the north shore of Lake Superior possessing attractive scenery of a different character It is therefore suggested that the opportunity for establishing one or more national parks or domains should not be neglected. Two such Parks of ample dimensions, one to the east and the other to the west, might now be selected. The most easterly should undoubtedly embrace Lake Nepigon, to the north of Lake Superior, and the other should take in possibly one hundred miles square of the finest mountain scenery in the Rocky Mountain zone. Such parks, with the marked salubrity of the climate, would attract visitors to frequent them. Rendered perfectly easy of access by the Railway, and with assurance that the life to be found there was marked by comfort at no extravagant cost, these resorts would, especially in the heat of summer, bring many within their boundaries on the score of health and recreation. Sportsmen and crowds of tourists would flock thither, some to hunt the grizzly, the cariboo or the bighorn, others to fish the splendid speckled trout to be found in the mountain streams; many with alpenstock in hand to climb the glacier-covered heights, and all to enjoy the pure air and the charm of the scenery and the striking features of natural beauty nowhere else to be seen. Every year a limited expenditure in forming roads and bridle paths to the remote sections would render the localities more and more attractive. In no long time all the aid that art could furnish would be manifested in developing the landscape and in establishing retreats of quiet and repose amid some of the grandest scenes of wild nature. Evidently such improvements, being in the common interest, they should in some degree be borne by the Dominion. In itself it would be a national matter. It would require no large expenditure; the development should be gradual and systematic, and in a few years the Dominion would possess attractive spots of the rarest picturesque scenery, to be ranked among those remarkable localities which all look upon with pleasure, and which, by the number of strangers who would visit them would become a source of general profit. It is scarcely possible to estimate the amount of money circulated in this form in Switzerland. It really forms no inconsiderable part of the annual revenue of the Republic. Once a route of travel and centres of attraction of this character are established with ourselves, the profit derived would be equally considerable; and, taking the question in its commercial aspect, would repay any moderate outlay so incurred.

One important result of more than ordinary Imperial interest is attained by the construction of the Canadian Pacific Railway. Halifax, with its admirable harbour, is the headquarters of the North American fleet, and its dockyard is furnished with every accessory for refitting and repair. If the British fleet is to rendezvous in Pacific waters, it must be plain that the same opportunities for repair and renewal of stores must be extended, and in proportion that the distance from England is greater the more positive demand exists for a completely equipped dockyard on the Pacific Coast.

Naval and military men have come to the one conclusion on the subject: that the Imperial Dockyard should be as near as practicable to the terminus of the Railway. Indeed it must be evident to all, that where there is a naval station with war vessels on active service there must be the means of refitting and renovation, in a location central and accessible, and one perfectly defensible. It is held that the dockyard should be on an efficient scale, so that a ship of war which has found refuge in port, whatever her condition, can be replaced in her integrity and made completely serviceable.

Captain Colomb, in reference to Imperial and Colonial responsibility in war, has remarked "That " an absolute and pressing necessity exists for the " erection of a great Imperial dockyard at the other " side of the world which would relieve the pres- " sure on home dockyards, and fulfil duties they " cannot in war perform, and in peace offer com- " mercial advantages of construction and repair to " ships of the mercantile marine." The advantages of a naval station in British Columbia extends beyond the mere repairing and refitting of vessels. They can be best set forth in the words of Admiral Mayne, who reports that with respect to the fleet in Chinese waters:—" Our ships there,

"which are sometimes almost disabled from sick-
"ness, could reach the healthy climate of Van-
"couver in six weeks, and might, if required,
"be relieved by vessels of the Pacific Squadron.
"Vessels have been ordered to Esquimault from
"China with crews greatly debilitated, and after-
"wards returned with all hands in perfect health."

However well situated Esquimault may be for a Sanitorium, it cannot be looked upon as offering equally the proper site for a naval arsenal. Esquimault was selected, it is said, at mere haphazard for the purpose of an hospital during the Crimean war. It is an exposed situation, and its defence is complicated by the position of the city of Victoria in the neighbourhood.

The construction of the railway, with its terminus established at Port Moody, has totally changed all the circumstances which hitherto had obtained prominence. It is now held that the naval dockyard should be on Burrard Inlet, near the terminus. The site has been pointed out by Major-General Lawrie and advocated by him in a carefully written paper, in which both the question of the necessity of such a dockyard and the site itself are fully discussed.

The spot on Burrard Inlet described by General Lawrie, is held to be eligible in every point of view. It is defensible by land and by sea, with good anchorage in front. It is situated on the north shore, west of the North Arm, so far within the Inlet as to be unassailable by cruisers, except at the risk of their total destruction, unapproachable by surprise by land, and in close proximity to the terminus of the railway; while at the mouth of the Inlet batteries can be constructed to make entry next to impossible. It must also be borne in mind that Burrard Inlet is directly opposite to the coal fields of Nanaimo. Coal is even to be found on Burrard Inlet itself, and in modern naval warfare coal is an important article of equipment. Indeed, it may be said to take priority; for without fuel no vessel of modern construction can move from her anchorage. The supply of coal, therefore, becomes of primary consideration, and the source where it can be obtained is of special value and has jealously to be protected.

These views of naval and military men have been widely echoed by all who have studied the question. It is on all sides an accepted opinion that with the completion of the Railway, bringing British Columbia within twelve or fifteen days of England, the terminus on Burrard Inlet becomes the most important strategic centre on the Pacific Ocean.

CHAPTER XXV.

CONCLUSION.

England and Canada—Old and New Colonial Systems—Political Exigencies—The High Commissioners—Lord Lorne's Views—The Future—The French Element in Canada—Colonial Federation—The Larger Union.

Scarcely a season passes without the production of some volume of startling adventures. If romance of incidents have been sought in these pages the result must have been disappointing. Nevertheless I venture to think that the described journey, embracing one hundred and twenty degrees of longitude, which I twice passed over in seventeen weeks, must have some interest to many who are identified with the growth and development of the Empire.

If I have any dominant thought in putting these pages into type, it is the hope that they may aid, in however humble a manner, in placing in prominence the close relationship between Great Britain and British North America, and in showing how firmly and permanently it may be established.

Inferentially, it may be said that the feeling of attachment to the Mother Land, which is blended with hope for the future, is not confined to the Dominion alone, but is common to all the outlying Provinces, in whatsoever quarter of the globe they may be.

The part which Canada has to play in the aggregation of States which constitute the British Empire is a subject which has constantly crossed my mind when engaged on these notes. It is a subject which I can only approach with diffidence. Until late years there has been an active Imperial minority who estimate the value of colonies by a narrow standard. They regard them simply as possessions beyond the sea which, when they cease to yield direct returns of profit, should be considered as so many sources of weakness. It was not only with complacency that men of this stamp viewed their possible separation from the Imperial relationship; but they advocated a severance of the connection equally as a benefit to the community to be cut adrift as to the Mother Country, which would thus be relieved of an embarrassing and unprofitable responsibility. The early difficulties which were experienced in some of the colonies arose mainly from the blunders and mismanagement due to the fact that the principles of colonial government were misunderstood. The second Pitt was one of the first boldly to advance the theory that the gift of self-government to the colonies would serve to attach them to the Mother Country, and Fox gave expression to his conviction that the only method of retaining them was to enable them to govern themselves.

The old colonial system has passed away. It is now forty years since virtual self-government was given to Canada. The Colonial Legislatures became supreme in all matters which bore on national life within their geographical limits. The only attempt at control exercised has been on those points of legislation which had an Imperial bearing.

Since the days when the Colonial House of Assembly possessed the power of directing its own local affairs there has been an end of the heart-burnings and disputes which were never absent on any assertion of Downing street control. The concession of self-government in a few years not only quieted the public mind concerning much which had agitated it, but it admitted the settlement of the most difficult questions, such as the Seigniorial Tenure in French Canada and the advance of money on municipal security. It enabled each successive administration to devote its energies to the establishment of the great public works necessary to open out important lines of communication. The true principle of colonial government has thus been realized. Great Britain has adopted as a fixed policy and has faithfully adhered to the principle of giving to her colonies of European races, equally with the United Kingdom, the fullest liberty of self-government, entailing upon them the wise observance of their political duties. As a consequence a totally new character has been given to Provincial aspirations. The principle, even with enlarged powers, has been extended to the Confederated Provinces of the Dominion. Many prominent men have advocated an extension of the system. They claim that the Dominion should be represented in the Imperial Parliament. The difficulty must always exist that the Canadian, as a representative of his own country, cannot with propriety interfere with questions affecting the domestic and political condition of the people of the British Isles. Their internal affairs can only be constitutionally controlled by their own representatives in parliament at Westminster. The Canadian's interests are assured by his own institutions. It is the Parliament at Ottawa which controls the laws of the Dominion. Those who dwell in the United Kingdom might equally claim to interfere in the legislation of this country as the Canadian to vote on laws in the working of which he has no direct interest. It would be at variance with all right for a representative from this side of the Atlantic to cast a vote on questions of taxation and expenditure to which the Dominion in no way contributed.

It is only step by step that human institutions adapt themselves to political exigencies. The advance of opinion is slow. All change is pertinaciously resisted. The British Constitution has grown and been developed from the first century of its existence. It may not always have kept pace with the progress of events, but the advance has been steadily in the direction of good government. Why should it cease to adapt itself to human requirements? As the world moves onwards it will doubtless continue to expand and to improve, and as circumstances demand its elasticity will admit of extension. Certainly there are wonderful progressive agencies now at work, and the conditions of life are changing every year. We cannot doubt that some political organization will be arrived at by which the various units which make up the Empire, while maintaining full control over their own local affairs, will be held together by an alliance founded on mutual affection and a consensus of belief in the common benefit which all derive.

In the mean time matters cannot be left to chance, and the best possible provision must be made by which the Dominion may be represented at the Imperial centre. To a great extent the void is supplied by the presence in London of a High Commissioner. He is a member of the Canadian Privy Council and can speak with authority on the part of the Ministry of which, to some extent, he is a member. All special representations can be clearly and lucidly submitted through him, while he can receive and forward those confidential communications which are made public only when it is expedient to publish them. There is here a guarantee against misrepresentation or misunderstanding on both sides by means of an organization which is simple and natural.

In his address to the Royal Colonial Institute Lord Lorne referred to the appointment of a High Commissioner, resident in London, representing the Dominion. He alluded to it as "by far the "most important event which has occured in the "colonial history of the last few years. As the "first step taken by a colony and cordially accept-"ed by the Imperial authorities," to lead to an arrangement by which the Imperial policy will be directly guided.

Lord Lorne in no way overvalues the importance of the presence at the Imperial centre of a High Commissioner of ability and experience. The Dominion thus represented can submit on all occasions precise and correct information, and in matters of treaty with foreign powers can set before the Imperial authorities the considerations which directly affect our interests. We have but to think of what we suffered through the ignorance displayed during the Ashburton negotiations leading to a treaty which, in its disastrous features, could not be repeated to-day.

Until late years, except the few who by some strange chance obtained the official ear, the Canadian entrusted with official business with the home government felt that he was not included in the circles and courtesies of diplomacy. Then the ordinary Canadian who was present in London was made painfully to feel that he was far less favourably placed than the actual foreigner. The citizen of a foreign state had his Embassy to which he could address himself, but the Colonial Office seemed to have the door barred against the Colonist.

If the teaching of history has any weight the barriers between the British people on the two sides of the Atlantic should be entirely removed. By the appointment of a High Commissioner the connection between the Empire and Canada, so far as the individual is concerned, becomes more real. The great truth to bring to the mind of the Canadian who sets his foot on the soil of the parent state, be it England, Ireland or Scotland, is that it is his home; that he is in much the same position as he would occupy in any Province of his own land.

The office of the High Commissioner is common ground whereon all may meet. At this centre the Canadian registers his name, and his address is known to all who ask for it. It is at this office that all enquiries about him can be made. He is personally and cordially welcomed. His letters may be directed to the office. His friends may meet him in the public room as if in a national club. He is in the midst of all information, and if his business partakes of a public character he is on the spot where its bearings can best be learned. If he has legitimate claims to be brought into official relations with some Departmental Head the High Commissioner is present to obtain for him an audience. The days are gone when a Canadian of credit and *status* was placed in a position inferior to that of a visitor from a foreign nation.

There are many ways in which the High Commissioner can assist the views of those visiting England. He can intervene even in the courtesies of life. Cabinet Ministers in London have but twenty-four hours in a day, like other folk, and, similar to the Governor General, no one of them can hold himself at the beck of the first comer asking for an interview. But there are many duties in life performed from self respect and not through the prospect of profit. Few men of any position in Canada visit Ottawa without leaving their names in the visitors' book of the Governor General, even when it is impossible that the least attention can be extended to them. So in London it would be a courtesy to inscribe your name in the book of the Minister in whom Colonial interests centre. On the other hand, it could not be but agreeable to him to receive this act of homage from a Transatlantic British subject. To all of us with any right feeling it is no little of a pleasure to testify our respect even in this unpretending manner.

I have thought that it would be by no means without advantage if, during the sitting of Parliament, and periodically when in London, the Colonial Minister held an occasional *levee*, where colonists could be presented by some responsible personage. With us the High Commissioner would be held to introduce any one entitled to the distinction. The presentation would be itself sufficient guarantee of respectability everywhere exacted. The reception might be monthly, and no Minister of the Crown could devote a few hours in a twelve months to a more important purpose. The proceeding would be simple and without cost, and it would be productive of good. It would establish the fact that there exists a strong ground of sympathy which unites the members of a common Empire. There is no feeling so paralyzing as that which makes us think we are held in indifference. Turning back no great number of years in the history of Canada, a feeling had crept on many of us that the Mother Country had become completely careless whether we remained within the fold of her Empire or passed out of it. Owing largely however to the social and statesmanlike qualities of the two last Governors-General that feeling has passed away. We do not now view ourselves in that dreary and disheartening condition. It may be said that there is much of sentiment in all this; but sentiment plays a stronger part in national feeling than the mere *doctrinaire* will admit. No true statesman will ignore the fact. There are few who possess the slightest knowledge of history but must recognize the presence and strength of sentiment in national life. In Canada we feel that from England have sprung all true theories of liberty and personal freedom which have so much advanced the world Not even the Roman citizen in the best days of the Empire could feel greater pride than any one of us in the possession of the right of declaring himself a British subject. The sentence itself is, as it were, the aegis under which he is protected and by which he is included in the first rank of national honour.

All that can be said respecting the degree of relationship between Canada and the Mother Country applies with equal force to the connection between every British possession and the Imperial centre.

Lord Lorne, in his address before the Royal Colonial Institute, has dwelt upon this subject with much power.

"These islands have thirty-five millions of people, Canada has now about five millions, Australia will soon have four millions. Britain has, for the small area she possesses, great resources in coal and other wealth, but it may be well for her to remember how little of the earth's surface she possesses in comparison with her children. The area of Canada and of the Australian States is so vast, the fertility of the soil is so remarkable, the healthfulness of their climate is so well proved, and the rapid increase of their white population is so certain that within the lifetime of the children of gentlemen here present their numbers will equal our own. In another century they must be greatly superior to us in men and material of wealth. How foolish, therefore, will our successors in England deem us to have been if we do not meet to the fullest degree possible the wishes of those growing States. They have a filial affection for their Fatherland. They will retain a brother's feeling for us if we are friendly to them in the critical time of their coming manhood. Days may arrive when we shall implore their assistance, and when the alliance of those Powers, grown into maturity and strength, and under very possible circumstances the strong arbiters of our own destinies, shall be ours through the wisdom we may show to-day."

That a closer union between the different outlying members of the Empire and the parent land is desirable, has passed beyond the stage of argument. The basis on which the relationship will rest is certain and known. It is that of affection and common interest. It may, however, be difficult to define the precise arrangement by which its accomplishment can be attained. The unity of the Empire is one of the leading considerations of the day. Its dismemberment cannot be thought of. Even in those more general interests which are common to the whole human race, it is desirable that this vast Empire, marked by progress and humanity of purpose, should be maintained in its integrity; an Empire world-wide in its extent, with a population of three hundred millions of souls.

All the difficulties which naturally lie in the way of inter-communication between these scattered possessions have been removed by science. The ocean is the common link of intercourse, and because it is so constituted Great Britain must remain its mistress to safeguard it.

If it be a marked feeling of this common nationality that a firm union should knit together into one whole the several separated communities, to each one there must be assigned special duties and functions, which may be difficult but yet must be quite possible to determine when all are animated by one dominant sentiment.

Lord Lorne conceives that a legislative union would be impracticable. At the same time he favours an organization in which the Mother Country and each division of the Empire would meet as a collective body. Each self-governing colony or group of colonies might be represented by their High Commissioner or by members appointed on some established principle. In allusion to this consideration Lord Lorne adds:—

"Your diplomacy in commercial matters must take into account the vastness of Imperial sway, and it must be thoroughly representative, not of this little island only, but of the great continents or parts of continents which are content to be under the same flag with you for the sake of mutual advantage. It must be an Imperial, not alone a British, Commission which discusses trade arrangements. The confederation of the Empire, which has been spoken of as possible in the future, must be expressed by no central and unwieldy parliament, representing lands separated from each other by the width of the world; but it must be represented by a council of envoys, who, by working together for each part, may consummate treaties and enforce agreements. No country like Canada would now allow the out-voting of her representatives which would take place in a parliament in London."

It has been remarked that the Empire must maintain its naval supremacy, and in this policy the Dominion, with her recognized nursery for seamen can render important service.*

The great importance of this principle rises into special prominence when we bear in mind that the opening of the Railway to the Pacific will lead to a great increase of British mercantile marine in these waters. The construction of a system of submarine telegraphs will also follow at an early day. They will be established across the ocean to Japan and connect with China. They will be extended to India, to Australia and New Zealand. Great Britain may then be in close relations with her possessions in every quarter of the globe by lines of communication under the protection of her flag without passing through an acre of foreign soil.

*The fisheries, only in their infancy, already employ 60,000 men and boys.

Egypt, owing to its geographical relationship with India and Australia, is constantly a source of anxiety. Lord Wolseley gave as his opinion that the destruction of the Suez canal could be effected by the means of a few old canal boats loaded with stone or one effective torpedo exploded in a well selected spot. Notes of warning in other forms have frequently been given. Three years ago an insurrection in Egypt, out of the fold of Imperial policy, but claiming consideration from the aspect it assumed with regard to Indian interests exacted British interference. Two-thirds of the available naval power of Great Britain was called into service to keep open the canal. Given then the possibility that the canal may at any hour be rendered unnavigable and the telegraph destroyed, what other conclusion can there be than the words of Lord Wolseley, that it is suicidal to depend on the route through Egypt as the means of communication with the East.

The Imperial character which this consideration gives to the lines of communication now being constructed by Canada is indisputable. They offer a constant reliable communication with the Eastern possessions of Great Britain when European complications shall assume a threatening attitude, or when Egyptian difficulties have led to the stoppage of the navigation of the Suez Canal. Canada will consequently add greatly to the common safety by the completion of her national Railway from the

Atlantic to the Pacific seaboard. Its two termini have the common excellence of possessing within command inexhaustible coal deposits, where ships may be supplied and naval arsenals may be established on any scale. The Railway itself passes through a territory a great part of which east of the Rocky Mountains is not surpassed in fertility by any soil in the world, while immediately north of the line the fertile belt presents a field for immigration for centuries, where bread and butchers' meat will be plentifully produced to meet the most extended requirements which the future may create. I have described the changes which have taken place in a few months, even under my own eyes, along the line. What districts of population and cultivation a few years of prosperity may create is beyond calculation.

We are taught by history that some four centuries back Columbus discovered this western land. But Cabot, of English birth, and under the English flag, was absolutely the first to land on the continent. We owe to another nation the early knowledge we possess of a large extent of Canada. The French were the first to penetrate the valley of the Saint Lawrence to the limit it is naturally navigable.

All nations are influenced by the events which

---

*Cabot landed on the coast of Labrador 24th June, 1497. Columbus did not see this continent till the following year. He discovered the West India Islands in 1492-3-4.

they experience, and no people were more moulded into a new development than the Anglo-Saxon race in the Eleventh century, when the Norman crossed the channel and wrung the sovereignty of the country from the reigning monarch. Traces of customs, of laws, of thought, of language, of feeling, of the character of those earlier centuries still remain. But in a few generations the descendants of those who fought in the battle near Hastings had no sentiment but for English soil. They had ceased to be Norman, and it was by the children of the conquering race that the liberties of the country were affirmed in the Great Charter.

In the Province of Quebec there yet remains the unmistakeable impress of its early settlement: of those Normans and Bretons who settled on the shores of the St. Lawrence and in Acadia, and of those who claim ancestry with the noble race which, south and east of the Loire, extending to Rochelle, so constantly battled for freedom of thought. One hundred and twenty years have passed since the last remnant of the power of France disappeared from the northern part of the continent. Great changes have taken place within this period. It was only step by step, in confusion and difficulty, that the present system of self-government became established: a truth evolved out of much complication and from want of the comprehension of Imperial and Colonial relations. The effect has been of imperfect accomplishment in much. This positive good has, however, been achieved, even if in other respects the consummation has been incomplete. The whole of the inhabitants of the several Provinces are united by the one feeling of advancing the common prosperity, and the French Canadian is found in the advanced ranks when the progress of the whole Dominion is in any way concerned.

Of the five great colonial empires which arose in the sixteenth and seventeenth centuries, Spain, Portugal, France, Holland and Great Britain, the British Empire is the only one which survives. The remaining powers possess but a few remnants of their once outstanding colonies. No one of them retains the character of its former strength. The loss of the thirteen colonies of North America a century back by Great Britain was a wound to the national greatness which it was feared by many would never be healed. It was a serious and painful separation which prudence and good government might have averted.

It is often no little of a benefit to each of us to pass through tribulation. Equally so with communities. The Mother Country in this struggle had much to unlearn before her possessions were wisely governed. It took nearly seventy years before the lesson bore fruit. But thoughtful men, step by step, won adherence to their sound policy. We have its result in the present prosperous condition of the Outer Empire, which now, apart from India, contains ten millions of the European race, little less than the population of the British Isles at the period of the American war.

In the last century powerful antagonistic forces were in operation: religious disabilities, commercial restrictions, a narrow franchise, an imperfect parliamentary representation, unwise trade regulations. Discontent followed. It was the interference with the commerce of Massachusetts with the West Indies which was one of the first causes of the severance of good feeling, so soon to be transformed into bitterness and hate. That these grievances no longer exist and that the several British Provinces enjoy free institutions, which it is to be hoped they will learn wisely to work; all this dates from that terrible struggle. Probably the lesson was only the better remembered that it was taught in blood and suffering.

No such repelling forces now exist. The causes of dissension have passed into oblivion. Commerce, science and increased intelligence have relieved the problem from the features which disfigured it. The Atlantic has ceased to be a cause of separation. It is a pertinent query, had these new conditions prevailed a century back, whether the Declaration of Independence would ever have been written.

The American revolution divided the history of the English speaking race into two streams. What will be their future course? They cannot flow in opposite directions. Are there any influences which will lead them insensibly to gravitate one to the other, until in process of years the waters will blend?

We may assert thus far, that however we may be unable to forecast the future, we can trace at this date an assimilation of thought in much, which a few years back could meet on no common ground. Such a result is visible on many occasions and in a thousand ways. In the words of Commodore Tattnall, who went to our rescue at the Pei-ho forts, "Blood is thicker than water." On all sides the movement is convergent.

The diffusion of the English race and the English language over the face of the globe is a result without a parallel. When Columbus and Cabot crossed the Atlantic the number of the English people equalled proximately half the present population of Canada. When Elizabeth ascended the throne it was about five millions. At the time of the American revolution the English population in the British Isles and in North America together numbered fifteen millions. The English-speaking population in all parts of the globe has now increased to a hundred millions, nearly equally divided between England, her Colonies and the United States.

The progress and well-being of the world is largely dependent on the prosperity and harmony of this rapidly increasing branch of the human family. That any of its elements should disintegrate, or that antagonism should take the form of hostility, is painful even to contemplate. There are no signs of any such tendency. There is a natural affinity existing between the children of the one parentage, with substantially the same theories of human duty, wth the like interests in the progress of art and science, by which our comforts are multiplied and human happiness increased. They enjoy equally free institutions, speak one language, with one literature, with common traditions, with a history one and the same for nearly the whole of the nineteen Christian centuries. The aims of the two great sections of the race are identical, and whatever political institutions in either case may prevail, it is an object worthy of the highest ambition of the most enlightened statesmen to bind these peoples in a perpetual alliance of union and friendship and common interest.

We may look hopefully to the closer union of all countries where our language is spoken as a consummation to be desired in the general interest of mankind. In the meantime as Canadians and British subjects our first duty is the strengthening and consolidating of the State to which we owe allegiance. It is the peculiar privilege of Canada to make manifest her earnest desire to build up and uphold the Empire of which we are an integral part, an Empire without a parallel in the world's history.

INDEX.

ACADIA, 106.
Acadians called on to take oath, 114; deportation of, 108, 115.
Ainsworth, 361.
Aix-la-Chapelle, peace of, 113.
Albany, Duke of, 74.
Alexander, Sir Wm., 105.
Alexandra Steamer, 333.
Aleyn Simon, Vicar of Bray, 77.
American Bar, London, 74.
Amherst, N. S., 16.
American war, its unfortunate character, 437.
Anne, Queen, her statue, Minehead Church, 82.
Annapolis, 105; Stone inscription, 105 n.
Argall, Capt. Samuel, 105.
Argyle, Duke of, 36.
Ashburton treaty, 125; its commercial effect, 126
Ashcroft, 315.
Astoria, 342.

BAD WEATHER AT SEA, 91.
Baker Mount, 357.
Baptiste. 297; Guide up Eagle Pass, 302.
Battle Creek, 235.
Batt's Hotel, 41.

Bear Creek, Selkirk range, 264.
Beauséjour Fort, N, S., 115.
Beaver Meadow, Kicking Horse, 244.
Beaver River (Columbia River), 250.
Belleisle, Straits of, 98.
Beresford, Lord C., R.N., 75.
Biard, Jesuit, 104.
Billings Station Irrigation, 370.
Bismarck, 373.
Blackfoot Crossing, 218.
Blanchard, 344.
Blucher, Marshal, his toast, 113.
Bluff Lake, Eagle Pass, 300.
Bois Brulés, 192.
Bow River, 222; crossing, 224, 226.
Bozzeman, 368.
Bozzeman tunnel, 369.
Brandon, 206.
Bray, 76.
British Association, 374; its proceedings in Dublin in the matter of a paper on standard time, 376.
Bristol channel, 80.
British Columbia, 6; known as New Caledonia, 342; Discovery of gold, 343; Political history, 344; House of Assembly first called, 344;

Vancouver Island incorporated with, 345; included in Dominion, Number of Senators and members allowed, 345; Population, 1870, 346; Physical geography, 346; Products, 351; Scenery, 353; Indians, 385.
British Empire, part which Canada has to take in, 421.
British family, main characteristics the same, 3.
Brockville, 144.
Brophy, Mr., 325.
Buffalo at Calgary, 226.
Burdett-Coutts, Baroness, 330.
Burnside, 204.
Bury, Lord, 65.
Brett, John, 103.

CABINET MINISTERS, IMPERIAL, 427.
Cache Creek, 315.
Calgary, 219.
Cambie, H. J., 318, 320.
Cameron, Duncan, 191.
Campana, S. S., 150.
Campbell, Mr., 290.
Campbellton, N. B., 18.
Canada influences yet traceable of its early settlement, 435; duty to the Empire; 439.
Canadian Alpine Club, its formation, 269, 301.
Canadian Camp, Wimbledon, 64.
Canadian Canals, 133, 140.
Canadian Government retained portion of the railway work in its control, 395.
Canadian Pacific Railway, its Montreal terminus, 141; its branch to Ottawa, 142; line to Winnipeg, 171; energy in construction of work, 394; principle governing location, 405; proposition to leave work on north shore Lake Superior unfinished, 406; positive reasons why that section should be constructed, 407; reasons for its present location through mountains, 410; height of passes, 413.
Canadians abroad, 72.
Cape Breton, 110, & n 113.
Cariboo waggon road, 319.
Castle Mountain, 232.
Cedars, large diameter, 299.
Central Pacific Railway, 413.
Chalmers, Colonel, 19.
Champlain, Samuel, 103, 129; knew of Lake Superior, 162.
Chaplin Station, 210.
Charles, I., 105.
Chinamen, 316.
Church service on Polynesian, 93.
Clark's Fork Valley, 366.
Climate British Columbia, 346.
Clyde River, 132.
Cobourg, 145.
Cochrane Ranche, 224.
Collingwood, 151.
Colonial Government, true principles of, 422.
Colomb, Captain, 457.
Columbia River, 253; feature of its territory, 257; descent to Beaver River, 259; junction with Ille-celle-waet, 290; not an American citizen north of it in 1846, 364; thoroughfare of Hudson's Bay Co., 364; river leaves line Northern Pacific, 364.
Columbia Valley, 352.
Commerce (early) of Canada, 139.
Concert, 99.
Cook, Captain, coasted Pacific Ocean, 340.
Corbett's Eating House, 35.
Coquetlon River, 328.
Cornwall, Lt.-Governor, 315.

INDEX. 443

Cornwallis, 114.
Coteau de Missouri, 210.
Critchelon, Major, 263.
Croft, Archer, 64.
Cromwell, Lord Protector, 106.
Cross Lake, 176.
Currie, Mr., 290.
Curry, Thomas, 185.
Custer Fort, 371.
Custer, General, his command and its extermination, 371.
Cypress Station, 212.

D. Mrs., of Toronto, the one lady at table, 91.
Dalles, The, 361.
Dansmuir, Mr., 338.
Devil's club, 262; poisonous effects, 312.
Dinner on Steamship, 91.
Divide Northern Pacific Railway, 367.
Dominion of Canada, 7.
Douglas, Fort, 193.
Douglass, Governor, 343.
Downing Street in Colonial matters—invariable cause of difficulty, 422.
Drake visits Pacific Ocean, 340.
Driard House, 338.
Dry dock—its advantages 416; construction recommended at Burrard Inlet, 418.
Drynock, 316.
Dufferin Lord, his speeches at Empire Club, 65, 143, 318.
Dufferin, Lady, 74, 143.
Du Luth, 163, 180.
Dunbar, Mr., 228, 230, 235.

EAGLE LAKE, 172.
Eagle Pass., 253, 298, 303.
Eagle River, 301.
Engineers, their career, 123; cheerfulness under privation, 242.

English Channel Steamers, 90.
English Society, its reserve and hospitality, 54.
English-speaking races, their duties to each other, 437; their population, 438: happiness and progress of the world dependent on their concord, 439.
Evening on board ship, 88.
Exmoor, 81.

FAILURE IN PROVISION SUPPLY, 291.
Fargo, 374.
Fine Weather at Sea, 95.
Fires, 233, 247.
Fisheries Exhibition, 72.
Fisheries, Canadian, 73; number engaged on them, 432n.
Fleming, Sandford Hall, 269, 277.
Fog whistle, 26.
Forest trees, immense size, 330.
Fort Colville Indians, 289, 297.
Fort William, 164, 169.
Frozen River, 325.
Frozen Snow, 274.
Fuca de, tradition he discovered Vancouver Island, 340.
Fur trade, 168.

GALLATIN, 368.
Galinee's Map, 162.
Galt, Sir Alexander, 22.
George, Prince of Wales, 119.
Georgia, Straits of, 334.
Georgian Bay, 152, 156.
Gillam, Capt. Zachariah, 183.
Glaciers, 240, 265, 273.
Glasgow, 34, 132.
Glendine, 372.
Glyndon, 374.
Goddard's Hospital, 76.
Gold Mining, 174; British Columbia, 313.

Gordon, Willie, 35.
Graham, Mr., 228.
Grant, Rev. Dr., 120, 178, 203; holds service at Hillsdale,232; holds service at the Columbia, 256; loses his watch,262, 277; service on the Ille-cellewaet, 282, 285; service at Shuswap Lake, 308, 314, 319, 326; leaves for Winnipeg,374.
Grant, General, his message to Congress, 407; its threat, 408.
Great Western Railway, England, 55, 80.
Greenwich hospitality, 71.
Griffin's Lake, 304.
Guildford, Park near, 46.
Gulf of St. Lawrence, 4.
Gun shot signals, 288.

HALIFAX, its harbour, 11; its pleasant society, 13; arrived at, 101; founded, 114; again arrived at, 119; a winter shipping port, 134.
Hall, Rev. C., 24.
Halliburton, Mr. R. G., 105n.
Hamlin, Mr., 314.
Hannington, Mr., 317.
Harrison River, 325.
Helena, 368.
Henderson, Sir Edward, 122.
Henley Regatta, 62.
Hennepin, Father, 163.
Henry VIII., 103.
Heron, 366.
High Commissioner of Canada, advantages of his presence in London, 424, 426.
Hill, Mr., 228.
Hill, Mr. A. J., 331.
Hill, Mrs, 332.
Hillsdale, 228.
Holte, Mr., 194.
Hopson, Governor, 114.
Horses on the route, 241; their names, 243; unable to proceed further, 274.
Hudson's Bay Co., 45, 167, 183; admirable treatment of Indians, 382; special arrangement of supply, 388.
Hudson's Bay Territory, French attempt upon, 184.
Hunter, Mr. Joseph, 306, 315.
Hurd, Major, 245, 249.

ILLE-CELLE-WAET, valley of, 272; passage through on foot, 276-278; painful advance of party, 283; Lower Canyon, 285.
Indian population: its decrease, 381; estimated present population of the Provinces of the Dominion, 382; cost of support by Government, 382; difficulties in way of civilization, 384, 391; aptitude for many positions, 385; those of British Columbia in many respects skilful, 385; their love of truth, 387; fidelity to engagement, 388; measure to be introduced in House of Commons, 390.
Indians, Blackfoot Crossing, 218.
Indians, Micmac, New Brunswick, 19.
Indians, Swift Current, 211.
Intercolonial Railway: Chief Engineer, 12; national work, 135.
Irving, Mr. Henry, 64.

JACKASS MOUNTAIN, 318.
Jam of Timber, 287.
James I. at Maidenhead, 78.
Jesus Hospital, 76.
Jogues, 168.
Joliet, 163.

KALAMA, 358.

INDEX. 445

Kaministiquia River, 165, 180.
Kamloops, 311.
Kamloops Indians, 304.
Kanaka Bridge, 326.
Kane's illness, 234.
Keefer, Mr. George, 317, 319.
Kennedy, Governor, 345.
Kicking Horse Pass., 287, 366.
Kingston, 145.
Kirke's expedition against Quebec, 105.

La Corne's Fort, 115.
La Jonquiere, 114.
Lake George, 159.
Lake Huron, storm, 157.
Lake St. Peter, 131.
Lake of the Woods, 174.
Lake Steamer accommodation, 155.
Land's End, 56.
Land, character of, West of Winnipeg, 411.
La Salle, 163.
Lawrence, 108.
Lawrie, Major-General, recommends Burrard Inlet as site for dry dock, 418.
La Verendrye, his discoveries, 181, 209, 368.
Leigh Dove, 235, 334.
Lefroy, General, 381.
Leopold, H. R. H. Prince, 20.
Lepage, Madame, 20.
Lepage, Mr., jun., 100.
Lery, De, 102.
Levée suggested: to be held by Imperial Colonial Minister, 423.
Light, Mr., 122.
Liverpool, 33, 40.
Livingstone, 369.
Location circuitous, 124.
Locomotives, changes effected by, 397.
London, its attractions, 44; hotel life, 48; its heat, 61.

Longueuil, Baron de, 212.
Lorne, Lord, 143, 379; his views as to the High Commissioner, 425; address Colonial Institute, 429; his views as to the Imperial connection, 431.
Louise, H.R.H. Princess, 20, 144; at British Columbia, 350. 379.
Louisbourg taken, 112; 2nd conquest, 113; its destruction, 115.
Lowell, Mrs., 75.
Lytton, 316.

Macdonald, 189.
Macdonell, Capt. Miles, 189.
McDougall, 290.
McDougall, David, 225.
Mackenzie, Hon. A., 65, 77; description of extent of exploration, 400.
Mackenzie, Sir. A., 182; discovered Mackenzie River, 342; first recorded white man to cross Rocky Mountains by land, 342.
McLean, 295.
Macleod, Mr. H. F., 315.
McMillan, Mr., 275, 277.
McMillan, 290.
Moredone, 373.
Maple Creek, 213.
Marquette, 163.
Maquena, 341.
Mascarene, 111.
Massachusetts against cession of Nova Scotia, 106; commerce preyed upon, 107.
Massacres, York and Oyster River, their lessons, 107.
Masse, 104.
Mayne, Admiral, 417; his report on the salubrity of Vancouver Island, 418.
Meaford, 152.
Mears, purchased territory near

446 INDEX.

Nootka Sound, 341.
Medicine Hat, 216.
Metapedia River, 20.
Meuron Point de, 170, 196.
Meuron de Regiment, 195.
Minas, attack of troops there, 113.
Minehead, 81.
Miramichi fire, 1825, 17.
Missiquash River, 114.
Missouri, Valley of, 368; Bridge at Bismarck, 373.
Moberly, Mr., Survey, 261; exploration Ille-celle-waet, 267 and 267n.
Moisture excessive, 300.
Moncton, 121.
Montreal, routes from Quebec, 127; canals to West, 133.
Montreal, city of, 5, 140.
Moose Jaw, 208.
Moosomin, 207.
Morley, 225.
Monts, de, first effort colonization, 103.
Mountain scenery, 227, 231, 238-241; on the Columbia, 255; Beaver River, 264, 279, 294, 304.
Mount Cascade, 228.
Moville, 30, 87.
Mowat, Hon. Oliver, 45.
Mullan Tunnel, 367.
Musgrove, Governor, 345.
Muskeg, 172.

NANAIMO, ITS COAL FIELDS, 419.
Naval supremacy of England, influence of Canadian Pacific upon it, 416.
Narrows, 334.
Neebish Rapids, 458.
Neilson, Mr., 234.
Neilson, Hon. John, 134.
Nepigon Fort, 180.
Newfoundland, 1.
New Westminster, 328, 337.

New York in London, 75.
Naxouat, 107.
Niagara, 149.
Necomeu Slough, 325.
North Pacific S.S., 357.
Northwest Company, 168-186.
Northwest settlement, 379.
Northwest trade, early records, 18?.
Northern Pacific Railway, reasons for returning by 355; its history, 356; height of passes, 613.
Nova Scotia, first colonization, 103; held by Cromwell, 105; demanded by French, 106; route or British province, 118.

OCEAN VOYAGES PAST AND PRESENT, 2; Polynesian, 84; present comfort, 85.
Ogilvie, Senator, 225.
Old Wives Lakes, 210.
Onderdonk, Mr., 320.
Oregon Pioneers, 363.
Oregon Question, 1846, 364.
Ottawa, 143.
Otter, Col., 64.
Owen Sound, 152.

PACIFIC SLOPE, people deficient in Eastern energy, 359.
Pack train, 235.
Padmore, 226.
Parisian S.S., 22, 97.
Parks, national establishment recommended, 415.
Parliamentary discussions as to the Canadian Pacific Railway, 401.
Party, its unfortunate influence, 402.
Passamaquoddy Bay, 104.
Penobscot, 104.
Pie à Pot, 210.

INDEX. 447

Pipon, Major, 122.
Point de Meuron, 170.
Polynesian S.S., 83.
Pond Peter, 185.
Pontgravé, 104.
Port Arthur, 165.
Port Moody, Burrard Inlet, 330.
Port Royal, capture of, 107, 108.
Portage la Prairie, assembly of force there, 193, 204.
Portland, Oregon, 359; its bad hotel, 360.
Poutrincourt, 104.
Potlach, 306, 390.
Provisions non-arrival, 295.
Provisions obtained, 305.
Pullman car, its comfort, 16.

QUEBEC, CITY OF, 127; ITS TRADE, 134; supports North Shore Railway, 135.
Quebec, Province of, duty regarding North Shore Railway, 135.
Quebec, late Government of, policy, sale of North Shore Railway, 137.

RAILWAY, APPEARANCE OF ON THE PRAIRIE, 217.
Railway delays, 166.
Railway mail train, 14.
Railway travel. Mr. L. D., 52; its comfort, 90; ease of modern travel, 394.
Railways, their social and political influence, 396.
Rapids, St. Lawrence, 139.
Rat Portage, 173; its bad fare, 175.
Rathdrum, 365.
Raymbault, 168.
Red Lion, Henley, 63.
Red River plain, 373.
Red River settlement, 189; Governor's proclamation, 196;

settlers called upon to abandon it, 192; broken up, 194.
Regina, 208.
Representative Government, its abuses, 404.
Representation in Imperial Parliament by Colonies impracticable, 423.
Richardson, 372.
Robinson, Major, 122.
Robertson, Collin, 192.
Roche de la, Marquis, 102.
Rocky Mountain, first view, 218.
Rogers, R. C. Archbishop of Chatham, 92, 99 100.
Rogers, Major, 222, 230, 249, 254; discovers pass, 268, 277.
Rogers' Camp, 250.
Rogers, Mr. Albert, 254, 277.
Ross, Mr. James, 222.
Route, uncertainty as to, 229.
Royal Academy, 64.
Royal Commissions, their importance, 401.
Royal William, pioneer steamer across Atlantic, 24.
Russell, Lord Alexander, 120.
Ryswick, peace of, 107.

SACRIFICE OF BRITISH TERRITORY, 365.
Sage, Mr. Dean, 21.
Sailors' Orphan Concert, 29.
Salisbury, Marquis of, Speech at Kings College, 59.
Sanbon Water Shed, 373.
Sand, its troublesome Character on the North Pacific R.R., 362.
Sand Point, 365.
Sault St. Mary, 159.
Savannah SS. Pioneer across Atlantic, 24.
Savona's Ferry, 312.
Scenery Remarkable on Canadian Pacific R., 414.
Scoby, 290.

INDEX.

Scotchman, absence of all memorial of, 77.
Seattle, 357.
Sea Sickness, 23, 88.
Sea Voyage, 23; Sunday service, 24; impatience of passengers, 29;
Section A, 171.
" B, 172.
" 15, 175.
Self-Government to Colonies, its concession the removal of difficulty, 422.
Selkirk, 176.
Selkirk Range, front view of, 249; ascent, 260; summit, 266.
Selkirk, Lord, 187; early attempt at emigration, 188; joined Hudson Bay Co., 188; opposed by Northwest Co., 189; Red River settlement, 189; hurries to Red River, 194; proceeds to the Kaministiquia, 196; his character, 197; death, 198.
Semple, Governor, 194.
Seven Oaks, affair 17th June, 194.
Seymour, Governor, 329, 345.
Shaginappy, 225. n
Shirley, Governor, 112.
Ship Building, 2.
Shuswap Indians, 272, 295.
Shuswap Lake, arrive at, 303.
Sicamouse Narrows, 309.
Simms, 372.
Sinclair, Mrs., 327.
Sioux, their conduct in Canada, 387.
Skunk Cabbage, 262, 253.
Slave River, 326.
Smith, Mr. Marcus, 329.
Snake River, 363.
Snow Storm, 177.
Soil on the Plains, 209.
Soil, Moosejaw to Qu'Appelle, 213.
Somerville, Mary, 28.

South Thompson River, 309.
Spain, seizes country of Nootka Sound, 341.
Spellman's Camp, 233.
Spokane Falls, 365.
Spurgeon's Tabernacle, 45.
Spuzzem, 320.
Stage coach, the old, 89.
Standard Time—Meeting of railway managers to determine, 375; proceedings taken by Congress United States, 378; date when came in operation, 379.
Start for the Mountains, 202.
Stephen, Mr. Geo., President C. P. R., telegram from, 42.
St Croix, fort of, 104.
St. John, city of, its fires, 17.
St. Mary's Bay, N. S., 103.
St. Lawrence River, dredging near Quebec advantageous, 136.
St. Paul, 374.
S. Swithen's day, 79. n
Stony Indian's, 242. n
Subercase, Governor, 107.
Suez Canal, its exposed state, 433.
Summit Creek, 235.
Sunday in the Mountains, 230, 255.
Superior, Lake, 161; north shore connection indispensible, 408; progress of work, 395.
Supplies to the Columbia, 223.
Swift Current, 211.
Syndicate Peak, 271.

TACHÉ, ARCHBISHOP, 205.
Tacoma, 357.
Tattuall, Commodore, 438.
Telegram, ocean, its non-receipt, 42; receipt of recalls civilization, 313.
Telegraph extension over Chi-

nese seas, 432.
Telephone, 320.
Thames at Monkey Island, 78.
Three Rivers, 130.
Three Valley Lake, 302.
Thunder Bay, 164.
Thunder storm, 177.
Toronto, 146.
Townsend, Rev. Mr., 19.
Trail through Kicking-Horse, 239; on the side of precipice, 258.
Travel, difference of present mode and that of last century, 396.
Trent River, 82.
Truro, N. S., Prince of Wales' visit to, 15.
Tseng, Marchioness, 74.
Tupper, Sir Charles, 22, 65.

UMATILLA, 363.
Union of the several component elements of the British Empire a necessity, 430.
Union Pacific Railway Co., 413.
United Kingdom, 34.
United States hotel life, 49.
Urquhart, Captain, navigates by sound, 333.
Utrecht, treaty of, 184.

Vancouver Island, 6.
Victor Lake, 301.
Victoria, 330.
Verden, 207.

Voyage across Atlantic, 98.

WAIT A BIT, 259.
Wales, Prince of, 75.
Wallace, Mr., 79.
Wallula junction, 363.
Warren, Admiral, 112.
Watershed Gulf of Mexico and Hudson's Bay, 373.
Watteville regiment, 195.
West of England, its flora, 81.
Westminster, treaty of, 106.
Whist often a penalty, 25.
White fish, 159.
Wild fruit on Selkirks, 269, 280.
Wilderness, entry into, 277.
Williamette River, 359.
Wilmot, Mr., 325.
Wilson, George, 230.
Windsor, visit near, 75; forest, 76.
Winnipeg station, 177.
Winnipeg, 179; its low level, 198; unprofitable land, 204,
Wolseley, Lord, his views of Suez Canal, 433.
Wright, Mr. Charles, 217.
Wright, Mr. S. B., 308.
Wright, Mrs., 308.

Yale, 321;
Yellow Head Pass, its advantages, 409.
Yellowstone River, 363; park, 368.
Young, Hon. John, 132.

NOTE.

The ceremony of naming Collingwood, which has been described at page 151 as having taken place in 1851, should have been referred to the 14th January, 1853. It was at this date that the meeting took place, when the locality in question, protected from the north by a few islands near the shore, then known as the "Hen and Chickens," was formally named Collingwood by the Sheriff of the County of Simcoe.

www.ingramcontent.com/pod-product-compliance
Lightning Source LLC
Chambersburg PA
CBHW032000300426
44117CB00008B/839